P9-DVU-920

DATE DUE

JE 2 '00			
AP 03 '01			
MAY 0 7 2009			

DEMCO 38-296

Sally Hemings &
Thomas Jefferson

❦

History, Memory, and Civic Culture

Jeffersonian America

Jan Ellen Lewis and Peter S. Onuf, Editors

Sally Hemings & Thomas Jefferson

❦

History, Memory, and Civic Culture

Edited by Jan Ellen Lewis and Peter S. Onuf

University Press of Virginia
Charlottesville and London

Riverside Community College
Library
4800 Magnolia Avenue
Riverside, CA 92506

E 332.2 .S24 1999

Sally Hemings & Thomas
    Jefferson

The University Press of Virginia
© 1999 by the Rector and Visitors of the University of Virginia
All rights reserved
Printed in the United States of America
First published 1999

♾ The paper used in this publication meets the minimum requirements of the American National Standard for Information Sciences—Permanence of Paper for Printed Library Materials, ANSI Z39.48-1984.

Sally Hemings and Thomas Jefferson was designed and typeset in
Dante by Kachergis Book Design, Pittsboro, North Carolina;
and printed on 55-pound Glatfelfter Supple Opaque and bound
by Thomson-Shore, Dexter, Michigan.

Library of Congress Cataloging-in-Publication Data
Sally Hemings and Thomas Jefferson : history, memory, and
    civic culture / edited by Jan Ellen Lewis and Peter S. Onuf.
        p.   cm. — (Jeffersonian America)
        Papers originally presented at a conference held Mar.
    5–6, 1999, at Monticello and the University of Virginia.
    Includes bibliographical references and index.
        ISBN 0-8139-1918-5 (cloth : alk. paper).— ISBN 0-8139-1919-3
    (pbk.: alk. paper)
        1. Hemings, Sally Congresses. 2. Jefferson, Thomas,
    1743–1826—Relations with women Congresses. 3. Jefferson,
    Thomas, 1743–1826—Relations with slaves Congresses.
    4. Presidents—United States Biography Congresses.
    5. Afro-American women—Virginia—Albemarle County
    Biography Congresses. 6. Women slaves—Virginia—
    Albemarle County Biography Congresses. 7. Miscegena-
    tion—Social aspects—United States Congresses. 8. United
    States—Race relations Congresses. I. Lewis, Jan, 1949– .
    II. Onuf, Peter S. III. Series.
    E332.2.S24   1999
    973.4´6´092—dc21   99-33901
    [B]   CIP

Withdrawn Community College
LRC and
4800 Magnolia Avenue
Riverside, CA 92506

To Our Friends and Amigos

CONTENTS

❧

ACKNOWLEDGMENTS

The Conference that led to the publication of this book was held at Monticello and the University of Virginia on March 5 and 6, 1999. "Sally Hemings and Thomas Jefferson: History, Memory, and Civic Culture" was made possible by the generous support of the College of Arts and Sciences, Melvyn P. Leffler, dean; the Corcoran Department of History, Michael Holt, chair; the Institute for Public History, Phyllis Leffler, director; the Office of President John T. Casteen; the Office of Provost Peter Low; the University Press of Virginia, Nancy Essig, director; and the Thomas Jefferson Memorial Foundation (Monticello), Daniel P. Jordan, executive director.

Julian Bond, chairman of the NAACP and professor in the history department of the University of Virginia, moderated with characteristic grace and authority a public panel session at the conference. The panel included most of the authors in this volume as well as Dr. Eugene Foster, the retired University of Virginia pathology professor who coordinated the DNA tests of Jefferson, Hemings, and Woodson descendants. Gene handled questions (and some abuse) with great dignity and good humor; he also was a welcome participant in seminar sessions on earlier drafts of the essays collected in this volume. Thanks to other nonauthor panelists for their contributions: Gertrude Fraser of the University of Virginia's Department of Anthropology; Scot French, assistant director of the Carter G. Woodson Institute for Afro-American and African Studies, University of Virginia; and Brenda Stevenson, Department of History, University of California at Los Angeles. Richard A. Samuelson, a graduate student in the Department of History at the University of Virginia, served ably as conference coordinator.

Seminar sessions were held at the International Center for Jefferson Studies at Monticello. Many thanks to Dan Jordan and to James Horn, the Saunders Director of the ICJS, for their gracious hospitality. Phyllis Leffler, Jim Horn, Joseph C. Miller of the University of Virginia's history department, and Jerry Handler of the Virginia Foundation for the Humanities made valuable contributions to our seminar discussions.

Good friends and critics James Oakes of the Graduate Center of the City University of New York and Herbert Sloan of Barnard College, Columbia University, provided thoughtful readings of earlier versions of these essays. Their comments helped us formulate some of the themes elaborated in our introduction.

Special thanks to Nancy Essig, acquisitions editor Richard Holway, managing editor, Ellen Satrom, and the able staff of the University Press of Virginia for their enthusiastic commitment to the project. With the Press's support (and prodding) we have been able to bring this collection to publication in only a few months. We are most indebted to our wonderful authors: without their timely cooperation, the "fast-track" publication of *Sally Hemings and Thomas Jefferson* would not have been possible.

Jan Ellen Lewis and Peter S. Onuf
May 1999

Sally Hemings &
Thomas Jefferson

❧

History, Memory, and Civic Culture

Hemings-Jefferson Family Tree

Thomas C. Woodson* *(1790–1879)* —— 11 children
& *Jemima*

Harriet *(1795–1797)*

Beverley Hemings *(1798–1822+)*

daughter *(1799–1800)*

Harriet Hemings *(1801–1822+)*

Thomas Jefferson *(1743–1826)* &
Sally Hemings (1773–1835)

Madison Hemings *(1805–1877)*
& *Mary Hughes McCoy*

son *(d. infancy)*

Sarah Hemings *(1835–1884)*
& *Reuben Byrd (?–1863)*

Thomas Eston Hemings
(1838–1863)

Harriet Hemings *(1839–1925)* &
James Butler (1835–1887)

Henry Spears (1842–1918)

Mary Ann Hemings *(1843–1921)*
& *David Johnson (?–1923)*

Catherine Jane Hemings
(1844–1880)
& *George Washington Hale*
(1845–?)

William Beverly Hemings
(1847–1910)

James Madison Hemings *(1849–?)*

Ellen Wayles Hemings
(1856–1940)
& *Andrew J. Roberts (1851–1927)*

Eston Hemings Jefferson
(1808–1856)
& *Julia Ann Isaacs (1814–1889)*

John Wayles Jefferson *(1835–1892)*

Beverly Frederick Jefferson
(1839–1908)
& *Annie Maud Smith (1845–1882)*

Anna W. Jefferson *(1837–1886)*
& *Albert T. Pearson (1829–1907)*

Source: Based on public, family, and church records and on oral history. Created by Lucia Stanton, Monticello.
*According to E. A. Foster et al.'s 1998 genetic study ("Jefferson Fathered Slave's Last Child," *Nature* 196 [5 Nov. 1998], 27–28), Jefferson's paternity of Eston Hemings is almost certain and that of Thomas C. Woodson is unlikely. Descendants of Madison Hemings were not tested. In 1999 Dr. Foster and his associates ran DNA tests on another line of the Woodson family; the results were not yet available when this volume went to press.

Introduction

Jan Ellen Lewis and Peter S. Onuf

In November 1998, when *Nature* magazine published a brief article reporting on DNA tests that strongly suggested that Thomas Jefferson was the father of his slave Sally Hemings's last son, it was both news and no news at all. The *New York Times* ran a front-page article and followed up with a feature and several op-eds. *U.S. News and World Report* put the story on the cover. Oprah Winfrey staged a family reunion between Jefferson's white descendants and his black ones. For a few months, the DNA test and its implications were the stuff of public discussion and even a bit of controversy, although it never rivaled the season's biggest story, the impeachment of President Bill Clinton.[1]

At the same time, for many people, particularly professional historians, the story was something of a nonevent or even an anticlimax. For years, most of the students we have taught, as well as good numbers of our colleagues, have believed that Jefferson was indeed the father of Sally Hemings's children. At most, the scientific evidence, which in itself is far from definitive, only confirmed what traditional sources as well as our professional judgment had suggested: some sort of long-term relationship existed between Jefferson and the slave woman who for almost two hundred years, since 1802, when James Callender first published the charge in the *Richmond Recorder* (see Appendix B), had been rumored to have been his concubine.

Yet no one who relied upon biographies of Jefferson or even most of the books written by professional historians would have known that there was an emerging consensus among historians of the period or a widespread belief among the public that Jefferson was the father of Sally Hemings's children. With few exceptions, almost all the Jefferson biographers and most of the historians—particularly white ones—who have had occasion to write about the Jefferson-Hemings story have either insisted that a liaison was either impossible or highly unlikely or declared themselves agnostics on the issue.

Among historians, then, until the fall of 1998, there was something of a paradox: While most of those who have written about Jefferson and Hemings have cast doubt upon the likelihood of a sexual relationship, the many more who have assumed such a relationship have not bothered to publish their thoughts. How can this paradox be explained?

It appears that if historians have not written about the Jefferson-Hemings liaison, it is because they have not thought it important. Whether or not there was such a relationship did not seem to them to have much bearing upon our understanding of history or of Jefferson himself. Consider Winthrop D. Jordan's reflections in "Hemings and Jefferson: Redux" about the less than one-half of one percent of *White over Black* that he devoted to Jefferson's relationship with Sally Hemings: "I thought arrogantly that I had broader and more important things in mind."[2] By and large, only those biographers who are deeply invested in Jefferson himself have written about the possibility of such a relationship, and then primarily to cast doubt upon it.

Hence, we confront not only a paradox but an irony: Historians, rather than biographers, have been most in tune with public opinion, believing generally, at least in recent years, in the possibility and even the likelihood of a sexual relationship between Sally Hemings and Thomas Jefferson. Yet biographers, more than historians, have found the issue of compelling interest. The significance of the DNA evidence, then, is twofold: It has forced a realignment of public perception and academics' interpretations, bringing to the fore the implicit alignment between historians and the public, while forcing into the shadows those biographers who had argued against the possibility. At the same time, the DNA evidence has challenged historians to explain the significance of an issue that the public, both black and white, has always found of great interest.

That is the purpose of this volume: for historians to reflect upon and begin attempting to explain the significance of the liaison between Thomas Jefferson and Sally Hemings.

On March 5 and 6, 1999, with the support of the University of Virginia, Monticello, and the University Press of Virginia, we brought together a group of specialists in early American and African American history and the history of race relations to offer their thoughts to each other and the public on "Sally Hemings and Thomas Jefferson: History, Memory, and Civic Culture." The essays in this volume represent this group of historians' reflections.

The moment was, and continues to be, enormously liberating, much more than we had anticipated. We knew that the public was intrigued by the question of the Jefferson-Hemings relationship, but we were dismayed by much of the commentary. Our original impulse was to encourage historians to try to shape public opinion, not by speaking in the sound bites of contemporary opinionizing, nor necessarily to offer the sort of perspective that will only be available after years of additional reflection and research. We hoped that historians would be able to suggest which fields of research now appeared most fertile, how this new piece of evidence might shift our perspective on a variety of topics, such as the history of race relations, and what the use of this new sort of evidence meant for traditional historians' methods. Two years ago, we published a review essay suggesting that Thomas Jefferson had come to serve as an American synecdoche; that is, he stood for the whole of American history and culture, and surely this was an inappropriate burden for any historical figure. "If Jefferson was wrong," the historian James Parton had written in 1874, "America is wrong. If America is right, Jefferson was right." We detected, in several recent studies, an attempt to place Jefferson in his historical context rather than to elevate him as an icon, standing in isolation from his time and place.[3] We hoped that post-DNA considerations of Jefferson and his world would follow this trend.

We were hopeful, but still we did not know what to expect. Before DNA the Jefferson-Hemings relationship had attracted little interest from professional historians. Whatever their suspicions, most scholars assumed the question would never be definitively resolved and probably wasn't worth worrying much about anyway. But those who gathered in Charlottesville soon discovered that this new piece of information in fact opened up new ways of looking at and thinking about a wide range of topics we recognized as "important"—from race relations, to the history of sexuality, to the way we practice history. New ways of imagining the past and new areas of research seemed to open before us. Moving beyond the "did-he-or-didn't-he" question, we encountered uncharted terrain: the social world that Jefferson and Hemings inhabited and, indeed, created.

That social world provides the context for reconsidering the sources of the original story of a Jefferson-Hemings liaison. Joshua Rothman has asked a simple question, one that had somehow eluded previous historians: How was it that James Thomson Callender, the scandal-mongering newsman who has been reviled for almost two centuries, got so much of the basic story right? Philip Morgan, who had originally been skeptical of the allegations, has extended his research into interracial sex in the British Atlantic. Together, Rothman and Morgan suggest that interracial sex, particularly between white men and black or mulatto women, was much more common in Virginia (let alone the Low Country or the Caribbean) than historians had previously supposed.[4] By sharply dividing the social world of the slave South into black and white, we have missed seeing both the sometimes distinctive experience of mixed-race African Americans and the role that whites (such as Thomas Jefferson) played in it. Lucia Stanton and Dianne Swann-Wright's moving account of the family stories of the descendants of Thomas Jefferson and Sally Hemings gives us a sense of the complicated history of mixed-race Americans, ones for whom racial identification might be a matter of personal choice.

How has this world, the one created by sex across the color line, escaped historians' notice? To be sure, in recent years some historians have been turning their attention increasingly toward the world that black and white created together, while others have been studying interracial sex. But these investigations have until now had little impact on Jefferson studies. Specialists continued to insist that Jefferson's personality—"his deepest urges were more self-protective and sentimental, than sexual"[5]—or pronouncements—"the quiet frenzy of Jefferson's dedication to beauty and refinement reflected an urge to hover above the squalor and horror of the slavery that existed below him on his mountain top"—made it "implausible that he had a love affair with one of his slaves."[6] Of course, if Jefferson didn't do it, then some other white man on his plantation did, but ironically, the obsessive attention to Jefferson has simultaneously deflected attention away from those other white men and the mixed-race children they fathered. Although those who have attempted to defend Jefferson have necessarily placed the blame for fathering Sally Hemings's children on some other white man (usually one of Jefferson's nephews, Peter or Samuel Carr), they have not considered the implications of that conclusion: Whoever the father of Sally Hemings's children might have been, Jefferson's Monticello was a mixed-race community, inhabited not only by whites and dark-skinned African Americans but also by a significant number of light-skinned slaves who were related to Jefferson in one way or another.[7]

If historians have missed seeing this world, perhaps it is because Jefferson himself threw us off the track. It is not only Jefferson's evasion of the truth, which Jan Lewis analyzes, or the subsequent eagerness of Jefferson scholars to take him at his word, which Clarence Walker and Annette Gordon-Reed consider, but Jefferson's own discussions of race that have misled us. As Jordan notes, Jefferson "seemed to have a temperamental tendency that led him insistently to slice his world into twos," and that tendency is reflected in his writings about race. In Jefferson's famous comparison of black people and white in Query XIV of the *Notes on the State of Virginia* (Appendix D), he wrote about racial difference in, literally, black and white terms, almost always to the detriment of black people. Reading these passages, one might think that Jefferson lived in a community in which the lines of racial difference were clear and sharp, rather than one with large numbers of mixed-race people, some of whom were his kin.

What we now know, or, rather, recognize about the racial composition of the Monticello community compels us to take another look at Jefferson's writings on race. Perhaps we are now better able to recognize them as an ideology, that is, an American ideology of race that was, as Jordan demonstrated in *White over Black*, being created by Jefferson and others at the turn of the nineteenth century. Of course, there are many ways to define ideology, but if one thinks of it as a form of miscommunication, then Jefferson's views on race were surely ideological: Living among people of a range of colors, several of whom were the children and grandchildren of his father-in-law, and one of whom would shortly become his concubine and the father of his children, Jefferson wrote as if everyone around him were either black or white.

We are now able to ask, as well, what the function of this ideology might have been. Werner Sollors suggests that it has served a political function, helping to assure that political leaders in the United States have been drawn, much more than in other nations with comparable populations, from among white, male Protestants. He draws our attention to the steady din of gossip about interracial sex that has accompanied American politics. Like Rothman, Sollors suggests that this gossip has functioned not so much to police behavior as to render interracial sex, and the claims it might enable blacks to make because of it, illegitimate. Like Jordan and Sollors, Walker draws our attention to the intimate connection between race and sex. As Walker notes, those who insisted that Jefferson could not have had a liaison with Hemings were making normative statements not only about race but about sex as well. To say, for example, that Jefferson was too "feminine" to have had sex with Hemings is to define the norms for both men and women, both heterosexual and gay.

In this context, it is no accident, according to Gordon-Reed, that the historian Fawn M. Brodie was reviled for suggesting that Jefferson had enjoyed a long-term relationship with Sally Hemings. To be sure, some of Brodie's psychoanalytic interpretations may have been tenuous, but all those who write about human behavior draw, if not so obviously, from the insights of either psychoanalysis or psychology. Jordan, for example, had written that Jefferson's "opinions were . . . sometimes quite directly the product of his repressions."[8] Gordon-Reed suggests that the opposition to Brodie's book was in part political, a refusal to let a white woman who relied upon the testimony of a black man (Madison Hemings) write the historical record. Her larger point is that whites have not been willing to let blacks define reality for them. In this case, it has meant that whites have claimed for themselves the right to define the iconic Jefferson. He must be the doting father described by his daughter Martha and not the indifferent one described by his son Madison. It has meant that the image of Monticello that must come to mind is the one Rhys Isaac has called the "first Monticello," the one Jefferson imagined as a retreat for himself and his white family and friends, rather than the "second Monticello," in which Jefferson fathered a family by his slave Sally Hemings. And if we believe that "reality" is in some measure socially constructed, it has meant that blacks have been largely excluded from the process of defining what it means to be American. It has meant that the narrative of American his-

tory has been written by whites, just as the structure and rules of politics—here defined most broadly as the exercise of power—have been established by whites. To overturn the received wisdom about Jefferson's
private life, then, is, according to Gordon-Reed, Isaac, Sollors, and Walker, in a fundamental way to challenge the distribution of power in our nation, for it is to challenge—and attempt to rewrite—what Sollors calls
"the legitimizing national myths" of the United States.

Several essays in this volume reflect upon what new national stories,
ones written by blacks as well as whites, might look like. As Gordon S.
Wood notes, "offsetting or undercutting the symbolic meanings" of historical figures such as Jefferson "by situating them in the peculiar circumstances of a very different past is no easy matter." He reminds us that
"false heritages are precisely what many people in the society want and
perhaps need." The reassessment of Jefferson occasioned by the DNA evidence, however, gives us the opportunity to write new stories, to hear
different voices. That is precisely what Lucia Stanton and Dianne Swann-
Wright do in their account of the Hemings family history. The descendants of Thomas Jefferson and Sally Hemings inhabited a world that was,
to use Sollors's phrase, neither black nor white, yet both.[9] It was a world
in which racial—and family—identity was both a matter of social ascrip-
tion and painful choice.

"To be a person is to have a story," Isaac writes. "Not to be allowed a
story is to be marked for obscurity and oppression." Part of what the contributors to this volume do is to tell other stories, ones to put beside the
stories that have been told by and about Jefferson. Thus this volume is entitled *Sally Hemings and Thomas Jefferson,* in the hope that juxtaposing Sally
Hemings's history with Thomas Jefferson's will enable us to rewrite the
history of the nation. Many of the essays in this volume conclude, explicitly or implicitly, with questions about what this new multiracial narrative
of American history might look like.

At the same time, both Wood and Jack N. Rakove remind us that because such a narrative is a central element of our civic culture, rewriting
it will be very difficult. Nor should historians think that it is in their exclusive power to write or rewrite the nation's legitimating myths. Rakove
helps us understand the nation's complex engagement with Jefferson (and
now with the story of Jefferson and Sally Hemings). Jefferson has been
such an appealing figure in part because of his confidence in the future,

and his eloquent and often-expressed hope that we might transcend the limitations of the past, that is, the limitations imposed upon us by history itself. In this sense, Jefferson confounds history and historians both, for he holds out the hope that we can escape exactly those conditions that historians insist we must understand: historical context, complexity, and the constraints that are imposed upon the individual by the collective weight of the present and the past. Rakove suggests that recent criticisms of Jefferson for his failures, in particular his deep involvement in the institution of slavery and the racism that sustained it, is in some measure a projection onto him and his generation of our failures to resolve the question of race. We—contemporary Americans, both black and white—are deeply disappointed in Jefferson for his failure to solve America's race problem. At the same time, because of our impulse to throw off the traces of history, we find inspiration in his commitment to equality, his hope, and his optimism.

Perhaps this is why, like Isaac, so many of us want to see signs of hope in the story of Sally Hemings and Thomas Jefferson. Perhaps their story can be the basis for a new narrative of racial reconciliation. That seems to be the way much of the public is interpreting the DNA evidence. Although the Thomas Jefferson Memorial Association, the organization of white Jefferson descendants that oversees the family graveyard at Monticello, recently decided not to "rush a decision" about admitting into membership the descendants of Sally Hemings, some members of that group are more welcoming. One observed that "Clearly, Jefferson loved her, and love is what counts." At Monticello to bury her own mother and meet for the first time her distant Hemings kin, this Jefferson descendant said that when families accept their diversity, "it's a beautiful thing. . . . It could heal racism in our country."[10] Such optimism—if not the comfortable acceptance of diversity—is profoundly Jeffersonian.

It is also at odds with the historian's sensibility. As Rakove observes, historians "are tied to a belief in the inadvertent and unintended consequences of human action." Jan Lewis contemplates these consequences and, like Rakove, considers the moral implications of Jefferson's actions. Rakove concludes that although the Hemings-Jefferson relationship "complicates and enlarges the problem of understanding Jefferson's *private* life . . . it does not fundamentally alter the essential *public* dilemma." Lewis, however, questions this sharp division between private and public, showing how the lies told within the Jefferson family, out of the best of motives—to protect Jefferson's white family and maintain its privacy—entered into the public record and became part of the national legacy of racism that denied the Hemings children their immediate legacy and, by extension, all black Americans their symbolic one. For her, the best of motives—in this case, the love of a doting father, the affection of an adoring daughter and grandchildren—have unintended bad consequences. Rakove implicitly turns this formulation on its head. For him, Jefferson is a flawed individual (as presumably, more or less, are we all). Yet Jefferson's articulation of the fundamental principles of modern democracy—government only by the consent of the governed, freedom of conscience, the right to privacy, the independence of religion from the state—have outlived not only him but also his limited capacity to find in them a way to terminate slavery. In this sense, Jefferson's principles have had consequences beyond those he imagined, but not, one might hope, beyond those he might have wished for.

❧

Our title, *Sally Hemings and Thomas Jefferson,* suggests our priorities. But putting Hemings first also underscores our problem, for we don't know very much about her; the discrepancy with what we know about our other subject, Thomas Jefferson, is obviously enormous. To some extent, if we know so little about Hemings, we have no one to blame but ourselves. Well before the DNA results were publicized, in *Thomas Jefferson and Sally Hemings: An American Controversy*[11] Gordon-Reed showed us that historians and biographers had failed to examine the evidence on the Hemings-Jefferson relationship with critical detachment. Moreover, some of what we thought was true was false, and true stories were too easily dismissed as lies. As Gordon-Reed eloquently argues, Jeffersonian scholars have thus justified overlooking the single most telling and historically credible document, an interview with Sally Hemings's son published in the *Pike County [Ohio] Republican* in 1873 (Appendix A). Sally Hemings had a story of her own, one that she passed on to her son Madison and presumably to her other children. Yet even when this document is mined for evidence about Sally Hemings's life, as both Brodie and Gordon-Reed have done, we are still left knowing very little about Hemings. Greater knowledge—and understanding—of her life awaits further research and new efforts to reinterpret the sources we have at hand. To be sure, we will achieve a better understanding of Sally Hemings and her world when we have reconstructed the world that she and Thomas Jefferson inhabited, even if, as now seems likely, no new "evidence" emerges.

Until then, we would do well to remember that everything we know and can learn about slavery in Jefferson's Virginia and at Monticello illuminates the constraints, conventions, and culture within which Hemings sought to carve out a life for herself and her children. But if the brutal fact of her enslaved condition is the defining circumstance of her life, it has been too easy to ignore the fact that Thomas Jefferson was a slaveowner, even in accounts of their relationship. Perhaps slaveowning defined Jefferson in some fundamental Hegelian sense, but we have something more concrete, specific, and local in mind. The constraints on Jefferson were in no way comparable to those on Hemings: he owned her and her children. Yet Jefferson was implicated in and shaped by his social world, a white-and-black world grounded in and sustained by violence, but made habitable by community custom and interracial accommodations.

Historians have been more interested in the deeper structures and sociocultural imperatives of American slave societies than in seemingly more modest questions about how these societies actually "worked" in particular families and communities. Interracial sex constitutes a crucial link between these small worlds and larger social structures. Transgression of racial boundaries was endemic in Anglo-America, a fact of life that was reflected in colonial slave codes, in community custom, and in the secret life of families. Acknowledging the Hemings-Jefferson relationship forces us to engage with this complex reality.

The first section of this book, "Race, Sex, and History," opens with Gordon Wood's "The Ghosts of Monticello," his reflections on the historian's dilemma as he or she reconstructs the hidden world of interracial families and attempts to situate an American icon in this unfamiliar setting, a setting perhaps most accessible to us in literary works such as William Faulkner's *Absalom, Absalom!* What sort of civic responsibility does the retelling of this American story entail for historians? Wood's meditation on the complicated relationship between historians and a general public that craves "heritage," the stories that give people their sense of collective identity, introduces the themes that inform the essays that follow.

All our writers are dealing with "race and sex." Our next contributor, however, has earned the right to go first. Winthrop D. Jordan revealed the crucial importance of sex for the construction of race in his magisterial *White over Black;* anticipating biographer Brodie by several years, Jordan was also the first modern mainstream scholar to give credence to the Hemings-Jefferson story. Jordan's decision to tell the story has been vindicated, not simply because it has now been confirmed, but because it draws us into the particularities of a biracial world that defied—even as it was defined by—the black-and-white distinctions of the race relations.

What sort of world was this? Philip Morgan offers a broad comparative perspective on interracial sex in the Anglo-American world. His close look at the sexual histories of two white men—one in Jamaica and the other in North Carolina—reveals the extraordinary range of interracial relationships that were possible under slavery and thus provides a framework for our speculations about Hemings and Jefferson. If white men exercised their sexual prerogative everywhere, in more or less casual and brutal ways, they could also find themselves entangled in—and therefore constrained by—more sustained relationships with slave women. At our conference in Charlottesville, considerable controversy was generated by the question: Within the social and cultural contexts of their day, what sort of relationship *could* Hemings and Jefferson have had? Our readers will discover that there is no consensus, particularly on the choice of words, all loaded, to describe the relationship. Was it a kind of "marriage?" Was Hemings Jefferson's "mistress" or "concubine," and what do those terms signify? Language fails us, for the use of any term seems to reduce the horrors of systematic sexual exploitation to something commonplace and quotidian, even—in the case of "marriage"—something worthy of respect. Perhaps our sense of outraged decency tells us we should simply remain silent. What after all can we call Phibbah, the slave woman who apparently exercised such power over Morgan's monstrously libidinous Jamaican Thomas Thistlewood? Is there a danger of conceding too much to Thistlewood—or to Jefferson—in the language we use to describe their relationships with female human property?

Yet silence is clearly no answer. The discomfort we may feel in giving the Hemings-Jefferson relationship a name should be a threshold to better understanding, not an excuse for averting our gaze. We should recognize that our discomfort is an echo of the conflicted feelings this relationship and others like it inspired in their own time. The historians' problem may be that we know too little to judge; it may also be that we know too much, that we don't know how to make sense out of all the experiences and meanings imbedded in this story. Could it be true, as Gordon-Reed suggests, that too many of us for too long (even now?) have simply not *wanted* to acknowledge that there was a story, or that it could mean anything at all? Or perhaps, in wanting to see in the complex history of slavery simply the story of a man and a woman, we hope to discover some measure of love that might redeem—or deny—the brutal exercise of power.

The second section of this book, "Stories and Lies, Remembering and Forgetting," focuses on what white and black family members, their neighbors, and their descendants said—or might have said, or did not say—about the relationship. These stories have their own history, a history that not only gets us back to the relationship they describe, as close as we can ever get, but that also made and makes it meaningful.

With Joshua Rothman's essay, we circle in on Hemings and Jefferson, locating them in the context of their "neighborhood." While Morgan provides both a broad comparative framework and a close reading of two white men who left unusually rich documentation of their sex lives, Rothman splits the analytical distance. Jefferson and Hemings did not conduct their relationship, whatever it was like, in social isolation. What did the neighbors know? We would have no way of knowing (and could only speculate on the basis of neighborhood knowledge of other liaisons) if someone, namely the journalist James Thomson Callender, had not asked the question at the time (Appendix B). The convenient assumption that Callender, an embittered office seeker, was a liar has enabled detractors to discount his reports from the neighborhood. But what if Jefferson, not Callender, was the liar? Then, as with so much else in the Hemings-Jefferson story, everything looks different: a whole new cast of characters, Jefferson's neighbors, suddenly come into sharp focus. Of course, we have always known that Jefferson had "neighbors," but they never have been much more than ciphers, dim figures in a distant background for a conveniently decontextualized Jefferson. Listening to Callender's informants—and listening to the customary silence of neighbors who knew many such stories about local families, often including their own—we can begin to see that Jefferson was very much a man of a *particular* place and time, not simply of a generic world—the slave-holding South—where slavery was a tragic legacy and burden for masters as well as slaves.

Jefferson kept quiet about his relationship with Hemings. That is precisely what neighbors and family expected, even demanded. But Jefferson and Hemings were enacting a story, whatever silence surrounded them. Rhys Isaac's suggestive cataloguing of stories they *could* have told, the narratives in their own cultural traditions that gave meaning to similar relationships, is a speculative foray into a lost inner history. Yet it is also a valuable reminder that this lost history was at the same time as deeply familiar and conventional to its protagonists as it was to their knowing neighbors. But, of course, Jefferson and Hemings "knew" vastly different things, most of which is necessarily lost to us.

Jan Lewis describes Jefferson's complicity in family lies that survive to this day in the fulminations of DNA deniers. Over the years, these false stories have become deeply familiar and conventional, and they have helped define national norms not only for race relations but family life as well. Jefferson could not have fathered Hemings's children because he was too devoted a father to his white daughters. Jefferson could not have disgraced his white family by maintaining a black family under their very eyes. One or the other of Jefferson's nephews confessed to fathering Hemings's children. The data in Jefferson's Farm Book prove that he could not have been the father. The Hemings children were not Jefferson kin. All these stories are false, yet they have come not only to structure the lives of several families but also to undergird the Jefferson deification enterprise, entailing significant costs upon Jefferson (and his image) and his heirs, both black and white, both literal and symbolic.

By contrast, the true stories Sally Hemings told her children are largely lost. Lucia Stanton and Dianne Swann-Wright recount the family stories of the descendants of Sally Hemings's sons, Madison and Eston, and show how their relationship to Thomas Jefferson was sometimes barely remembered and sometimes suppressed. As these mixed-race Americans negotiated the color line, family genealogy was both a burden and a legacy, something to be escaped or perhaps privately cherished, but rarely—until recently—something to be publicly celebrated. Stanton and Swann-Wright conclude that the family traditions of the descendants suffered, in varying degrees, both from the complicated choices of individual family members and from their contemptuous dismissal by the larger culture. If the "heritage" of white Americans meant embracing the Jefferson family's lies, it also meant rejecting the true stories of this—and many other—mixed-race families.

In the third section, "Civic Culture," we turn to the stories that now circulate among Americans, stories that simultaneously and selectively connect us to and disconnect us from the past. Clarence Walker and Werner Sollors remind us that race-mixing has always been a taboo subject in American history. Yet it is a taboo that, like Jefferson's shadow family, is always there, at the boundary of sexual (and political) respectability. In fact, that taboo defines respectability, in the process policing both sexual behavior and political practice. What does the Hemings-Jefferson relationship "mean?" That question, for better or worse, is not the sole province of disinterested scholars, however well equipped we imagine we are to answer it.

It is an historiographical truism that historians can only talk about whatever can be talked about within their own historical circumstances. We may be bringing back some important news from the late eighteenth and early nineteenth century, but we are also, inevitably, projecting our own ambiguous and ambivalent values into hitherto dim and musty corners. Walker and Sollors both ask for a little more self-consciousness in this commerce with the past. Surely, they suggest, our collective sense of "heritage," the sum of all our family stories, is less brittle and more supple than hysterical defenders of "Thomas Jefferson" and other iconic nation-founders recognize.

As historians and citizens, we occupy an ambiguous position. As Jack N. Rakove notes, we cannot help making moral judgments, but as historians we, more than others, should understand that we cannot impose upon those in the past a responsibility for moral judgment we could not demand of ourselves in the present. Hence we may not share Conor Cruise O'Brien's belief that a disgraced and disgraceful Jefferson must be toppled from his pedestal in order to guarantee the civic health of the republic.[12] And we may agree with Annette Gordon-Reed that the fact of Jefferson's relationship with Sally Hemings, however troubling its implications may be, is not in itself disgraceful. Still, we do not believe that American nationhood should be premised on lies, however "noble." In his thoughtful essay, Rakove attempts to sort through these complex historical and moral issues, recovering a Jefferson who is "ours"—that is, a Jefferson for all of us, black and white, imperfect yet hopeful beings that we are. Is our conception of American nationhood so fragile that Jefferson has to be "right" about everything for America to be "right"? Can we seize the promise of the Jeffersonian legacy while acknowledging the flaws of its progenitor? These are not, Rakove suggests, merely rhetorical questions in these waning days of the twentieth century. Jefferson still lives, Rakove concludes, not so much as a flawed human being, but in his ideals—government by the consent of the governed, the right to an inviolable sphere of autonomy that protects privacy, conscience, and religion.

Jefferson's protean legacy, of course, has been put to a multitude of conflicting uses, as Merrill D. Peterson demonstrated in his classic study, *The Jefferson Image in the American Mind*.[13] But it may be a good time to insist that we also must now think of Thomas Jefferson *and* Sally Hemings. And the last word belongs to Gordon-Reed. In the wake of DNA, it will be easy enough for us to strike righteous and edifying postures on the "large issues" raised by the Hemings-Jefferson relationship. But as she writes, in our concluding chapter, "the most difficult issues are the seemingly 'small' ones." Let's start at the beginning, making some simple sense of this man we thought we knew so well. Consider this: "Thomas Jefferson had thirteen children, six of whom lived to adulthood. Some of his children were white and some of them were black. He had four sons born to him, three of whom lived to adulthood. He had three daughters who lived to adulthood, not two. Jefferson did not live in celibacy for the forty-five years after the death of his wife of ten years Martha Jefferson. He had a thirty-eight-year, apparently monogamous, relationship with Sally Hemings, an enslaved black woman on his plantation, and fathered a child with her when he was sixty-five years old."

The writing of history is always a dialectic between the particularities of time and place, the most minute details of a verifiable past, and the generalizations we try to make out of these facts. The DNA evidence that strongly suggests that Thomas Jefferson was the father of Sally Hemings's son Eston is one of those tiny details, in itself conclusive of almost nothing. But when it is put together with the other evidence at hand, and when its implications are confronted, we can begin to see new worlds, to craft new interpretations, to engage the past in new ways, and to ask the old questions anew. In this way, all of us are the heirs of the world Sally Hemings and Thomas Jefferson created, engaged in the individual and collective enterprise of trying to make sense out of the world that they have bequeathed us.

NOTES

1. Eugene A. Foster et al., "Jefferson Fathered Slave's Last Child," and Eric S. Lander and Joseph J. Ellis, "Founding Father," *Nature*, 196 (5 Nov. 1998), 27–28, 13–14; Dinitia Smith and Nicholas Wade, "DNA Test Finds Evidence of Jefferson Child by Slave," *New York Times*, 1 Nov. 1998; Barbara Murray and Brian Duffy, "Jefferson's Secret Life," *U.S. News and World Report*, 9 Nov. 1998, 58–69.

2. Winthrop D. Jordan, "Jefferson and Hemings: Redux," chapter 2 in this volume. The reference is to Jordan's *White over Black: American Attitudes toward the Negro, 1550–1812* (Chapel Hill, 1968).

3. Jan Ellen Lewis and Peter S. Onuf, "American Synecdoche: Thomas Jefferson as Image, Icon, Character, and Self," *American Historical Review*, 103 (1998), 125–36.

4. It should also be remembered that however many mixed-race children may have been born in the slave South, it is only through careful and scrupulous research that we can learn whether any white man fathered mixed-race children. Although the DNA evidence now comes close to proving that Jefferson fathered at least one of Sally Hemings's children, sometimes we will also discover that paternity charges cannot be sustained. As Philip Morgan convincingly shows, the long-standing assumption that Jefferson's mentor, George Wythe, fathered a mixed-race child is probably untrue. If Joshua Rothman's work asks us to remember that widely circulated gossip may have a basis in truth, Morgan's work reminds us that it also might not.

5. Joseph J. Ellis, *American Sphinx: The Character of Thomas Jefferson* (New York, 1997), 219.

6. Garry Wills, *New York Review of Books*, 40, no. 14 (12 August 1993), 6–10.

7. An exception is Douglas Egerton, "Thomas Jefferson and the Hemings Family: A Matter of Blood," *Historian*, 59 (1997), 327–45.

8. Jordan, *White over Black*, 471.

9. That is the title of Werner Sollors's most recent book: *Neither Black nor White, yet Both: Thematic Explorations of Interracial Literature* (New York, 1997).

10. Leef Smith, "For Black and White, a Monticello Homecoming," *Washington Post*, 16 May 1999.

12. Conor Cruise O'Brien, *The Long Affair: Thomas Jefferson and the French Revolution, 1785–1800* (Chicago, 1996).

13. Merrill D. Peterson, *The Jefferson Image in the American Mind* (1960; Charlottesville, 1997). For further commentary see Peter S. Onuf, "The Scholars' Jefferson," *William and Mary Quarterly*, 50 (1993), 671–99.

PART I

Race, Sex, and History

CHAPTER I

The Ghosts of Monticello

Gordon S. Wood

Reading the essays in this volume and, indeed, all the material pertaining to the Jefferson-Hemings relationship published over the past three decades or so, one has the acute sense of being in the midst of a Faulkner novel. As in Faulkner's *Absalom, Absalom!* (which was set in a fictional Jefferson, Mississippi), we have lots of stories, all told from different perspectives, all trying to get at an elusive truth about something that happened a long time ago, something that involves slavery and miscegenation—what Ellen Randolph Coolidge, Jefferson's granddaughter, called "the thing [that] will not bear telling."[1] In all these writings we have our own Miss Rosas, our own Mr. Compsons, our own Quentins and Shreves, each seemingly with a different story to tell, each trying, like Faulkner's characters, to make sense of what happened out of "the rag-tag and bob-ends of old tales and talking." Certainly some of the recent attempts of historians to reconstruct Sally Hemings's life from the most fragmentary sorts of data surpass in imaginative ingenuity the efforts of Faulkner's characters to put together a meaningful story. Even Faulkner's crucial phrases that define his characters' diverse interpretations seem relevant to this Jefferson-Hemings story—Miss Rosa's "without rhyme or reason or shadow of excuse"; Mr. Compson's "it's just incredible. It just does not explain"; Quentin's "if I had been there I could not have seen it this plain";

and Shreve's "an awful lot of delayed information awful quick." At times
Jefferson himself even seems to resemble Thomas Sutpen, with his "entire plan and design" for his life, always weighing, measuring, and calcu-
lating, which was the source of his "innocence" and his naive belief "that
the ingredients of morality were like the ingredients of pie or cake and
once you had measured them and balanced them and mixed them and
put them into the oven it was all finished and nothing but pie or cake
could come out." Reading about Jefferson and Sally Hemings and the
Monticello household, we feel the curiosity as the Canadian outsider
Shreve, wanting desperately to know about the South. *"What's it like
there. What do they do there. Why do they live there. Why do they live at all."*[2]

Faulkner's original working title for his novel was "Dark House," a title
that might be applied equally to Jefferson's mountaintop house. Monticello may not have contained as bizarrely gothic a household as that of
Thomas Sutpen, but it was certainly an odd place. The building itself, for
all its celebrated brilliance, was peculiar, to say the least. Located on a
mountaintop, in violation, as Rhys Isaac says, of all Palladian precedent, it
was expensive to build, not easily accessible, and deficient in water—a
droll and whimsical house that was scarcely habitable by anyone but its
builder. With Jefferson continually "putting up and tearing down," Monticello was always in an unfinished state, and this, said a visitor in 1802, gave
it an appearance of "general gloom" and "decay."[3] Jefferson may have
been a genius, but he was certainly an eccentric one. He lived so method-
ically at Monticello that people could set their watches by his movements.
As master, he could scarcely have been more self-indulgent. He enjoyed
his elaborate suite of first-floor rooms, while his visitors and family struggled up cramped and narrow stairways to their quarters. His continual
"putting up and tearing down" was done, he said, simply for the sake of
his own "amusement," and he spared no expense doing it—or anything
else, for that matter. He bought wines he could not afford and, according
to his slave Isaac Jefferson, even when he dined alone he sat down to lav-
ish dinners of eight covers and had as many as thirty-two covers for
guests.[4]

The contrasts between his innocence and the real world around him
are startling. Picture him secluded in his study, down on his knees poring
over his books, twenty on the floor at one time, optimistically plotting the
future of his country even as it was careening beyond his control and un-

derstanding. Or think of him wandering about his plantation, the meticulous record keeper, jotting down every little expense while remaining unaware of his overall financial condition and the immense debt he was incurring. Or even more disturbing, see the enlightened liberal, decrying the evils of slavery even as he bought, bred, and flogged his slaves and hunted down fugitives in much the same way as his fellow Virginia planters did. Or finally picture this man, railing throughout his life against the depravity of racial mixing, even as miscegenation permeated his home and as, it now seems likely, his own mulatto offspring grew up around him. He may not be Sutpen, but he is a very strange man.

In most respects, Monticello was not so odd. It was an ideal plantation of the Old South, a self-contained patriarchal enclave set apart from the hustle and bustle of the outside world. Like many other southern planters, Jefferson regarded his slaves as members of his "family," whom he as patriarch had responsibility to protect and care for. But like all such plantations of the Old South, the ideal had to be a hollow shell, no matter how kind or gentle the master. Jefferson was never able to free most of his slaves, and he justified this failure by saying that freeing them would be "like abandoning children": they could not survive outside his kindly rule. In the end, he died so deeply in debt that the "family" that he had nurtured and controlled for sixty years had to be sold and dispersed throughout the land. So like Sutpen's design, his estate fell apart, and he ended up abandoning his "children" after all.[5]

That many of us thought Jefferson was incapable of sexually using a slave like Sally Hemings is interesting, since, as we have seen from the remarkable ongoing studies by Lucia Stanton, the senior research historian at Monticello, Jefferson was in most respects a typical slaveholder. Although he always condemned slavery, he owned one of the largest slave populations in Virginia. Upon the division of his father-in-law's estate in 1774 he became the second largest slaveholder in Albemarle County. Thereafter the number of his slaves fluctuated around 200—with increases through births offset by periodic sales to pay off debts. Jefferson was known to be a good master, reluctant to break up families or to sell slaves except for delinquency or at their request. Nevertheless, between 1784 and 1794 he disposed of 161 people by sale or gift. Jefferson was averse to separating young children from their parents, but once slave boys or girls reached the age of ten or twelve and their working lives began, they were no longer children in Jefferson's mind and therefore could be separated from their parents.

Monticello was a working plantation, and Jefferson was eager to make it pay. His slaves may have been members of his "family," but they were units of production as well. Everywhere on his plantation he sought to eliminate pockets of idleness. If a slave was too old or too sick to work in the fields, he or she was put to tending the vegetable gardens or cooking in the quarters. When one of his former head men named Nace became ill, Jefferson ordered that he be "entirely kept from labour until he recovers"; nevertheless, Nace was to spend his days indoors shelling corn or making shoes or baskets. He was willing to prescribe lighter work for women who were pregnant or rearing infant children because they were actually breeding more property; thus, said Jefferson, "a child raised every 2. years is of more profit than the crop of the best laboring man." This was one of the times, he said, when "providence has made our interest and our duties coincide perfectly."[6]

"I love industry and abhor severity," said Jefferson in 1805, and he himself apparently never physically punished a slave. Yet, as Winthrop Jordan has pointed out, the coercion of the whip fundamentally lay behind the workings of his plantation. He certainly had no scruples in ordering disobedient slaves whipped; those he could not correct he sold, often as a lesson to the other slaves. Jefferson ordered one particularly unmanageable slave to be sold so far away that it would seem to his companions "as if he were put out of the way by death."[7]

Jefferson had a deep fear of racial mixing. While he had no apprehensions about mingling white blood with that of the Indian, he never ceased expressing his "great aversion" to miscegenation between blacks and whites. When the Roman slave was freed, he "might mix with, without staining the blood of his master." When the black slave was freed, however, he had, said Jefferson, "to be removed beyond the reach of mixture." Jefferson could never really imagine freed blacks living in a white man's America, and throughout his life he insisted that any emancipation of the slaves had to be accompanied by their expulsion from the country. He could not even contemplate any "blot or mixture" on any future territory that might become part of the United States. He thus wanted all blacks sent to the West Indies, or Africa, or anywhere out of the country. Whites and blacks had to remain "as distinct as nature has made them." The blacks' "amalgamation with the other color," he said in 1814, "produces a degradation to which no lover of his country, no lover of excellence in the human character can innocently consent."[8]

Although many historians had earlier doubted the Jefferson-Hemings sexual relationship precisely because of Jefferson's lifelong antipathy to racial mixing, they may have inverted the cause and effect. Because miscegenation was going on at Monticello and throughout the South, and, as now seems probable, he himself was engaged in it, his repeated expressions of revulsion at racial mixing may have become psychologically necessary to hide the reality. Or, as Joshua Rothman suggests, perhaps it was the fact that Sally was, in the slave Isaac Jefferson's words, "mighty near white" that allowed Jefferson to cross the racial lines he had so rigidly drawn.[9] Sally was a quadroon, but her children were octoroons, and thus were considered white by Virginia law and by Jefferson's extraordinary mathematical calculations worked out in a letter of 1815.[10] Perhaps for that reason he found it easier to free them and not her.

Whatever the reasons he used to justify a sexual relationship with a black slave, Jefferson certainly sought in every way to protect his conscience from the reality of his owning hundreds of human beings. Sensitive as he was, he had to numb himself to the world around him, close his mind in a way that distanced and dehumanized the black families, including presumably his own offspring, among whom he lived throughout his life. In the infrequent descriptions of his slaves in his correspondence, Jefferson, as Stanton points out, singles them out "for characteristics—trustworthiness or unreliability, intelligence or stupidity, sobriety or drunkenness—that bear entirely on performance."[11] To Jefferson the slaves could not be real human beings, never mind persons who might be equal to him and other whites. According to his grandson Thomas Jefferson Randolph, the presence of slaves often annoyed him; he wanted none of them near him when he rode or around him at dinner, and he designed his dumbwaiters for that reason. At the White House in Washington he preferred white servants when he could get them.[12]

Only by regarding his slaves as productive machines or as something akin to his farm animals could Jefferson justify what was going on at Monticello. As he reportedly told a visiting Englishman in 1807, the "Negro race . . . were made to carry burthens."[13] He thought of his slaves, as Jordan reminds us, "as a category of people rather than as individual persons," and he showed toward them and their native African languages none of the curiosity he paid to the Indians and their languages.[14] For Jefferson, most of his slaves were and had to be merely names in an account book and, as Stanton has indicated, "only first names, and diminutives at that."[15] He mentioned Sally Hemings only a few times in his writings, and then only in passing. Unlike some other planters with the children of slave concubines (as several papers in this volume demonstrate), he showed few signs of affection toward Hemings or her offspring. Even his supposed mulatto son Madison Hemings admitted that "he was not in the habit of showing partiality or fatherly affection to us children," although "he was affectionate toward his white grandchildren."[16] As Joshua Rothman points out, Jefferson never acknowledged his slave children publicly or privately and never made any effort to prepare for their financial futures. Apparently he did not even bother to teach them to read; the Hemings children had to coax the white children in the household to help them to learn to read. Although Jefferson allowed two of Sally's children to escape and freed the remaining two in his will, he otherwise treated them with remarkable coldness and detachment. As we know, Jefferson kept track of everything that went on at Monticello. In his Farm Book he dutifully recorded not only the new colts he acquired and the hogs he killed but also the births of nearly all his slaves, including Sally's children. If Jefferson was indeed the father of at least some of these children, as now seems likely, then what are we to make of his recording the births in this unfeeling, methodical way?

Maybe Faulkner could have explained it. He certainly would have understood Monticello and what went on there, and he would have understood as well our current fascination with the Jefferson-Hemings relationship. That relationship in some sense goes to the heart of what it means to be a southerner or an American. The central issue in Faulkner's novel *Absalom, Absalom!* is the fear of miscegenation. Thomas Sutpen had become the biggest single landowner and cotton-planter in his antebellum Mississippi county. Yet, as Mr. Compson pointed out, some people always suspected something shady about Sutpen's past. "There were some among his fellow-citizens who believed even yet that there was a nigger in the woodpile somewhere."[17] "A nigger in the woodpile" is not a phrase that any educated or sensitive person would use today, but it was a crude white vulgarity referring to some secret hidden in the past. The expression actually got its meaning from the racist fears of whites that they might have secret black ancestors deep in their past. To the extent that this expression has disappeared and those fears have eased, to that extent is America's racial situation better than it was in the past.

Throughout much of American history many whites objected strenuously to the slightest suggestion of miscegenation between Jefferson and his slaves. Not only did whites depict Jefferson as too morally superior for such behavior, but, as Werner Sollors points out, racial mixing of all sorts was regarded with abhorrence. Many of us tend to forget that as late as 1966 nineteen states still forbade interracial marriages. Who can forget President Harry Truman's vulgar query: "Would you want your daughter to marry a Negro?"[18] But that world is disappearing, and our current response to the Jefferson-Hemings relationship and the DNA findings suggests that a new world is trying to emerge.

The recent DNA findings by themselves are not the cause of these changes in our perspective on Jefferson. Such reassessments have been in the works for some time; indeed, they are responses to major changes in American race relations that have been underway for the past half century or so. Thoughtful reassessment of Jefferson and Sally Hemings really began with Winthrop Jordan's magnificent study of white American attitudes toward blacks in the period up to 1812.[19] For the first time a modern professional historian had seriously considered the possibility of the sexual relationship. Once Jordan had put the issue on the table it had to be dealt with by an older generation of historians, if only to refute it. In some ways Fawn Brodie's 1974 psycho-biography of Jefferson, path-breaking as it was, tended to derail the natural trajectory of America's coming to terms with the interracial relationship. Brodie's sentimental claims of a thirty-eight-year passionate love affair between Jefferson and his slave gave critics ammunition to discredit the possibility of any sort of sexual liaison.[20] Brodie actually wanted to celebrate the popular, positive image of Jefferson by saving him from accusations of racism and sexual exploitation. If Jefferson truly loved his mulatto slave, she believed, he could not have had as much antipathy to African Americans as others had suggested.

In 1979 Barbara Chase-Riboud turned Brodie's findings into a popular novel, *Sally Hemings,* that sold a million and a half copies.[21] With the change in sexual mores since the 1960s, the American public became more accustomed to being told about the sexual peccadilloes of public figures. By the early 1990s most Americans, if not most professional historians, were prepared to accept the likelihood of some sort of sexual relationship between Jefferson and Sally Hemings.

In 1992 at a conference held at the University of Virginia celebrating the 250th anniversary of Jefferson's birth the issue of race and slavery and the Sally Hemings relationship became central to the proceedings. Once the issue of miscegenation was raised at the conference panelists and members of the audience stumbled over themselves in their eagerness to discuss it and acknowledge its reality in American life. One of the panelists at the conference, Bernadine Simmons, a vivacious and outspoken black TV journalist from Richmond, electrified the audience by claiming that all the African Americans in the room were "mongrels." Miscegenation, she said, was not something that Americans want to talk about. But look at us, she said. "We did not get to be that way because God said it would be that way. . . . It got to be that way because people were miscegenating at all hours of the day and night." The late Armstead Robinson, then director of the Carter B. Woodson Institute for Afro-American and African Studies at the University of Virginia, chimed in with a claim made by a geneticist friend that 10 to 20 percent of the so-called whites in the southern states had some mixture of black blood. Others pointed out the way in which the offspring of miscegenation, like the light-skinned Hemings family, were given privileged positions in the big houses of the slaveholding planters and the manner in which these privileges have been carried into our own time in the class distinctions maintained among blacks.

Suddenly the truth or falsity of the Hemings affair at the conference became irrelevant compared to the undoubted fact that overwhelming numbers of white slaveholders had participated in miscegenation and that, acknowledged or not, many Americans today were living with various degrees of racial mixture. No scholar, even those who found the Jefferson-Hemings liaison implausible, could deny that Jefferson presided over a household in which miscegenation was taking place. Regardless of whether he himself was directly involved, he knew that white relatives or white members of his household or his Monticello staff were having sexual relations with his slaves. Despite their dismissal of the exaggerated portrayal of a romantic Hemings affair in the 1995 Merchant and Ivory film *Jefferson in Paris,* most historians were now primed to believe what several decades earlier they had stubbornly doubted.

With the publication in 1997 of Annette Gordon-Reed's powerfully argued book *Thomas Jefferson and Sally Hemings: An American Controversy,* the resistance of many historians to the plausibility of a Jefferson-Hemings liaison seriously began to crumble.[22] The DNA findings of E. A. Foster and his colleagues, published in *Nature* in November 1998, only seemed to clinch what was already becoming a widely accepted fact.[23]

As Dr. Foster has since repeatedly pointed out, there is still some small room for questioning Jefferson's relationship with Sally Hemings. It has been suggested that any one of the male line of a male slave fathered by Jefferson's father, grandfather, or paternal uncles could have impregnated Sally Hemings, and the DNA findings would be no different. In addition the DNA finding that the supposed first of Hemings's children, Thomas Woodson, was not Jefferson's creates a problem. Although the newspaper writer James Callender identified a "Tom" as the eldest of Jefferson's mulatto children in 1802, there is considerable doubt that this Tom ever existed, or if he did, that he was the son of Jefferson and Hemings. Yet there is a long oral tradition among the black Woodson heirs that Tom was real and was the son of Jefferson. So much has been made of the validity of black oral traditions and the ways white historians used to ignore them that this Woodson oral tradition cannot now be easily dismissed.[24]

Despite these problems, clearly the burden of proof has shifted: until otherwise disproved, Jefferson is now presumed to have fathered one or more of Sally Hemings's children. Indeed, what is remarkable is the alacrity and enthusiasm with which historians, including most in this volume, have now come to accept the truth of the Jefferson-Hemings relationship. Even Annette Gordon-Reed, as she says, was unprepared for a world "without serious opposition" to her beliefs.[25] So accepting of the sexual relationship are most historians now that it will be difficult for any future scholarly cautionary notes to get heard. The historical arguments are now likely to be not over the existence of the relationship but over whether there was any affection involved in it. The paucity of evidence on the question makes it precisely the kind of issue historians delight in arguing about.

All this suggests that the present cultural climate has changed radically from what it was forty years ago. "The taboos have been lifted," declared one American professor recently, and "talking about miscegenation in families is no longer considered the horrible shaming thing it was."[26] We now seem to be at a point not only, as Jordan says, where the one-drop rule of racial identity is in a "slow process of gradual dissolution," but also where many Americans, at least white Americans, are eager to believe in the rightness of racial mixing.[27]

Some black Americans welcome the Hemings relationship because it was part of a black tradition long denied, and it represents an assertion of black humanity and at the same time makes Jefferson humanly accessible. But unlike whites, they seem less willing to celebrate the relationship as a way of easing race relations in America. They understandably resist the implications of miscegenation and interracial marriage, fearing that racial assimilation will lead to the weakening if not the disappearance of black culture and identity. Many white Americans, on the other hand, seem to welcome these implications. These whites yearn for an end to our racial problem and see in interracial marriage the ultimate solution. Yet, as Lucia Stanton and Dianne Swann-Wright point out, this yearning is undoubtedly an example of the "tendency of whites to want to make the rules about race."[28]

Nevertheless, these DNA findings will likely complicate the future of our identity politics and our searches for authentic selves. Sally Hemings was no doubt a slave, although hardly a typical field hand; her racial identity is more problematic ("mighty near white"), and the racial identities of her children and descendants are even more confusing.[29] No essay in this volume is more poignant and more revealing of our current plight than that of Stanton and Swann-Wright. To learn, as these historians did, "that Sally Hemings's children and their descendants had been changing, reconstructing, or reinforcing their racial identities through all the generations from the time of slavery until the present" is to discover "the ambiguities and absurdities of racial definitions" in America. In some sense maybe all Americans, like the dozens of living Hemings' descendants, share a common "connection to Monticello." Perhaps for all of us and not just for Eston Hemings's descendants, "Thomas Jefferson remained a primary reference point."[30]

So for both black and white Americans, Jefferson, even in his relationship with Sally Hemings, is continuing to play the symbolic role in American life that he has always played. As Merrill Peterson told us decades ago, the image of Jefferson in American culture has always been "a sensitive reflector . . . of America's troubled search for the image of itself."[31] He remains a touchstone, a measure of what we Americans are or where we are going. No figure in our history has embodied so much of our heritage and so many of our hopes. It is not surprising therefore that he should now have become a new symbol for our multicultural and multiracial society.

In 1943 at the two hundredth anniversary of his birth, Jefferson—the symbol of democracy and equal rights in our war against fascism—was seen as the solution to our problems. During the subsequent half century, largely because of his slaveholding and his racial views, he became instead the source of our problems. Now once again the wheel has turned, and he and his relationship with Sally Hemings have become a new symbol offering perhaps the possibility of some sort of racial reconciliation. All these symbolic meanings constitute what English historian David Lowenthal calls heritage and French historian Pierre Nora calls memory.[32]

Every nation needs heritage and memories, but the problem with these popular symbolic traditions is that they often tend to overwhelm and distort the actual history of the past. We Americans have a special problem in this respect. Few nations put such stock in the ideas and behavior of a generation that lived two hundred years ago as we Americans put in our "Founding Fathers." And in doing so we make a great mistake. We seriously err in canonizing and making symbols of historical figures who cannot and should not be ripped out of their own time and place. By turning Jefferson into the kind of transcendent moral hero that no authentic historically situated human being could ever be, we leave ourselves demoralized by the time-bound weaknesses of this eighteenth-century slaveholder. All this is peculiarly the burden of being an American. We Americans continually ask ourselves what Washington or Jefferson would think of some current public event or policy. Can anyone imagine asking Tony Blair's government what William Pitt would think?

In the face of their fellow citizens' massive symbolic needs, what is the historian supposed to do? Many historians try to cut these historical figures off from the present, separate them from the accumulated two centuries of heritage and image making and locate them in their own historical context. Jefferson was, historians like to say, a man of the eighteenth century, a very intelligent, bookish, slaveholding Southern planter, who was enlightened and progressive no doubt for his time, but like all human beings possessing as many weaknesses as strengths, as much folly as wisdom, as much blindness as foresight. On most matters he could not share our ideas, indeed, could not imagine our world at all. Once we put Jefferson in the context of his time he becomes a much more ordinary human being, a victim as much as a protagonist of the events in which he was caught up.

Once Jefferson's career as plantation slaveholder is seen as the career of many other southern slaveholders, many historians assume that deification of the man will stop and that Americans will cease searching for legacies that supposedly pass directly from this eighteenth-century man to our present. No doubt Jefferson made many ringing statements on behalf of liberty, equality, freedom of speech, and freedom of conscience that have resounded throughout our culture, and indeed the world's culture, during the past two hundred years. We Americans quite sensibly renew our belief in these values by periodically reinvoking and rereading Jefferson's statements. Yet we ought always to remember that Jefferson's eighteenth-century statements have been glossed, mediated, expanded, and developed by two centuries of subsequent historical experience that is just as important in sustaining our values as the original statements themselves. The legacies we have received from the past are not and should not be seen as the products of a single man of the eighteenth century, or for that matter all the Founding Fathers put together; instead, our legacies are the products of our entire accumulated historical experience.

Yet we Americans have such a vested interest in the Founding Fathers, for our jurisprudence, if for no other reason, that offsetting or undercutting the symbolic meanings of these historical figures by situating them in the peculiar circumstances of a very different past is no easy matter. Those historians who attempt to do so run great risks of undermining whatever it is that actually sustains popular interest in the past. Take, for example, Pauline Maier's book on Jefferson and the making of the Declaration of Independence.[33] This book represents contextual history in the extreme. Maier sets out to recover the actual historical circumstances surrounding the creation of the declaration, circumstances whose mundane nature puts the origins of the declaration greatly at odds with the quasireligious character it later acquired. She explains, as no one ever has before, what precisely Jefferson meant when he said that his writing of the declaration was "not to find out new principles or new arguments never before thought of . . . but to place before mankind the common sense of the subject, in terms so plain and firm as to command their assent."[34] In other words, Jefferson never claimed to be the "author" of the declaration in the modern sense of the word. Maier picks up this point and runs with it; she cuts Jefferson down to size and makes him just one figure among many in 1776, and perhaps not the most important figure in the writing of the declaration.

There is a price to be paid, however, for this sort of severe contextual history. Maier is so committed to critical contextual history—in getting the story of 1776 right—that she has no sympathy whatsoever with the symbolic memory that has grown up around Jefferson over the past two centuries. She has no compassion for what later generations of Americans have done in distorting the actual historical origins of the Declaration of Independence, in glossing, expanding, and changing its original historical meaning, in other words, creating the popular heritage that presently surrounds the declaration. She describes all the ways subsequent generations embellished, misused, and refashioned the original historical character of the declaration, and criticizes all of them. Maier even condemns Abraham Lincoln's use of the declaration to condemn slavery as bad history. She writes that Lincoln's view of the past, "was a product of political controversy, not research, and his version of what the founders meant was full of wishful suppositions."[35]

Correcting the heritage that distorts and violates the authentic history of persons and documents in the past is presumably what we critical historians are supposed to do. That may be the appropriate posture when we are correcting obvious myths like the stories of Parson Weems about George Washington. But what about the uses that Lincoln and Martin Luther King, Jr., made of Jefferson and his statements about equality? By the precise standards of critical history these uses were part of a false heritage that it is presumably the responsibility of historians to correct.

Yet, as David Lowenthal and others point out, these distortions of heritage are precisely what many people want and perhaps need in order to keep the past alive and meaningful. We critical historians thus tamper with popular heritage at our peril. Can we really cut Jefferson and the other founding fathers loose from the present without losing something valuable to the culture? Is it even possible to do so? Is critical history what Americans really want or need? Historian Nell Painter discovered this problem in presenting her revisionist and historically accurate portrait of the famous ex-slave and abolitionist preacher, Sojourner Truth. Painter came to realize that audiences and readers did not want to hear about her revisions, however historically accurate they were. And at the end of her book Painter herself seems to concede that heritage is more important than history. "The symbol of Sojourner Truth," she says, "is stronger and more essential in our culture than the complicated historic person." "The symbol we require in our public life still triumphs over scholarship."[36]

The question historians have to ask is: What precisely is it we do, or are supposed to do, in writing about a heavily symbolic figure like Jefferson, and what is the relationship of what we do to the larger popular culture? We are just beginning to assess the implications of these latest DNA findings and the Hemings relationship for our understanding of Jefferson and his times. What are we to make, for example, of historian John C. Miller's statement in 1977 that if the Sally Hemings story were true, Jefferson "deserves to be regarded as one of the most profligate liars and consummate hypocrites ever to occupy the presidency"?[37] As Gordon-Reed suggests, if the story of Hemings were true, "all that had been written about Jefferson's private life and character would have to be re-examined."[38] Given the present passions and politics involved and the popular symbolic importance of Jefferson, a disinterested historical assessment of Jefferson will not be easy. But this volume points the way.

At the end of Faulkner's *Absalom, Absalom!* Shreve the Canadian asks Quentin why he hates the South. "'I don't hate it,'" Quentin said, quickly, at once, immediately; 'I don't hate it,' he said. *I don't hate it* he thought. . . . *I don't. I don't! I don't hate it! I don't hate it!"*[39] One can imagine the American public now asking a similar question—Why do historians hate Thomas Jefferson?—and historians answering in a similar manner, quickly, at once, immediately: We don't hate him! We don't! We don't! We don't hate him! We don't hate him!

NOTES

1. Ellen Randolph Coolidge, quoted in Jan Ellen Lewis, "The White Jeffersons," chapter 6 in this volume.

2. William Faulkner, *Absalom, Absalom!* (1936; New York, 1986), 143, 12, 80, 155, 214, 211–12, 142.

3. William Howard Adams, *Jefferson's Monticello* (New York, 1983), 34–36.

4. Isaac Jefferson, "Memoirs of a Monticello Slave," in James A. Bear, Jr., ed., *Jefferson at Monticello* (Charlottesville, 1967), 13.

5. Lucia Stanton, "'Those Who Labor for My Happiness': Thomas Jefferson and His Slaves," in Peter S. Onuf, ed., *Jeffersonian Legacies* (Charlottesville, 1993), 164.

6. Ibid., 155, 150.

7. Ibid., 158, 160.

8. Thomas Jefferson (hereafter TJ) to William Short, 18 Jan. 1826, in Paul L. Ford, ed., *Writings of Thomas Jefferson,* 10 vols. (New York, 1892–97), 9:361– 62; TJ, *Notes on the State of Virginia,* Query XIV, Appendix D in this volume; TJ to James Monroe, 24 Nov. 1801, TJ to Edward Coles, 25 August 1814, both in Merrill Peterson, ed., *Thomas Jefferson: Writings* (New York, 1984), 1097, 1345.

9. Joshua D. Rothman, "James Callender and Social Knowledge of Interracial Sex in Antebellum Virginia," chapter 4 in this volume.

10. TJ to Francis C. Gray, 4 March 1815, Appendix C in this volume. Stanton, "Those Who Labor for My Happiness," 163.

12. Sarah N. Randolph, *The Domestic Life of Thomas Jefferson* (Charlottesville, 1978), 328, 309.

13. Stanton, "Those Who Labor for My Happiness," 163.

14. Winthrop D. Jordan, "Hemings and Jefferson: Redux," chapter 2 in this volume.

15. Stanton, "Those Who Labor for My Happiness," 163.

16. "Memoirs of Madison Hemings," Appendix A in this volume.

17. Faulkner, *Absalom, Absalom!* 56.

18. Werner Sollors, "Presidents, Sex, and Race," chapter 9 in this volume.

19. Winthrop D. Jordan, *White over Black: American Attitudes toward the Negro, 1550–1812* (Chapel Hill, 1968).

20. Brodie built up much of her case for the love affair through speculative readings of limited evidence. For example, she made much of the fact that TJ in his journal of his travels in southern France in 1787 used the word *mulatto* only twice in describing the soil. Then the fourteen- or fifteen-year-old Sally joined the Jefferson household in Paris, and the result, said Brodie, was that the love-stricken Jefferson in his journal for a trip through northern Europe in 1788 mentions the word eight times. Did TJ write to his supposed mistress during his trips? No letters have been found, but Brodie found it significant that the letter-index volume for this year 1788 had disappeared—the only volume missing in the forty-three-year record.

21. Annette Gordon-Reed, *Thomas Jefferson and Sally Hemings: An American Controversy* (Charlottesville, 1997), 181.

22. Ibid.

23. Eugene Foster et al., "Jefferson Fathered Slave's Last Child," *Nature,* 196 (5 Nov. 1998), 27–28.

24. During the week of 8 March 1999, shortly after the conference that produced this volume was held, I received by express mail an elaborate packet of materials from the Woodson family, arguing for the truth of the Woodson connection to TJ. The family has launched a massive public relations blitz and offered to come to my university to make a two- or three-day presentation with four presenters.

25. Annette Gordon-Reed, "'The Memories of a Few Negroes': Rescuing America's Future at Monticello," chapter 11 in this volume.

26. "The Week in Review," *The New York Times*, 28 March 1999.

27. Jordan, "Hemings and Jefferson."

28. Lucia Stanton and Dianne Swann-Wright, "Bonds of Memory: Identity and the Hemings Family," in this volume.

29. Isaac Jefferson, "Memoirs of a Monticello Slave," in Bear, Jr., ed., *Jefferson at Monticello*, 4.

30. Stanton and Swann-Wright, "Bonds of Memory."

31. Merrill Peterson, *The Jefferson Image in the American Mind* (1960; Charlottesville, 1997), vii, 9.

32. David Lowenthal, *Possessed by the Past: The Heritage Crusade and the Spoils of History* (New York, 1996); Pierre Nora, "Between Memory and History: *Les Lieux de Mémoire*," in Jacque Revel and Lynn Hunt, eds., *Histories: French Constructions of the Past* (New York, 1995), 631–43.

33. Pauline Maier, *American Scripture: Making the Declaration of Independence* (New York, 1998).

34. TJ to Henry Lee, 8 May 1825, in Peterson, ed., *Jefferson: Writings*, 1501.

35. Maier, *American Scripture*, 206.

36. Nell Irvin Painter, *Sojourner Truth: A Life, A Symbol* (New York, 1996), 287.

37. John C. Miller, *The Wolf by the Ears: Thomas Jefferson and Slavery* (New York, 1977), 176. "To give credence to the Sally Hemings story," Miller added, "is . . . to infer that there were no principles to which he was inviolably committed, that what he acclaimed as morality was no more than a rhetorical façade for self-indulgence, and that he was always prepared to make exceptions in his own case when it suited his purpose."

38. Gordon-Reed, "'The Memories of a Few Negroes.'"

39. Faulkner, *Absalom, Absalom!* 303.

CHAPTER 2

Hemings and Jefferson: Redux

Winthrop D. Jordan

Nearly forty years ago I found myself having to write something about the relationship between two individuals, Sally Hemings and Thomas Jefferson. This obligation resulted from my engagement in a larger project, a history of attitudes on the part of one group of people toward another, specifically the English and their Anglo-American progeny toward Africans and their Afro-American descendants, primarily in British North America but also in the West Indies.

The result was a long book entitled *White over Black: American Attitudes toward the Negro, 1550–1812*.[1] I undertook this project for several reasons, only some of which I was fully conscious of at the time. Primarily, it then seemed to me a worthwhile topic that no historian had previously undertaken and thus was suitable for a Ph.D. dissertation. I was happily plunging into an historiographical void, aided only by histories "of the Negro" written by such scholars as Lorenzo Johnston Greene and John Hope Franklin. These professional scholars were then deliberately and cruelly marginalized because they were "Negroes" and dealing only with what were presumed in the historical academy to be unimportant matters.

At first I thought I was also going to deal with white attitudes toward American Indians, but I quickly drew back as I began to realize that my focus on blacks presented a much larger topic than I had at first realized.

Yet, after ruling these Indian peoples out, they kept coming back into my discussion about Negroes because white Anglo-Americans seemed so persistently to have been convinced that they were a radically different kind of people than those who came from Africa.

As an undergraduate I took no history courses. Instead, I followed the less rigorous route of a broad-gauge major in "social relations," which included individual and group psychology as well as sociology and cultural anthropology. I knew that since childhood I had been interested in "prejudice" and "stereotypes," but I was not fully aware about the source of this interest. It simply never occurred to me to wonder *why* there was a large picture of a group of rifle-shouldered Negro soldiers and a white man on a horse hanging over my grandparents' mantelpiece.[2] That picture was simply there. It was not until my dissertation was nearly completed that one of my elderly grandmothers told me that "thee knows that we went over in the carriage to his house where that nice Mr. Garrison bounced me on his knee."

Since then, I have been pushed into much greater appreciation of the powerful influence of such family memories, although it is only recently that such realization has come to intersect more consciously with my life as a professional historian and the present question about Sally Hemings and Thomas Jefferson.

The book that emerged eventually from my dissertation was begun before but for the most part was written during the civil rights crises of the late 1950s and early 1960s. No one that I knew was unaware of these headlined developments. I did not read a daily newspaper or a weekly news magazine, partly because I thought I did not have the time but also because I was convinced that doing so might warp my assessments of documents written several centuries ago. As I wrote in the preface, "I have attempted . . . to avoid reading widely in the literature of the present crisis because it is frequently so tempting to read the past backwards—and very dangerous."

Only a few years previously, my thinking about intergroup relations had been profoundly shaped by another but clearly related matter, the Holocaust in Nazi-dominated Europe. Revelations about the vicious horrors and enormous dimensions of that tragedy shook me powerfully as a fourteen-year-old. My emotional reactions to the Holocaust have never gone away, and I think today that they probably influenced, in a manner that even now I do not fully understand, my perceptions about "race relations" in my own country, the United States. I know that *White over Black* was composed partly with an underflowing spirit of admonition about the fact, as it seemed to me, that this nation's problems with such relations were deep, longstanding, and seriously dangerous for all concerned.

That book included a chapter of fifty-three pages about Thomas Jefferson. Entitled "Thomas Jefferson: Self and Society," that chapter attempted to deal with what was then for me the surprising fact that Thomas Jefferson wrote more extensively and more negatively than any other of his important contemporaries about the natural mental capacities of "negroes." Yet at that time, during the early 1960s when I was reading and writing about the matter, it became clear that despite Jefferson's negative assessment of blacks, he had also genuinely yearned for their freedom even while he derogated their suitability for it.

Of the sixteen chapters in that book, the discussion of Jefferson was the only one that focused on a single person. As a subset of the larger project, the chapter deliberately commented on the interaction between one person and his larger society concerning the concept of race in the United States. Later, as further evidence turned up concerning racial attitudes, it became clear that Jefferson's conflicting viewpoints were widely accepted among his contemporaries, despite the fact that the fundamental contradiction he posed—between the evil of slavery and the inherent inferiority of its black victims—was a desperately uneasy one. This contradiction stood out, especially in light of his then well-known and now famous earlier words about what he had called "that equal Creation" (as he wrote in his draft of the Declaration of Independence) having resulted in all men being created equal.

Jefferson's most extended remarks about blacks appeared in the only book he ever wrote, *Notes on the State of Virginia,* which he began before the War of Independence was fully over in North America and first published in the new republic that called itself the United States of America in 1787–1788. His remarks were both passionate and relatively brief, and they comprised only a few pages of his book. Nonetheless, they reverberated among his contemporaries and even after his death in 1826, a death that at the time famously coincided with the death of John Adams on the same fiftieth-anniversary day of July 4, 1826. Both during Jefferson's lifetime and after, some commentators found his judgment accurate, others off-target, and still others outrageous. But when I was pursuing my project more than a century and a half after Jefferson set forth these opinions, it became clear that his words were widely read at the time and were—as historians often say rather imprecisely—"influential," since many other writers cited and commented on them.

I began this research about Jefferson by reading his *Notes on the State of Virginia,* and then most of the modern biographies of Jefferson. From that platform I plunged into the more comfortable ocean of his own published writings, first into Julian Boyd's magnificent *The Papers of Thomas Jefferson,* which alas then did not yet bring him chronologically even to becoming Washington's Secretary of State, and thence into Ford's *Works,* Lipscomb and Bergh's *Writings,* Cappon's *Complete Correspondence between Thomas Jefferson and John Adams,* and Betts's *Jefferson's Farm Book.* At that point I stopped examining Jefferson's own writings and made no effort to search out his unpublished manuscripts, my energy having collapsed under the weight of distressing awareness that over time Jefferson had written more letters than I could read, perhaps ever but certainly for my then present purposes.

During the later stages of reading and writing, I found myself trying to forget what his biographers in the twentieth century had written about him and even at times regretting that I had read them. With the considerable sense of relief brought by reading more and more of Jefferson's own words, I became acutely conscious that my view of them was different from those of his leading biographers. I began to think and have now come close to concluding that biography as a genre of history is a perilous enterprise because it usually (although not always) so rigidly fences the boundaries of inquiry as to preclude wider questions concerning the culture in which the individual lived.

At the time I wrote, however, it seemed to me that some of what Dumas Malone had written, in the 1951 second volume of his magnificent and widely acclaimed biography, showed signs of being a modernized version of Jefferson's ideas about his own life and relations with other people. Sometimes Malone seemed almost to parrot Jefferson's personal views, the ones that Jefferson held in his most optative moods.

In that volume, entitled *Jefferson and the Rights of Man,* Malone offered the following description of Jefferson's social reception upon his return from his lengthy diplomatic mission in France to his presumed "retirement" at Monticello. This event took place in 1789, at a time when Jefferson mistakenly supposed that he had no ambitions for further public service.

He got home two days before Christmas. The news of his coming, which he sent ahead in order that the house might be ready, had spread like wildfire through his farms, and the slaves had asked for and received a holiday. Their joyful reception of the Master and his daughters constituted a scene like no other that Martha [his daughter] had ever witnessed. Accounts differ as to whether the slaves actually unhitched the horses and pulled the carriage up the last ridge of the mountain, but there can be little doubt about what they did when it reached the top. They carried the Master to the house in their arms, some blubbering and some laughing, kissing his hands and feet and the ground beneath him. To their simple minds it seemed that he had come home to stay.[3]

This description, written about fifty years ago by a highly regarded biographer, powerfully suggested to me that I ought to continue my study of white attitudes toward blacks into the recent history of this country. This suicidal urge was effectively squelched by realization that such an enterprise would take nearly forever. Yet Malone's words heightened my convictions about the longstanding persistence of these negative attitudes. Had I been competent to parse such remarks, written in the mid-twentieth century, I might have offered the following paragraph:

When Malone wrote, about 1950, the prose was different, but the underlying premises about black Americans and their presumedly superior owners remained very similar to what they had been a century and half before. The words had altered rhetorically and were much more fully veiled, but the underlying assumptions still stood with their stark durability. Malone's passage deserves close attention. Today, we would distort Thomas Jefferson's world if we found anything odd in the biographer's description of Jefferson's sending ahead word that the house should be "ready." And surely we should avoid trying to modernize such phrasing as "like wildfire" into "through the grapevine," since the biographer was exactly on target about such communication among slaves. Joyful greetings of returning masters were not uncommon at American slave plantations, and they also took place in England when the servants welcomed returning squires. Yet we should not neglect the fact that Christmas-time was a customary holiday for slaves in late eighteenth-century Virginia. The reiterated capitalization of the term "the Master" was Malone's creation, not Jefferson's. As an account of an historical episode, Malone's writing disintegrated toward the end into imaginative assertions unsupported by evidence about which he, as a good biographer, was uncertain. He lapsed from his customary tone of certainty about historical evidence into such phrases as "there can be little doubt about what they did. . . ." Then, at the end, Malone, as a great admirer of Jefferson, offered a picture of the slaves' responses to Jefferson's arrival that rings now much more of the nineteenth and first half of the twentieth century than of Jefferson's time. There are other, very believable accounts of slaves welcoming home their owners, but Malone's description of Jefferson's slaves as "some blubbering" and "some laughing" while carrying Jefferson "in their arms" and "kissing his hands and feet and the ground beneath him" immediately brought to mind some older accounts about a much earlier and more famous entry into Jerusalem. More pertinently, in terms of both geography and time, this description conveyed an overwhelming whiff of magnolia blossoms that belonged more to the period of the Lost Cause and to such creative inventions as *Gone with the Wind* than to Jefferson's eighteenth-century culture. It was capped by reference concerning Jefferson's slaves to "their simple minds."[4]

It was this last phrase, especially, that pushed me from the springboard of biography into the ocean of Jefferson's own words. I hoped to achieve a more neutral and more distant stance about the historical record, but I realized then and now that my reading of this record may have been partially and perversely shaped by what were at the time the purportedly best modern biographical assessments.

I read Jefferson's letters chronologically, and by the time I got to the first decade of the nineteenth century I had nearly forgotten about Sally Hemings. James Callender's accusations concerning Jefferson's relationship with "Dusky Sally" intruded themselves much like an unwelcome, obstreperous, and thoroughly noxious gate-crasher bursting into an otherwise serious and sedate salon. My first hope was that I would not need to deal with Callender's politically and personally motivated malicious accusations because they were so transparently the work of a scandalmonger. I thought arrogantly that I had broader and more important things in mind. Like most historians then, I may have felt at first that James Callender ought not be taken seriously, since he was clearly less than a role model for historical accuracy and, even more plainly, was out for himself and decidedly not a nice person. I ended up writing five pages on the question of Sally Hemings and Thomas Jefferson, which amounted to less than a half of one percent of that book.

Those few pages included nearly as many words about the significances of the charges as about their probable truth or falsity. When I said that "the charge has been dragged after Jefferson like a dead cat through the pages of formal and informal history," I recall doubting whether even nine lives would be enough to save that poor animal. And now, here we are, still talking about its fate.

As I look back, while writing that chapter even the thought of mentioning the Hemings matter seemed a distraction, one that might best be ignored on grounds of not being pertinent. On further reflection, I began to realize that something had to be said about the purported affair, especially in light of what I had otherwise concluded about Jefferson's relationships with women.

I investigated one obvious evidentiary point about Callender's charges, because I realized with some astonishment that apparently no professional historian had bothered to inquire about where Jefferson actually was at the probable times Sally Hemings became pregnant. The birthdates of most of her children were readily available, and his own voluminous correspondence provided a remarkably complete record of his physical location during the years 1795 to 1808. Leaving aside the years in Paris, where her first child seems to have been conceived, I calculated that he was home at Monticello nine months before each birth and that he had been away for about two-thirds of the time during those years. New evidence shows that my calculations were somewhat inaccurate but not wildly off the mark. This former discovery seemed to me suggestive, both about Jefferson and about modern historical treatments of the subject, but obviously it provided no firm proof of paternity. His presence at Monticello might well have resulted in rearrangements concerning who occupied what room and most certainly would have altered the pattern of visits to the plantation not only from distant admirers and acquaintances but also from relatives and friends from the neighborhood. Yet the facts about actual paternity seemed to me far less important than his public pronouncements about the racial varieties of humankind and the relationship of these pronouncements to Jefferson's inner psychic world.

Two important books published after my brief assertion that Jefferson was physically present at the places and times Sally Hemings conceived her children have contributed to my skepticism about leaving such topics solely in the hands of biographers. In 1974 Fawn Brodie referred to "the elaborate chronologies made by Jefferson scholars which . . . demonstrate that" Thomas Jefferson and Sally Hemings were "in the same house nine months before the births of each of her seven children, and that she conceived no children when he was not there."[5] Much later, in 1997, Joseph J.

Ellis wrote that Brodie's "new evidence in fact came from Malone" and that "Malone's research revealed that Jefferson was present at Monticello nine months prior to the birth of Sally's children." But the latter statement is misleading, since Malone himself to my knowledge never publicly discussed such chronology in connection with Hemings. Ellis suggested that Jefferson "was often away at Philadelphia or Washington."[6] What I wrote in 1961 and published in 1968 included a more precise analysis of Jefferson's whereabouts. In the single sentence I devoted to the question, I got the total number of Sally Hemings's children wrong, having dismissed the infant conceived in Paris and not knowing about the recently discovered one, born in 1799, who also died in infancy. I reported my own calculation of dates directly from Jefferson's letters and from Betts's *Jefferson's Farm Book,* not from Malone's "Chronologies," which at the time did not extend to the period of most of her pregnancies. I calculated the timing of his absences with greater precision than Ellis when I wrote that during the years 1795 to 1808, "though he was away from Monticello a total of roughly two-thirds of this period, Jefferson was at home nine months prior to each birth." Recent research, based partly on materials not then available to me, shows that he was at Monticello almost exactly 50 percent of the time and that the probability that this conjunction of his visits to Monticello and Sally Hemings's conceptions having occurred by chance is about 1 percent.[7] The question then and now still seems to me much best framed in such a way, within the concept of probability. I wish I had possessed the mathematical skills to do so.

My few pages on Sally Hemings and Thomas Jefferson immediately followed a much longer discussion in the same section of that chapter, which was entitled "Thomas Jefferson: White Women and Black," about his relationships with and attitudes toward women. This was at a time when the concept of "gender" had not yet become popular among historians, but without foreknowledge about this later development I did manage to place the issue in what now seems its proper context. As I was convinced then, "The facts of the [Hemings] matter require attention not because Jefferson's behavior needs to be questioned but because they are of some (but not very much) help in understanding Jefferson's views about miscegenation and, far more, because they shed light on the cultural context in which he moved and of which we are heirs."

Jefferson's relationships with women of whatever race seemed to me rigidly strained and not consistent with the norms that prevailed in his own class and society. His love for his wife was readily apparent. Yet his grieving for her, after her early death, seemed to me to have had in its prolonged intensity not only the ring of self-pity but a feeling of injustice inflicted on the living survivor. Not long after his wife's death, he wrote his daughter, also named Martha, a detailed missive about her own proper role; it included the lofty admonition that "nothing is so disgusting to our sex as a want of cleanliness and delicacy in yours." However many of Jefferson's eighteenth-century counterparts may have shared his views, few if any such fathers issued instructions to their daughters in similarly imperial tones.

More than most of his contemporaries, Thomas Jefferson bifurcated the worlds of women and of men. Of course his own culture provided ample basis for such division, yet Jefferson's posture seemed unusual even by the standards of the day. One can gain a sense of his eccentricity—in the literal sense of that term, meaning off-center—by comparing him with two other individuals who may serve as radically different examples of how gender distinctions could be handled in that culture of the American Enlightenment. At one extreme, there was William Byrd of Virginia, who after quarrels with his wife adopted as a method of reconciliation the practice of "rogering" her at such venues as his pool table.[8] At another, there was John Adams's relationship with Abigail, between whom there were disagreements but few if any signs of outright conflict and thus no signs of such creative intervention. Read in one way, these two extreme examples can be seen as caricatures of Jefferson's world, yet both of them embodied and indeed represented a sense of engagement and intimacy between members of the opposite sex that Thomas Jefferson seemed unable to feel.

At the time when I was trying to write about the attitudes of white Americans toward blacks, I made no such gross comparisons, but I did think that Thomas Jefferson's views about differences between men and women powerfully shaped his ideas about racial distinctions, and vice versa. He seemed to have a temperamental tendency that led him insistently to slice his world into twos. This temperamental stance was transparent in many arenas, such as those that are now referenced by the words *gender, race,* and *politics.* I thought that exploring this temperamental bent was crucial to understanding his thinking.

With his "politics," this view of the world had been commented upon occasionally but had received less attention than it had deserved. When combined with his powerful felicity with the pen, his stance made him a marvelously effective revolutionary in a monarchical-versus-republican situation. Conspicuously, after its famous prologue, his draft of the Declaration of Independence consisted of paragraph after paragraph of "He has"s and a litany of dichotomous statements about the events leading to the American Revolution, of the alleged attacks by King George upon his people, and of attacks by a party of one upon the party of the whole. On the eve of another revolution, he framed his analysis of French society into such terms as *hammer and anvil* and *sheep and wolves*. Sometimes he could draw back, but only by completely denying such dual distinctions, as with the famous words of his first inaugural address: "We are all republicans: we are all federalists." These latter clauses have often and rightly been acclaimed for their conciliating nature, but they also reveal an inability to recognize a wide range of differing shades of opinion. There are numerous other examples. In the realm of politics, Jefferson always saw human society without the graded shadings of chiaroscuro. Rather, he saw them in terms of—as the phrasing goes—black and white.

Widely and justly hailed in his own time and ever since for his devotion to freedom, Jefferson—even more than most of his fellow revolutionaries—thought of freedom as the very opposite of slavery. He never deviated from his conviction about the necessity of eventual freedom for blacks. Yet he remained convinced of the need for removing freed slaves and, indeed, the much smaller number of blacks who were already free as the result of the numerous private manumissions that had been legislatively permitted in Virginia toward the end of the Revolutionary War. Having assured himself about the absolute necessity for such removal, he was never able to decide on the crucial questions about the problem—the sometime, the somehow, and the somewhere. In later life, when he self-consciously muted his public expressions of his antislavery convictions, he lapsed into a feeling of hopelessness. He simply could not find a way to achieve this goal, although he predicted disaster if the nation failed to reach it.

Nor did he change his mind about the specter of racial intermixture. Only six months before he died, in 1826, he wrote of his "aversion" to "the mixture of colour" that might come about in his country.[9] Nor did he alter his opinion about the low intellectual capacities of Africans and African Americans that his derogations of Phillis Wheatley and Benjamin Banneker had earlier made clear.

Thomas Jefferson's more direct experiences with people of African descent provide a different but congruous picture. Like most his of slaveholding contemporaries in Virginia, Thomas Jefferson was neither conspicuously cruel nor benevolent. As for his own enslaved workforce, he melded theory and practice in the then customary ways. He simply assumed that his numerous slaves constituted the mass of people necessary to provide the requisite support for his public services, his intellectual curiosities, and his hobbies, such as playing the violin and tinkering with useful inventions. He did not take these other lives into account when he had a telescope mounted at Monticello so that he could view the construction of his beloved university. Virtually none of his contemporaries, of his status, would have thought he was wrong in taking this view not only of the new University of Virginia but of the slaves who were doing much of the actual work of building it.

Yet here again, in an important sense, Thomas Jefferson was eccentric. In his huge production of letters and private records, he did not customarily write about his slaves as individuals, partly because he was temperamentally not a diarist and partly because he was away in public service from his farming operations for such long periods of time that he could not know most of them as separate persons. In this respect, the diaries of William Byrd and Landon Carter stand in marked contrast. Jefferson did not seem to know as individuals most of the people who supported his extravagant style of living. He allowed himself to become more and more deeply committed to this style, which included a nearly insatiable appetite for the best books and wines from France. It was this appetite, as well as the general and disastrous decline of Virginia's agricultural economy, that drove him in later life ever more deeply into debt and drove him also to load work upon his slaves in a desperate effort to get out from under the weight of debt that he did not want to saddle upon his recognized children. Yet in the end, he did just that. He died leaving himself and his children more deeply mired in debt than any other president. Throughout his life, he had voiced his determination to keep his slave families together. But in the end, almost all his slaves were sold at auction, with friends and families scattered and separated from each other as well as from their home grounds.

He recognized these slaves as a necessary support for his manner of living, but his interest in them was always more theoretical and programmatic than personal. Considering slaves as a category of the human species, he described their condition in America as "miserable," but he thought of them as a category of people rather than as individual persons. He made one of his most personal comments about the people he owned when he wrote instructions about his "nailers." These slaves were the some "dozen little boys from 10. to 16. years of age" whom he set to making nails as a profit-making venture during his presumed retirement at Monticello beginning in 1794. Later, not long before his first inauguration as president of the United States, he wrote from the new capital that his nailers ought not be whipped except in extreme cases because whipping tended "to degrade them in their own eyes."[10] This lofty instruction to his son-in-law remains especially revealing in light of the detailed records he kept of each individual nailer's effectiveness at production. Daily he weighed and recorded the poundage of iron rods in and the poundage of nails out for each individual nailer by name. While we can sympathize with a debt-ridden man desperately trying to extract financial profit from the font of his livelihood, a man who was encased in eighteenth-century assumptions about correct order, we can also hear in his instructions something admiring biographers have missed—Thomas Jefferson knew at a level he was unwilling to acknowledge that he lived as owner and master in a social and economic world that was fundamentally driven by the whip, as well as by the threat of sale for misbehavior.

As for his hard driving of his slaves, I should separate myself from what I wrote some forty years ago. I failed at that time to recognize the importance of fundamental changes that were taking place among the nation's African American people and particularly among those with whom Jefferson had the most intimate contact: those he owned. The world of his slaves was changing during his lifetime. My few short remarks about Sally Hemings and Thomas Jefferson were tainted by a lack of understanding about these changes, because these comments did not account for the fact that in his later years the sense of cultural distance between Virginia's slaves and slavemasters had rapidly diminished.

By the time he became a large slaveholder, most or all of Jefferson's slaves spoke English as their native language. Two years before the Declaration of Independence, the colony of Virginia effectively and permanently banned importation of slaves from Africa. Jefferson did not refer to any of his slaves as having been born in Africa and probably he did not own any who had been. Yet surely they spoke their own English with their own West African accents, rhythms, and sentence structures. Their owner never took any interest in these creolized versions of English, nor, indeed, in native African languages, although it seems likely that as a youngster he had heard at least a few of the latter actually spoken. This lack of curiosity is especially striking in light of his well-known scientific interest in Indian languages. Surely, Indian languages in one sense seemed closer to home to Jefferson. They were native to his country, in contrast to distant Africa, but in actuality he had grown up in much closer proximity to African than Indian manners of speaking. Yet he never commented on this subject. He lamented deeply losing his large accumulation of notes on the languages of the American Indians through the vandalism of thieves on his final journey home from Washington, D.C., in 1809, but with the original languages of American slaves he remained unconcerned. His posture on this subject was encapsulated by his remarks in *Notes on the State of Virginia*. There he wrote a long appendix, "Relative to the Murder of Logan's Family," and favorably compared the "Speech of Chief Logan" to "the whole orations of Demosthenes and Cicero," while pronouncing in three lines that the poems of young Phillis Wheatley were "compositions published under her name" and "below the dignity of criticism."[11] On this matter of oratorical and literary ability, Jefferson invited American Indians into the pantheon of white European accomplishment and at the same time slammed the door on the possibility that black Africans might enter.

Although Thomas Jefferson was not then or since widely acclaimed as a literary critic, the difference in these two assessments seems to me to epitomize his views of what were for him the only other two pertinent races of humankind. With Indians and whites, as he explained publicly, there should and would eventually be an intermixture, resulting finally in a melding that would end the conflict between the two groups of Americans. With blacks he retained his "aversion" to the possibility of this process. He remained determined to call for the transformation of three perceived groups of peoples into two.

The question of voice—of speech and accent—has more to do with Sally Hemings and Thomas Jefferson than might at first appear, despite his never having commented on this or anything else about her except once noting that she had given birth to a child. Lacking tape-recordings, we can only surmise. But given her ancestry and training as a lady's maid, it seems probable that her language sounded to Jefferson very much like his own. Surely it was distinct from what must have sounded to him like the guttural speech of the great majority of his slaves who had been put "into the ground" as field workers and even very different from the male members of the Hemings family whom he had elevated to various roles as craftsmen. Whether other household Hemings slaves spoke with the same tone is a matter of conjecture.

My previous treatment of Jefferson's itch for dichotomy seems to me now to have been not entirely on target. I approached the question of a Jefferson-Hemings sexual relationship without attending to two social factors that I now think may have had more importance than I realized at the time.

One is the matter of "color." It now appears odd that in a book called *White over Black,* which emphasized the historical importance of skin complexion for the perception of racial differences, that the author should have failed to pay much attention to this factor when dealing with the purported relationship with Sally Hemings. She was very light-skinned, and so were many members of her family and, much more, her children.

When I wrote, it seemed to me that in Jefferson's eyes Sally Hemings may have seemed nearly "white" to him, without altering his assessment that she stood in a separate category as a slave. Today, I think her diction may have been nearly as important as her color in shaping his thoughts about who she was. He treated all members of the Hemings family as standing in a different category than all his other slaves, and many reasons for this have been adduced. As I look back now, given my continuing conviction about his tendency to bifurcate the world, there is both illogic and logic in this view that Jefferson may well have regarded Sally Hemings as close to his own kind both in color and voice even while she was clearly so distant in both status and gender. It was the same kind of confused "reasoning" that remains with us today, confusion that results when a society develops a "one-drop rule" of racial definition and is at the same time faced with the fact of increasingly common melding over the generations.

Often, over a long period time in various states, there have been various attempts to define the difference between "white" and "black" in legal terms, with such fractions as one-quarter/three-quarters and one-eighth/seven-eighths. According to Virginia law, Sally Hemings's children were "white." But in Virginia and throughout this country, such statutory attempts at classification have customarily been disregarded in social practice. In this country, more than any other, the governing social principle remains dominant over legal definition. For in both public and private eyes, if a person appears, in physiognomy, to have any African ancestry, that individual is classified as "black." If they are not so perceived, they are "white." As a matter of daily assumption and practice, this one-drop rule about appearance trumps the law. My conviction about this derives partly from the recent publicity about the living people who regard themselves as descendants of Hemings and Jefferson, but also from more personal experience. After publication of *White over Black,* I met and heard from many people who thought I must be "black," while all my life I had been regarded and treated as "white." "In order to understand your book," one correspondent wrote, "I need to know whether you are white or black."

Perhaps the Jefferson-Hemings affair may best be considered in light of such tragically destructive confusions. Since Jefferson throughout his life was temperamentally susceptible to such clashes of logic—most obviously as a slaveholder and advocate of human equality—he may have sensed that with Sally Hemings he was entering a separate and private world where his customary dichotomizing rules did not apply. Here was space in which he could find a separate kind of comfort because the prevailing rules were not fully in place.

Such a view of his inner workings might also help explain the details of the effective but furtive manumissions of her children, and eventually of Sally Hemings herself. There were no formal deeds bestowing freedom. In various ways the children were allowed and assisted in quietly slipping-and-sliding out of the rigidly dichotomous world of slavery into a different realm of freedom where over time some became "white" and some became "black."

Today, also, I would place much greater emphasis on Jefferson's sense of cultural distance between most of the people he regarded as black and those he thought of as white. His sense of that distance must have diminished during his lifetime, but he left no direct evidence about his feelings about this development, as most people then (and for the most part now) ordinarily did not. So we are left to guess, without explicit evidence, that Thomas Jefferson found Sally Hemings at least enough one of his own to permit a sexual relationship. Her appearance, dress, demeanor, and diction may well have been sufficiently close to his world to permit him to engage with her intimately, with whatever complicated combinations of such emotions as affection and dominance we will never know.[12]

The one-drop rule that reigned in Jefferson's day and until quite recently in this country is currently undergoing a slow process of gradual dissolution. One has only to watch television to see it. Signs of this silently creeping development were becoming evident in the 1960s, although much less clearly then than now. At a time when white segregationists were vociferously denouncing the awful prospect of "amalgamation" and "mixture of the races," black male college students were embracing, more privately, the slogan "sleep white and marry black." The tangled ambiguities, or cross-ruffs, or whatever term properly describes this intermingling of such confused assessments will not go away soon. But surely these destructively explosive perceptions and postures will not be around forever, even though it is equally clear that they are not going to totally evaporate soon.

In this respect, perhaps recent developments are pulling us back toward a small part of the world Thomas Jefferson lived in. If so, the inevitable melding—in the long term—of the purportedly different peoples who constitute this nation is ironically anticipated by one of its most important founders.

What is important historically about the Hemings-Jefferson affair is that it has seemed to so many Americans to have mattered. This latter fact, rather than what actually happened between the two persons, still seems to me to constitute the best and proper ground from which to consider disclosures of the present day.

NOTES

1. Winthrop D. Jordan, *White over Black: American Attitudes toward the Negro, 1550–1812* (Chapel Hill, 1968).
2. The Saint-Gaudens friezed statue of the (black) Massachusetts 54th still stands facing

the Massachusetts statehouse. I learned much later that my grandmother's father had done much to recruit the regiment and that her uncle had become its commanding officer when Col. Shaw was killed at Ft. Wagner.

3. Dumas Malone, *Jefferson and the Rights of Man* (Boston, 1951), 246.

4. At the time, I did not know that Malone's account paraphrased a mid-nineteenth-century biography of Thomas Jefferson (hereafter TJ) that quoted at length a remembrance by Jefferson's daughter, Martha Jefferson Randolph. The "blubbering" and the "kiss[ing]" of the ground were her words. The terms "like wildfire" and "'the old master'" were those of the biographer, Henry S. Randall, *The Life of Thomas Jefferson*, 3 vols. (Philadelphia, 1865), 1:552–53. A slightly later account by Jefferson's great-granddaughter, although it differs on some details, also paraphrases some of the same terms; Sarah N. Randolph, *The Domestic Life of Thomas Jefferson, Compiled from Family Letters and Reminiscences* (New York, 1871), 152–53. Neither of these nineteenth-century accounts mentions or hints at "their simple minds." I am grateful to Lucia C. Stanton, senior research historian at the Thomas Jefferson Memorial Foundation (Monticello), for these references.

5. Fawn M. Brodie, *Thomas Jefferson: An Intimate History* (New York, 1974), 296.

6. Joseph J. Ellis, *American Sphinx: The Character of Thomas Jefferson* (New York, 1997), 304.

7. Fraser D. Neiman, "Monte Carlo Evaluation of the Relationship between Thomas Jefferson's Visits to Monticello and Sally Hemings's Conceptions," *William and Mary Quarterly* (forthcoming). Dr. Neiman is director of archaeology at Monticello; he kindly sent me a copy of this paper at the suggestion of Lucia C. Stanton.

8. A more recent study, Kenneth A. Lockridge, *On the Sources of Patriarchal Rage: The Commonplace Books of William Byrd and Thomas Jefferson and the Gendering of Power in the Eighteenth Century* (New York and London, 1992), reaches somewhat similar conclusions, although with rhetoric so distended that the conclusions often seem inflated.

9. TJ to William Short, quoted in *White over Black*, 467.

10. TJ quoted in Jordan, *White over Black*, 432–33, except for "boys," which is quoted in Lucia Stanton, "'Those Who Labor for My Happiness': Thomas Jefferson and His Slaves," in Peter S. Onuf, ed., *Jeffersonian Legacies* (Charlottesville, 1993), 153.

11. TJ quoted in Jordan, *White over Black*, 437, 477–78.

12. At the conference of authors and editors participating in this book (March 1999 at Monticello and the University of Virginia), usually there was considerable agreement. But on this question about the *affect* that prevailed between Hemings and Jefferson, there was not. I did not contribute to the occasionally heated discussion, which centered on such terms as *rape, concubinage,* and *marriage.* I thought it very unlikely that anyone today will ever know enough about the emotional contents of the Hemings-Jefferson relationship to understand it thoroughly and that such labels do little to help our understanding.

CHAPTER 3

Interracial Sex in the Chesapeake and the British Atlantic World, c. 1700–1820

Philip D. Morgan

On Saturday, 24 January 1730, forty-year-old Mann Page was dying. A distinguished member of Virginia society—educated at Eton and Oxford, a councillor at age twenty-three, twice married to daughters of prominent families—he was perhaps best known for the house he built, Rosewell, probably the largest mansion in the colony. On his deathbed, Page summoned John Clayton to draft his will. The dictation took about ten hours; by its end, the draughtman's hand was weak and trembling and Page had only two hours to live. Whenever Page's wife, doctor, or servants entered the bedchamber to minister to him, the dictation stopped. He "would not suffer any person to be in the Room," recalled Clayton, "except a little Mulatto Boy of about eight years old which he kept there to call other people when he wanted them." Who was this boy? Could it have been Page's son? If Page was not the father, presumably some other white man at Rosewell was responsible. And if not Page's son, how had the boy earned his master's special trust and favor? The mulatto boy's status and paternity are a mystery, but interracial sex had unquestionably occurred at Rosewell.[1]

In 1744 another Virginia councillor, the sixty-six-year-old "Hon[ora]ble" John Custis Esquire, otherwise known as John Custis IV, successfully petitioned the governor and council for permission to free a five- to six-year-old slave boy "Christened John but commonly called Jack, born of the body of his Negro Wench Young Alice." Four years later, Custis acknowledged to his white son, Daniel Parke Custis (who was then thirty-eight), that he was "very melancholly" at the illness of the "dear black boy Jack." Should Jack die, the old man lamented, he was sure he would soon follow suit; the boy's death would break his heart and bring his "grey hairs with sorrow to the grave," because his life was "wrapt up" in this black boy. On the day the elderly father penned this letter, he wrote a deed of manumission for Jack, incorporating the date of the license acquired from the governor and council four years earlier.[2]

Three days after recording the manumission, Custis made provision for the now nine- to ten-year-old boy. He deeded him 250 acres, along with cattle, hogs, sheep, tools, as well as Alice, Jack's mother, and her increase, and Jack's choice of four slave boys of his own age. In addition, Custis entered into a bond of £500 sterling, so that after his death, his executor would pay Jack, until he reached adulthood, the following annual items: an allowance of £20; six Princess linen shirts; a new coat, waistcoat, and breeches of strong warm cloth; two pairs of stout shoes; two pair of stockings; a hat worth five or six shillings; a "first coat" of osnaburg; a fat beef; four fat hogs; and four barrels of Indian corn. Custis meant for Jack to live well.[3]

A year later, in 1749, Custis continued to make provision for Jack. He bought a small piece of land, sixteen and a half acres in size, on Queen's Creek, adjoining Queen Mary's Port. Matthew Moody of Williamsburg was to hold this tract along with the 250 acres already deeded Jack in trust for his use; if Jack died without heir, the land would pass to George Kendall of Northampton County, where John Custis had been born. In November, Custis, now near death, made his will, confirming the deed of manumission and elaborating on his wishes for Jack's maintenance. As soon after his death as possible, Custis wanted his executor to build a handsome dwelling house according to a plan drawn up by his friend and fellow councillor, John Blair, on the small tract near the head of Queen's Creek. This house was to be furnished in middling planter style: with one dozen high Russia leather chairs; one dozen low Russia leather chairs; a Russia leather couch; three good feather beds, bedsteads and furniture; and two good black walnut tables. When Jack reached his majority, the house, a good riding horse, and two able working horses would be his. Custis gave Mrs. Anne Moody, the wife of Matthew Moody, his picture of Jack. Jack was to live with Daniel Parke Custis until he reached adulthood and was to be well maintained out of the profits of the estate already given him.[4]

Jack did not enjoy these benefits for long. On 9 September 1751, John Blair noted that about one or two in the morning "Col. Custis's Favourite Boy Jack died in about 21 hours illness." Then aged about twelve or thirteen, Jack had come down with a pain in the back of his neck, had been bled and shortly thereafter died. Some haggling occurred between George Kendall and Daniel Parke Custis over who had rights to the property destined for Jack. In 1752 the York County court noted that no evidence of "meritorious service," the only legitimate reason for freeing a slave after the passage of a law to that effect in 1723, had ever been offered in Jack's case. The court seems to have been questioning the special favor enjoyed by John Custis in freeing Jack. Kendall must have been confirmed in his ownership, for in 1753 Daniel Parke Custis bought the 266½ acres meant for Jack from Kendall for £350 Virginia currency.[5]

What is to be made of this tale? Although John Custis never acknowledged paternity, he almost certainly fathered Jack. Deeply unhappy in a nine-year marriage, and a widower for the last thirty-four years of his life, Custis was about sixty-one years of age when Jack was born. In all the letters, deeds, and indentures, Jack is always referred to as a "negro" or as "black," never a mulatto. Custis never expressed any concern for Alice, Jack's mother. The extent of his favor was the consigning of Alice and her increase to Jack. But Custis expressed great emotional concern for the boy, provided for him handsomely, and had his portrait painted. A supplicant on behalf of Daniel Parke Custis, John Custis's son, mentions winning the father's favor by presenting Jack with a horse, bridle, and saddle in Daniel's name. Remarkably, Custis acknowledged his love for Jack to his white son, and in his will he committed Jack to his half-brother's care. This provision occurred after John Custis reportedly tore up a previous will that had disinherited Daniel in favor of Jack.

Custis chose carefully when he sought people to look after Jack's interests. Matthew Moody, who held all Jack's land in trust for him, was a tavern keeper at Queen Mary's Port and also operated a ferry at Capitol Landing. He lived near, if not next to, the land on which Custis planned a house for Jack. A number of free blacks also lived at Queen Mary's Port. As Moody almost certainly dealt with a number of free black watermen in his position as ferry keeper, Custis might have supposed or known that Matthew and Anne treated free people of color fairly. For this reason, perhaps, Anne was deemed worthy of Jack's portrait; and it too might have served as a pledge, guaranteeing that Anne would safeguard the boy both in image and in reality. Similarly, Custis's decision to have his friend, John Blair, design Jack's house, may owe something to Blair's open mind. Matthew Ashby, a free black man who purchased his wife and two children and then secured their freedom, appointed Blair, "his good friend," as his executor.

Shadow families seem to have run in the Parke-Custis clan, and in others too, as will become evident. Custis's famous father-in-law, Daniel Parke II, who left Virginia to become the governor of the Leeward Islands, also left behind his wife Jane. He had taken a mistress in England, with whom he had a child. In the Caribbean, he had affairs with married women, and in his will bequeathed all his estate in the islands to his daughter, born to the wife of a member of the Antiguan assembly. His sexual behavior was one reason an angry mob of Antiguans murdered Parke in 1710.[6]

These stories of two prominent Virginians reveal how difficult, if not impossible, it is to establish the facts of interracial sex. Page may have fathered a mulatto boy, although the evidence is far from conclusive; Custis was almost certainly, although not definitively, the father of two sons—one white and the other presumably a mulatto. These two portraits suggest caution in any pursuit of the reality and myths of interracial sex in the early modern Chesapeake.[7]

Despite the difficulties of disentangling truth from fiction, this essay will attempt to explore the incidence and character of interracial sex in the Chesapeake region. It will tell stories of individuals, not just for the human interest that such tales convey but because truth often resides in the intimate details of singular lives. The essay is divided into four parts. I focus first on George Wythe for two reasons: his supposed interracial liaison is a classic example of a tale becoming "fact" by mere dint of repetition; Wythe also brings us closer to his most famous student, Thomas Jefferson. Attention then turns to broader patterns of interracial sex in the Chesapeake and to a greater range of individuals. This second section distinguishes sex between white women and black men from that between white men and black women. It also differentiates private practice from public opinion, particularly singling out traditions of interracialism in specific families, as well as identifying the broader contours of community sentiment and sanctions. In a third section, I set the patterns of interracial sex in the Chesapeake in a larger Anglo-American context, largely by reverting to a focus on individuals, highlighting the sexual behavior of Thomas Thistlewood and of William Thomas Prestwood, who will serve as Jamaican and Carolinian counterpoints, respectively, to our Chesapeake exemplars. I conclude by bringing the essay's findings to bear on the relationship of Sally Hemings and Thomas Jefferson.

❧

George Wythe was a witness to two of John Custis's indentures providing for the boy Jack. Thus, the famous teacher and jurist apparently saw the consequences of interracial sex at close quarters. He also is commonly assumed to have had a long-standing interracial liaison himself. What is the truth of this story?[8] Its veracity is all the more intriguing because Wythe was, according to many, a paragon, a model of probity, an early modern Aristides, and also a role model for Jefferson. Contemporaries described him as approaching "nearer to perfection than any man I ever saw"; as possessing "dove-like simplicity and gentleness of manner"; as upright, virtuous, learned, distinguished and beloved; as casting "light upon all around him"; and as the "most virtuous and illustrious of our citizens." No enthusiast for Virginians, the traveler Andrew Burnaby was nevertheless impressed by Wythe's "inflexible rectitude and integrity of principle, as would have dignified a Roman senator." Another witness, describing a near eighty-year-old and seemingly senile Wythe as prone "to answer the calls of nature" publicly in city streets, nonetheless testified to an "unsullied dignity" that had "gained the Esteem of all his Citizens." None waxed more eloquently than Jefferson, who referred to his mentor's "spotless virtue"; "a purer character has never lived"; he was "the Cato of his country," whose language was chaste and integrity above reproach. Did such an exalted and exemplary man have an interracial affair?[9]

The evidence in favor of such a proposition is as follows. A month after the death of his second wife, on 15 September 1787 Wythe freed Lydia Broadnax, his cook and housekeeper. Four years later, he moved to Richmond where Lydia continued to cook and keep house for him. At his death in 1806, Wythe had a fifteen-year-old mulatto boy, Michael Brown, living in his household. In his will, Wythe reserved the rents from his Richmond home and the interest from his bank stock for the support of "my freed woman Lydia Broadnax, and my freed man Benjamin [freed on 25 January 1797, when Benjamin was then more than forty-five years old], and freed boy Michael Brown" during the lives of the first two and after their deaths in trust to Michael. Finally, a half century after Wythe's death, Dr. John Dove, who claimed to have been present during the sickness (from an apparent poisoning) and death of Chancellor Wythe, declared that the judge "had a yellow woman by the name of Lydia who lived with him as wife and mistress as was quite common in this city fifty years ago with gentlemen of the older time. By this woman he had a son named Mike who was not only free looking but very intelligent & the Judge took great pleasure in educating him & made him an accomplished scholar." The case seems watertight.[10]

But more detailed probing raises questions. When Wythe freed Lydia Broadnax in 1787, she was more than forty-five years of age. He freed her shortly after his second wife's death, perhaps at his late spouse's request. At least by 1797, Lydia possessed a house in Richmond, and two years later she was taking in boarders. She continued to cook for her former master, but apparently lived elsewhere. She even hired her time in these years. She seems, then, to have been no mistress during Wythe's Richmond sojourn; indeed, it seems more likely that she was married to Benjamin, the other freed adult mentioned in Wythe's will. William DuVal, Wythe's Richmond neighbor, said, "Never had a man a more faithful servant" than she; another friend described her as "Aunt Lydy." Furthermore, Michael Brown was fifteen years old at the time of his death in 1806. Since Lydia would have been about fifty in 1791 when Michael was born, it seems highly unlikely that she was his mother, as Dr. John Dove claimed. In the early 1790s Henry Clay referred to her as "an old negro woman," again suggesting the unlikelihood of her being a recent mother. In addition, Dove's testimony is erroneous in a number of factual matters and he was apparently not present when Wythe died (he was only fourteen at the time). Moreover, a property dispute seems to have occurred between the Wythe estate and the estate of James Dove, the doctor's father, perhaps accounting for the son's malicious gossip.[11]

No contemporary testimony suggests Wythe had an interracial liaison.

Of the fourteen witnesses who testified to Wythe's poisoning, not one mentioned that Lydia Broadnax was his mistress or that Michael Brown was his son. No newspaper reported any such gossip. Wythe would have been about sixty-five when Michael Brown was born; he had no children with either of his two wives. Fawn Brodie claimed that "for a white man to leave a house and grounds to his mulatto housekeeper, and bank stock to her yellow son, and to ask none other than the President of the United States to be responsible for the boy's education seemed such an obvious advertisement of the boy's paternity that it left many of the citizens of Richmond aghast." According to Brodie, so appalled were Richmond citizens that they rushed to defend Wythe's murderer, who was in turn hastily acquitted, so that Wythe's paternal gesture could be repudiated. But Richmond citizens were not aghast; they mourned Wythe. His body lay in state in the hall of the House of Delegates, before "a great concourse of citizens" witnessed his burial in St. John's Church cemetery. Wythe's murderer was freed only because no black could testify against a white person. William Wirt recalled that Wythe "was universally beloved in the society of Richmond." In Virginia more newspaper column inches were devoted to Wythe's death than to Washington's seven years earlier, an indication of his exalted place in people's affections.[12]

Wythe was renowned for his benevolence toward African Americans and his antislavery convictions were well known. In a chancery suit of 1798 concerning the efforts of Robert Pleasants, a leading Quaker opponent of slavery, to free the slaves conditionally manumitted by his father, Wythe took the unprecedented and radical step of awarding profits to any slave who had been wrongfully held in bondage—a decision that was soon overruled. In private, too, Wythe acted on his principles. After his second wife's death, he divested himself of most of his slaves either by gift or by manumission. In the late 1780s he freed not only Lydia but Polly, a girl, and Charles, a man. In 1791 William Munford argued that it was impossible to comprehend Wythe's "divine virtues without living in his house." Would you believe it, he wrote to a friend, that Wythe was teaching Jimmy, his slave, to write? In 1797 Wythe freed Jimmy (James) as well as Ben. The wife of Judge Cabell reported that Wythe was educating Michael Brown much the same way he had Jimmy. She reported, "To test the theory that there was no natural inferiority of intellect in the negro, compared with the white man, he had one of his own servant boys and one of his nephews both educated exactly alike." Such seems to have been the reason for Michael Brown's presence in Wythe's Richmond household.[13]

So who was Michael Brown? There is no evidence that he was a former Wythe slave, manumitted by his master. Rather, Brown was a common family name among free blacks in Richmond. In 1784, for example, Dr. Robert Brown freed two children, Sally and Billy, who took his surname. Most intriguing, William DuVal, Wythe's neighbor and executor, freed a Nancy Brown, her three children, and grandchild. In 1797 DuVal sold a lot to a woman named Ann Brown, who was most likely a free black. There is no Michael among the roughly twenty individuals DuVal freed in Richmond and Henrico County, but the association between Wythe and DuVal and the latter's connections to free blacks named Brown is tantalizingly suggestive. Might not DuVal have found an orphan named Michael Brown for Wythe, or perhaps persuaded a free black family to let their son be placed with the chancellor to be educated? When Wythe, dying of poison, heard that Michael Brown had predeceased him, he is reported to have said, "Poor Boy," not using the possessive, or acknowledging Michael as his son. To be sure, Wythe in his will recommended "the freed boy Michael Brown" to Jefferson's patronage, but that act can be explained by Wythe's belief that Jefferson was an appropriate mentor. Jefferson "sincerely" regretted the loss of Michael Brown, "not only for the affliction it must have cost Mr. Wythe in his last moments, but also as it has deprived me of an object for attentions which would have gratified me unceasingly with the constant recollection & execution of the wishes of my friend." Jefferson evidently had no qualms about incorporating another mulatto into his household.[14]

Lydia Broadnax had long been known to the Jefferson family. In 1778 Martha Jefferson gave Mrs. Wythe's cook (presumably Lydia) eighteen shillings. After Wythe's death, Jefferson learned that Lydia had a small miniature, a silhouette, of his idol. He asked to borrow it so that he could get it copied by Charles Willson Peale. Lydia was prepared to hand over the original in return for a copy, but Jefferson was content with his imitation. In 1807 Jefferson sent $50 to Lydia after she asked him for assistance. In 1820, when she wrote her will, she gave all her property to Philip Wythe and Benjamin Wythe, free boys of color, grandsons of her late sister Letty Robertson. The Wythe name continued in these two boys, but they were not Lydia's children. Rather, they appear to have been the children of Isaac Judah, a prominent Richmond Jew whom Lydia named her executor, and Lydia's niece, perhaps Maria or Betsy, the two slaves Judah freed in his will.[15]

Unlike Mann Page for whom evidence of fathering a mulatto boy is scanty at best or John Custis for whom the evidence is more compelling though not conclusive, the preponderance of evidence in Wythe's case points against his having an interracial liaison. His attachment to his housekeeper, his benevolence in freeing slaves, and his educational experiment in testing the intelligence of a mulatto boy have been misinterpreted. Apparently, Wythe fathered no shadow family, although shadowy rumors have swirled around him ever since. Part of the contrast among the three men may owe something to generational differences. Custis and Page, born in the late seventeenth century, came of age in the early eighteenth century, when interracial liaisons were viewed with a fair measure of forbearance; Wythe, born in 1726, lived into the early nineteenth century, when aversion to interracial sex ran much deeper. These broader patterns of practice and changing contours of sentiment need to be sketched.

❧

Although most interracial sex in the eighteenth-century Chesapeake was between white men and black women, sex between white women and black men was not unknown. In the late seventeenth and early eighteenth century, perhaps more white women than black women gave birth to mulatto children. Certainly, many white servant women were prosecuted for the offense, and a number of free black men married white women. But, as the number of white servant women and proportion of free blacks dwindled over the course of the eighteenth century, this form of interracial sex declined, although it never ended entirely. Thus in 1729 Sarah Clarke, an indentured servant, arrived in Westmoreland County and during her servitude gave birth to "two Mulatto bastard Children." By 1775 Thomas Clarke, Sarah's grandson, was suing for his freedom, and one planter in Westmoreland was sufficiently interested in his case to reconstruct the Clarke family history. Similarly, in 1770 Thomas Jefferson tried to secure freedom for Samuel Howell on the basis that he too descended from a white woman, probably a servant. Much earlier in the century, Howell's grandmother was born a mulatto, "begotten on a white woman by a negro man." Edward Tarr can stand as an example of a free black married to a white woman. In 1754 he purchased a 270-acre farm in Augusta County and served as the local blacksmith to an extensive white clientele. He participated vigorously in the social and economic life of his predominantly white neighborhood and was married to a Scot named Ann Moore.[16]

White women faced legal strictures and hostile opinion for living with black men. In 1731 one white woman in Northampton County accused another of being "a Negro whore and Negros strumpet [who] . . . would have Jumpt over nine hedges to have had a Negroe." Slanderous speech about interracial sex was now more commonplace. Seven years later, Tamar Smith, a white woman living in the same county, served a six-month imprisonment and paid a fine of ten pounds for marrying a mulatto man. In 1763, after a decade of turning a blind eye to Tarr's relationship with Moore, an Augusta County grand jury, apparently inspired by an enemy of Tarr's, presented her for "living and Cohabiting with a Negro called Ned." Two years later she was convicted of the offense and received a punitive fine. In 1764 a Virginia master claimed that a white woman had "decoyed" away his male slave, with whom she had a child. By aiding and abetting a runaway, this woman compounded her crime. Five years later, the wife of a prominent gentleman of Calvert County, Maryland, committed the cardinal sin of giving birth to a black child. Her husband registered his disgust in the local newspaper, by railing at her for "pollut[ing]" his bed. In 1785 the members of a Baptist Church in Stafford County, Virginia, registered their strong displeasure at the behavior of Susan Leftrage, who scandalously had committed fornication "by cohabiting with a negro." In the mid-1790s William Faris, an Annapolis watchmaker and silversmith, noted two local scandals in his diary. The first concerned a report that Captain James West had called off his marriage to Peggy Whitaker when he discovered Peggy's sister had a mulatto or black husband. The marriage seems to have taken place three months later, perhaps because Lydia Whitaker, Peggy's sister, was proved to have married a white man. The second concerned a young white woman named Nancy Quynn who left for Frederick County, Maryland, accompanied by her brother Allen because "the town says she is with child and not of her own color." Rumors of relations between white women and black men were enough to bring disgrace.[17]

Yet general hostility to unions between white women and black men could coexist with a measure of local toleration. In 1795 Absalom Fears, a yeoman farmer, who then owned two hundred acres in Prince Edward County, Virginia, permitted his daughter Elizabeth to marry a fellow yeoman, James Dungey. The married couple soon settled on two hundred acres of their own, purchased by Dungey next to his new father-in-law's farm. The Fearses were white, and James Dungey was black—or, more precisely, mulatto. As with the Parke-Custis clan, interracialism was a tradition in the extended Fears-Dungey family. James and Elizabeth Dungey's son Absalom, named after his white grandfather, took a white woman as his partner in the late 1820s. In the late 1810s the household of Elizabeth's brother, William Fears, contained a free black man named James Fears, a blacksmith. The Fearses were no doubt unusual in their open acceptance of an interracial marriage within the family, but their white neighbors seemingly came to terms with the match. As Melvin Ely writes, "white officials referred to Elizabeth as 'Mrs. Dungey'; her marriage had not cost her that everyday honorific." The Dungeys played a full role in community life—even getting permission to reroute the local road so that it would come by their house and having it maintained at county expense—and seem to have been accepted as an integral part of local society.[18]

Divorce petitions in early national Virginia also demonstrate that some white women who were either married or about to be married to white husbands were willing to engage in sex with black or mulatto men. From 1803 to 1820 eleven white men filed petitions for divorce accusing their wives of interracial adultery. The birth of a mulatto child, normally conceived before the marriage, was the usual grounds for the petition. Husbands usually labeled their wives as "degraded" and themselves as outraged and embarrassed. The wives were usually contrite, although Betsy Mosby of Powhatan County spiritedly declared that she "had not been the first, nor would she be the last guilty of such an act, and that she saw no more harm in a white woman's having a black child than in a white man's having one, though the latter was more frequent."[19]

Although a constant but low-level incidence of sex between white woman and black men occurred throughout the century, interracial sex in the early modern Chesapeake, as Betsy Mosby rightly observed, was predominantly between white men and black women. The former practice was often tolerated; the latter was tacitly accepted, sometimes openly permitted. In the late seventeenth century a white man in Lancaster County lived "without disguise" with a mulatto woman and promised her marriage but died before he could make good on his promise. In the first decade of the eighteenth century a Northern Neck planter, Stephen Loyde, openly recorded the birthdates of his two illegitimate children. As he noted in his diary, both were born "of Rachel a negro woman." Some masters preyed on slave women, who were clearly viewed as fair game for men's advances. William Byrd II approached slave and servant women indiscriminately. Even as a sixty-seven-year-old he played "the fool with Sally." John Hartwell Cocke, friend to the sage of Monticello, recalled that, in Jefferson's day, many masters had slave families, cited "Jefferson's notorious example," and also identified the "damnable practice" of bachelor plantation owners keeping slave mistresses, a practice he thought more common in Virginia than elsewhere.[20]

A certain measure of easy-going, promiscuous behavior on the part of white men was taken for granted. That slave women wore little clothing may have encouraged white men to see them as accessible. Young white men were expected to sow their oats in the slave quarters. Eighteen-year-old Ben Carter reportedly took a young maid named Sukey into the stable "and there for a considerable time lock'd" themselves together. Six months later, the Carter household "whispered" with rumors that Ben had broken into the nursery in order to "commit fornication with Sukey (a plump, sleek, likely Negro Girl about sixteen)." The casual humor attached to white male–black female sex is intimated in a letter from Judith Sheppard to her brother-in-law, Philip Sheppard. She begins "Dear Black Philip," and jokes with him about his trip to Prince Edward County to "pay his addresses" to a Miss Agness W. She reports that Philip's brother, her husband Joseph, had "laughed very much at the manner in which you contracted Agness." In a previous letter Philip apparently had said that he wanted very much to see his "lovely, divine and angelical fair A-SS." Joseph's response was to say "you might see a *brown* one without going to P. Edward." To cover her modesty, Judith adds, "you must not think I had anything to do with the expression, more than having the impudence to write what he said."[21]

For the most part, masters were not especially concerned about their overseers' liaisons with slaves, as long as general order prevailed. Father John Ashton, chaplain to Charles Carroll, complained that one of Carroll's overseers had become intimately involved with a female slave who lived with her husband and children. Carroll found Ashton's interference irritating. Removing the slave woman from the quarter required finding another "good house wench" to replace her. Acknowledging that "the crime of adultery is certainly great"—and thereby tacitly recognizing the slave marriage—Carroll doubted that altering the slave woman's situation would prevent it. He supposed that the overseer was "too fond" of the slave woman. Carroll concluded irritably in Latin to the effect that the gods will punish religious offenses, lamented ever sending for a priest, and expressed the typical planter claim that he wanted to keep the slave woman "in our family."[22]

Some masters became, as did Thomas Wright of Campbell County, "much attached" to their lovers. In Wright's case, his "very black" woman Sylvee bore him four mulatto children between 1780 and 1793. He eventually freed Sylvee and the children, providing for her after his death. In 1791 he freed "his Robin" (as he called eleven-year-old Robert, his eldest son), told friends that the boy would be his heir, and gave him a horse to ride to school. The proud father boasted that his son—usually described as a "light" or "bright" mulatto—was one of the "strongest negro fellows" in the county. After Thomas Wright's death in 1805, Robert Wright inherited his father's plantation and six adult slaves; a year later he married a white woman—again indicating how interracialism followed family lines. Robert's marriage was contrary to law but aroused no controversy among his neighbors. Indeed, when his marriage foundered in 1816, many solid white citizens endorsed his divorce petition, testifying that Robert was "an honest, upright man, and good citizen." Although his petition failed, Robert Wright persuaded another white woman to live with him until his death in 1818.[23]

George Calvert, a notable Maryland figure, had a long-lived interracial liaison and fathered a large shadow family. George's father was an illegitimate but acknowledged son, and George's sister married John Parke Custis, who was John Custis IV's grandson—so illegitimacy and interracialism again ran in the family. After his father's death in 1788, George Calvert, aged twenty, assumed the management of his father's slaves in Prince George's County, Maryland. He soon formed a relationship with a slave named Eleanor Beckett, otherwise known as Charlotte or Nellie, of Native American and African ancestry. Their first child, Anne, was born in

1790; the second, Caroline, was born three years later. Both would later take the Calvert surname. Calvert and Eleanor had at least three more children together—Cyrus, Charlotte, and John. In 1799 George married a white woman, Rosalie Stier, and they had nine children, the firstborn sharing a name with his second-eldest slave daughter. Two years after his marriage, Calvert freed ten of his slaves, including Eleanor Beckett and her five children. His black family continued to live on the plantation for another decade. Rosalie never mentioned their existence, although it is difficult to imagine that she was unaware of their presence. By all accounts, George and Rosalie lived a happy married life for twenty-one years; George described himself as "lost" and "afflicted" when Rosalie died at age forty-three. Apparently, Eleanor Beckett married William Norris, an Englishman, about the same time Calvert married Rosalie Stier. It seems to have been an arranged marriage. Norris is said to have died of a broken heart after finding out that his wife was still bearing Calvert's children. In the second decade of the nineteenth century, after Norris's death, Calvert relocated the Beckett family to land he owned in Montgomery County. In the early 1820s, after Rosalie's death, Calvert reaffirmed the freedom of Eleanor, their children, and then grandchildren, and also proceeded to free other of Eleanor's children—perhaps his children. Thus in 1822 he freed two young mulatto women, Charlotte and Sophia Norris, both born about 1803. Several years later, he freed Matilda Norris, another mulatto, born about 1805. These could have been Eleanor Beckett's daughters by Norris or by Calvert while she was living with Norris. In 1827 he freed a mulatto man named William Beckett, about twenty-one, presumably another of Eleanor's children. In all, Calvert freed twenty-three members of the Beckett-Norris clan.

The second generation of mulatto Calverts continued the tradition of interracial liaisons. About 1812 Caroline Calvert, as she called herself—George Calvert and Eleanor Beckett's second-oldest daughter—met Thomas Cramphin, Jr., a seventy-two-year-old planter and landholder who had served three terms in the Maryland legislature. Cramphin, who had never married, took Caroline as his common-law wife. They lived together for about nineteen years and had nine children. Cramphin must have been about ninety when he fathered his last child. In his 1824 will, Cramphin acknowledged that Caroline was living with him and had given birth to his children. He provided handsomely for her and delegated his

end George Calvert" the trustee for the support and edu-
nd Caroline's children. Three of Thomas and Caroline's
ge's grandchildren—shared names with George's white

attern of naming is evident in Stephen Hughes's family,
who lived in Jefferson country, Albemarle County. In 1798 Hughes, a
planter who owned more than 1,000 acres, freed a slave woman named
Chancy and her five children, Elizah, Louisa, Hastings, Johanna, and
Sophia. Peter Marks, a prominent Albemarle businessman who had
owned Chancy and her five children, had sold them to Hughes three years
earlier. Chancy may have been the Marks's mulatto daughter. Three of
her five children, fathered by Hughes, shared the names of Marks's white
children. When Chancy became free, she and her oldest son Hastings,
then taking the surname Hughes, moved to a plot of land adjoining
Hughes's property. In 1801, she gave birth to Mary Hughes and three years
later to Betsy Hughes, yet again borrowing names of Peter Marks's white
children, further indicating the entanglement of white and black families.
Thirty years after her birth, Mary Hughes would marry Madison Hemings, a former slave of Thomas Jefferson, thus becoming the daughter-in-
law of the mulatto half-sister of Jefferson's wife. The interracial web became intricate and extensive in Albemarle County.[25]

The network of interracial connections also radiated out from Monticello. As Lucia Stanton notes, "several and perhaps all of Betty Hemings's
daughters formed relationships with white men." In the late 1780s, one of
those daughters, Mary Hemings, the sister of Sally Hemings, was hired
out to Thomas Bell, a white merchant in Charlottesville, whom Jefferson
described as "a man remarkable for his integrity." Bell indicated his fair-
ness to people of color by managing the money of Nancy West, the mulatto daughter of a white planter and later common-law wife to a Jewish
merchant in Charlottesville. After a few years of working for Bell, Mary
asked to be sold to him, along with the two children he had fathered. Jefferson complied, and Bell later freed his family. Residing near the court
square in Charlottesville, Thomas and Mary Bell were an interracial couple. When Bell died he willed most of his estate to his wife as a life estate,
with the property ultimately going to their children, Robert Washington
and Sarah Jefferson Bell—the names again suggesting the connections to
prominent Virginia families.[26]

The examples of the Wright, Calvert, Hughes-Hemings, and Bell-Hemings clans suggest an easy acknowledgment of interracial liaisons in the late eighteenth century, but this impression is somewhat misleading. White men's liaisons with black women could be tolerated, especially if carried out discreetly; but public condemnation easily surfaced. Discretion, for example, was expected of clergymen; thus, the Reverend Patrick Lunan of Nansemond County found himself roundly condemned for, among other things, his solicitation of "Negro and other women to commit the crimes of fornication and adultery with him." Community standards were often given an idealized gloss for the benefit of outsiders. Travelers to the late eighteenth-century Chesapeake reported that a man's reputation could be ruined by fathering a mulatto child. Such a man "would be scorned, dishonored; every house would be closed to him; he would be detested." Another visitor noted that public opinion was firmly against miscegenation, so much so that "no white man is known to live regularly with a black woman." In 1784 a Maryland woman broke off her intended marriage because of "the Tale of a Tale about a Negro Woman and several children" in her prospective husband's past. Another woman contested the story, saying the mistress was "not a black woman but a mustee and is a very pretty woman with only one child." Apparently, a mustee was a more acceptable mistress than a black woman. Strong admonitions against interracial sex were backed up by laws, and some attempted to tighten the legal sanctions. In 1803 a Norfolk newspaper carried a petition requesting a law to prevent "any white woman from haveing a black husband and to prevent white men from haveing black or yellow wifes or sleeping with them." If such occurrences were discovered, the petition continued, both parties should have thirty-nine lashes on the bare back. Many inhabitants of the commonwealth, this report noted, believed that more injuries flowed from the vice of interracial sex than from gambling. A year later a grand jury in Petersburg complained of free blacks and mulattoes coming to town, many of whom "come only for the purpose of Prostitution to the ruin of the morals as well as of the Health of the younger part of the community," and sought action to curtail the alleged practice.[27]

In their wills, whites rarely mentioned special provisions for children sired with black women. In a study of 3,190 Maryland wills between 1634 and 1713, Debra Meyers found only a handful that suggest white paternity of mulatto children. Perhaps the "negro boy Thomas" that Thomas Gerard wanted baptized and for whom he set aside 1,000 pounds of tobacco to pay for his education was his son. But the only explicit case occurred in 1682 when Timothy Goodridge left his entire estate to his friend, Phoebe Loftus. Goodridge stipulated that his four mulatto children were to serve Phoebe until they turned thirty-one. The same applied to any other children conceived or born to Joane Sangoe (presumably a black woman) before he died. Similarly, a search of eighteenth-century York County, Virginia, wills turns up little. An exception is in 1781 when Thomas Jarvis, then aged forty-one and a small slaveholder, provided that his "mulatto boy Billy whom I believe to be my son" should be set free. Jarvis wanted Billy bound to James Honey, a cabinetmaker in Williamsburg. He also desired his executors to purchase two mulatto children, Billy's brother Johnny and sister Franky, belonging to Nathaniel Burwell, to set them free. Jarvis gave Billy two slaves and the balance of his estate. Billy was about thirteen when Jarvis died. In 1810 he would be described as "a bright mulatto."[28]

Even when manumissions were at their most liberal in the early national period, few concerned children whose white fathers admitted parentage. Of about nine hundred individuals manumitted in the towns of Alexandria, Fredericksburg, Norfolk, Petersburg, Richmond, and Williamsburg in the early national era, only six children were freed by fathers who acknowledged paternity. One of the fathers, Joseph Ashlin, who manumitted four children in Richmond in 1807, seems to have been ashamed of his behavior. "It has been my misfortune," he contritely declared, "from and by a connection carnally with a woman of colour, to bring into creation" four children named William Barrett, Salley Barrett, Frances Barrett, and Cyrus Barrett. Only Cyrus lived with his father; the other three resided with separate masters. All four presumably took the surname of their mother, not their father. Noting that Virginia now prohibited "a general emancipation," Ashlin begged, solicited, and prayed for his children's freedom on the basis of his "peculiar situation." In the previous year in Norfolk, R. Demoiter freed his two mulatto children. Since he was almost certainly a French refugee from Santo Domingo, he was probably acting according to Caribbean rather than North American norms.[29]

In the islands, masters openly lived in unions with slave women and often provided for their mulatto children. In Edward Long's condemnatory words, white men tended to "riot in goatish embraces." Black concubinage was part of the fabric of the social landscape. The magnitude of the difference between mainland and island is captured in Virginia merchant John Hook's ruminations about his brother Duncan, then resident in Jamaica. In a 1779 letter, John writes metaphorically of Duncan's fall from grace, of "a blot" on his "Escutcheon," of a "ship wreck" that "is not only disgracefull but in time will be a bitter sting to all those Gentlemen who forms such connections." The practice (of establishing an interracial family) "is too fashionable in Jamaica," he continues, "and is held in deserved contempt universally through this continent." Despite his strong feelings, however, he will not press the issue with Duncan "from motives of Delicacy," not meaning to "upbraid or insult his weakness." He is aware of the predicament of a man rearing a family "of whom he is ashamed" and yet "where his affections undoubtedly is placed." The ties of nature "bind mankind," John knows, "in spite of every effort to the contrary." But, he declares, any man with "a single spark of sensibility" will forever rest uneasy, thinking "how much better would it have been for him to have married a white woman." Virginia mores, as expressed by John Hook, were the opposite of those prevailing in Jamaica.[30]

A brief consideration of one Caribbean master will help confirm the difference between island and mainland customs and thereby put the Chesapeake experience in perspective. Almost as soon as he arrived in Jamaica in 1749, Thomas Thistlewood, an English immigrant, noted in his diary that an elderly Kingston man that he met had "a genteel mulatoo girl" as his mistress. Living openly with slave or free mulatto concubines was normal island behavior, and Thistlewood accommodated readily, never attempting to marry a white woman but confining his attentions to black women. Restrictions on white women in the islands were, if anything, even more rigid than on the mainland. John Stedman recognized the region's double standard when he observed that "any European female [who] had intercourse with a slave . . . is forever detested and the slave loses his life without mercy—such are the despotic laws of men over the weaker sex." Thistlewood was once shocked to hear a report of a Mrs. Cocker who "made free with one of Michigan's Negro fellows!" He registered his surprise, "Strange, if true," but he thought the story believable.[31]

Thistlewood exemplifies the white man as sexual predator. His sexual exploitation widened and deepened over time as he made sexual advances on a growing number of women. He seems to have targeted African women, perhaps because they were especially vulnerable, with fewer attachments among the slave men; perhaps they seemed more exotic to him. He was surrounded by more Africans than Creoles, but he also gravitated toward the newcomers, having sex with four times as many immigrant as native slaves. He also singled out girls. Casual exploitation is suggested by the time (usually afternoons on a sugar estate on which he was overseer, and then mornings when he established his own estate, with Wednesday always the most popular day) and place (often a field or structure associated with the working environment) of many of his sexual encounters. This was opportunistic predation, exploiting women when and where they worked. Compulsive experimentation is suggested by his coupling just once with two-thirds of all his many partners. Finally, Thistlewood often had sex with runaway slave women he captured; they were truly defenseless.[32]

White men extended their dominion over black women to the bed as one way—perhaps the best way, from their perspective—to demonstrate their mastery. The sex act served as ritualistic reinforcement of the daily pattern of social dominance. Nowhere was this more nakedly apparent than in the islands. Thistlewood on occasion had sex publicly, noting the presence of individual slaves or in a few cases of many slaves. He sometimes saw and often heard of assaults by whites on slave women—a gang rape by four guests of one employer, a vicious sexual attack by a sailor on one slave woman, even the burning of a recalcitrant slave woman by two rejected white suitors. Thistlewood took advantage of his power to exploit women sexually on a massive scale. Throughout his thirties and forties, he had sex at least twice, usually three times, a week. Even in his sixties, he had sex on average every four days with between six and twelve women a year. In the last year of his life, when he was sixty-five, he had sex more than once a week; on ten occasions he noted that the sexual act occurred with the slave woman standing with her back to him.[33]

Slave women were not entirely defenseless in their encounters with sexual adventurers such as Thistlewood. Most of Thistlewood's sexual activity took place not at the workplace or outside but in his house. Presumably, he let it be known that he would welcome a visit from a particular slave. Slave women sometimes rejected Thistlewood's and other whites' sexual advances. Slave women could also take advantage of the need of most whites, even Thistlewood, for emotional attachment as well as sexual release. One of Thistlewood's subordinates, a bookkeeper, was so infatuated with his slave mistress that he hysterically abused her owners "in an extraordinary manner" when they punished her. According to Thistlewood, this slave woman led her besotted lover on a merry dance, pretending illnesses to get out of work, while the bookkeeper "humoured" and indulged her. Coobah, a privileged slave, had a frank view of sex, marking on a fellow slave's "smock bosom" the initials of three men who were then, respectively, her husband, her "sweetheart" (both slaves), and the one "she is supposed to love the best" (a white man). She ornamented the smock with three figures, apparently representing clouds—presumably indicating her dreams—and then appended the following ditty:

> Here's meat for money
> If you're fit, I'm ready
> But take care you don't flash in the pan.[34]

A slave woman's strategy and its risks are revealed in two incidents. John Thistlewood, Thomas's nephew who came to work under his uncle's tutelage in 1763, relates the first. One Sunday in 1765 Lettice, "a very likely wench of the Mandingo Countrey" who spoke "good English," visited John and tried "to perswade" him "if possible to ly with her." The woman explained that she was the mistress of a white man on a neighboring estate. Her master for some unspecified reason—perhaps impotence—was unable to provide her with a child. She told John that she "wanted to have a child for a master." Giving birth to a mulatto child, this African woman no doubt surmised, would be a way to consolidate her position and eke out favors. Being the mother to a white man's child would raise her status. She told John that she would come again the following night when she knew he would be working in the boiling house. The other incident arose from a seeming casual conversation Thistlewood recorded. One of his acquaintances reported that he had cut off his mulatto sweetheart's upper lip, close to the nose, in a jealous rage after she gave birth to "too dark" a child. The man added, "a Negroe should never kiss those lips he had." He apparently also kept two other women as mistresses: the sister of the one he had violated and a white woman.

The chilling lesson they had just learned no doubt had its intended effect.[35]

Most of Thistlewood's sexual encounters occurred with just a few women—about one in ten of all his sexual partners. These regular partners often extracted favors for sex. In one year two women made enough cash to buy a year's supply of food or two to three yards of fine cloth. Once on his own estate, he began paying considerable money for sex—between 1s 6d and 2s 6d on each occasion. Moreover, Thistlewood always had one woman to whom he was more closely attached than to any other. From late 1753 onward this woman was Phibbah, a Creole and a housekeeper. She made significant material gains through her association with Thistlewood. She owned pigs, poultry, and horses; she entered into an agreement with a nearby slave driver, who in return for furnishing a stallion for her mare was to have every third foal. She even owned another slave whom she sometimes hired out for wages. And she regularly lent large sums of money to Thistlewood. Their son John was freed at age two, and she too would finally gain her freedom after Thistlewood's death. Interracial sex was not only exploitation, it could occasionally involve exchange—however asymmetrical.[36]

Thistlewood's relationship with Phibbah cannot be adequately summarized as racial oppression on his part and the extraction of material favors on hers. It was both of these but much more. Consider Phibbah's actions when pregnant. During her confinement, she brought a slave woman for Thistlewood to "keep as a sweetheart." When he inevitably strayed to another woman, Phibbah had her property removed from his house, rejected his gifts, and remonstrated with him, obviously aggrieved at the insult she had received. She had affairs with other men, most particularly with her owner and Thistlewood's employer, no doubt a calculated rebuke to her philandering mate, whose jealousy was aroused but who could do little about it. After one tiff, she moved out and only returned when Thistlewood sent an emissary to intercede with her. She was able to travel without leave. She spoke up for other slaves. When a white bookkeeper drunkenly rounded on her "in a strange Billingsgate language," she gave as good as she got, with Thistlewood approving his mistress's stand, taking her side. Phibbah's major test came three years after their relationship began, when he decided, after arguments with his employer, to take a new job on a nearby estate. Although, as he put it, she "grieved very much" at his impending departure, and he conceded that he could not sleep at the prospect of leaving her, she refused to go with him. Instead, she embarked on a campaign to win him back. She visited him frequently, showered him with gifts, revealed that she was "sick" with longing for him, which elicited one of his few expressions of real emotion when he expressed pity and sympathy for her because she lived in "Miserable Slavery." He acknowledged that he was "mighty lonesome" when she was not there, and eventually he agreed to return. Phibbah had won a victory, but as with many small triumphs by slaves it was bittersweet, for Thistlewood arrived back not just keen to renew his association with her but also suffering a fresh bout of venereal disease.[37]

The one place on the British American mainland that had close affinities with the Caribbean was South Carolina. Many white Carolinians countenanced concubinage far more readily than did Chesapeake whites: it presented less danger to fundamental social distinctions, a lack of white women encouraged it, and religious sanctions against the practice had far less effect. A Frenchman was sure that the inhabitants of the Carolinas were "less scrupulous" about interracial affairs than their Chesapeake counterparts. Some visitors to the low country were shocked by the openness with which white men consorted with black women. In 1773 a New Englander visiting South Carolina observed that "the enjoyment of a negro or mulatto woman is spoken of as quite a common thing: no reluctance delicacy or shame is made about the matter." The one visitor who is on record as being surprised by the relative "privacy" with which interracial "conversations" were conducted was from the West Indies, where concubinage was even more extensive and more openly acknowledged than in the Carolinas.[38]

For a personal view of Carolinian sexual mores, the experiences of William Thomas Prestwood, who lived his first twenty-five years in South Carolina and the rest of his life in North Carolina, are instructive. Born in 1788, Prestwood became a teacher and surveyor. He kept a coded diary, extant volumes of which date from 1808. During his twentieth year, he noted eight sexual encounters with Binah, a slave owned by his mother, and one encounter with a white woman whom he "did not promise to marry." His sister "hinted" that she knew that "Bynah [was] his mistress," so his liaison was no secret, and he replied that he "would have two mistresses in twelve months." On another occasion, he recorded that a fellow white man "planned to steal" Binah from him, suggesting again a general interest in slave women. In October Binah told Prestwood that she was "breeding," and he gave her "powder," presumably an abortificient. He continued to have sex with Binah and by 1813 began using a symbol of an upturned *v* with a dot near the apex to signify their sexual encounters (a crude representation of her sexual being). According to his records, he and Binah had sex about six or seven times a year in the early 1810s; occasionally he had sex with other women (usually white women, it would seem). In early July 1817 he "heard" that Binah had a child, but nothing more was said. The diary is cryptic and laconic, but Binah seems not to have meant much to him, although he noted on one occasion telling a white man not to beat her.[39]

From March 1818 onward he began having sex with Celia Clarke, a white woman, whom he would eventually marry on 14 May 1820. Sex with Celia occurred regularly, on average about every three days, although he did not give up Binah entirely, recording ten sexual encounters with her over these two years and two months (as against 190 sexual acts with Celia). After his marriage, he rarely mentioned sexual encounters with his wife (usually only to record when they resumed after childbirth). Sex with Binah did not quite stop—there was one occasion in 1827 and another in 1829—but in 1831 she died and Prestwood did no more than note her burial. Sex was mentioned infrequently thereafter, until Prestwood turned sixty-one, when he began a relationship with a (presumably, white) widow known only as CR. The liaison lasted the remaining ten years of his life, and in that time he recorded 305 sexual encounters with her, from a high of about once a week in the first year to a low of about once a month in the last. Encounters took place mostly in fields, lofts, and closets, and most of the time encounters were "good" or sometimes "sweet" but occasionally failed. Despite this late flourish to Prestwood's sexual activity, he was no sexual athlete, certainly not in Thistlewood's league. Nor, despite his unusual mention of sex with a slave, are his interracial sexual encounters anywhere as extensive as Thistlewood's. Too much cannot be read into just two diaries, but the contrasts between mainland and islands, even Carolinas and Jamaica, seem as striking as the comparisons.[40]

❧

This sketch of patterns of interracial sex in the early Chesapeake and wider Atlantic world helps establish the context for understanding

Thomas Jefferson's relationship with Sally Hemings. Interracial sex took many forms in British America. In those cases where the male partner was white and the female black—the typical pattern for most of the eighteenth century—it ranged from deep commitment on the part of the white man to his black partner and mulatto children to the most outrageous forms of sexual abuse. Jefferson's behavior probably fell somewhere in the middle. It makes little sense to assert that Jefferson raped Sally or that their relationship was the functional equivalent of a loving marriage. A more nuanced picture, as evident in many of the relationships previously described, is possible.

On the one hand, the relationship between Jefferson and Hemings, as with all slaveowner-slave relationships, was ultimately a forced embrace. Jefferson owned and controlled Sally Hemings. Sexual access to slave women was one of the prerogatives of ownership. The word used by Madison Hemings (as well as by Isaac Jefferson and James Callender) to describe his mother (and also his grandmother) was *concubine,* which in Samuel Johnson's eighteenth-century dictionary was defined as "a woman kept in fornication." The word means literally to lie together. When John Adams heard the allegation of Jefferson's liaison with a slave woman, he was not surprised, identifying it "as a natural and almost unavoidable consequence of that foul contagion in the human character—Negro slavery." Modern notions of romance—seeing Hemings and Jefferson as America's premier biracial couple—should not be projected onto unions born of trauma, dependence, and constraint.[41]

On the other hand, such a relationship did not have to be based solely on heartless domination; it might have involved a measure of affection. Even Thistlewood, whose sexual relations with slaves were often brutal and coercive, was ensnared in the complexities of a genuine, albeit severely asymmetrical, relationship. It is surely in the realm of possibility that a widowed, middle-aged white man (who had pledged to his wife that he would never remarry) could be attracted to a fair-skinned African American woman, who was almost certainly the half-sister of his late wife. Marriages to close relatives were common in early Virginia, and marrying or cohabiting with a former sister-in-law was probably not altogether rare. The development of this relationship was all the more plausible in the mid– to late–1790s, as even Julian P. Boyd, the noted Jefferson scholar, acknowledged. A staunch advocate of Jefferson's upright moral character,

Boyd described the possibility of an interracial liaison offensively and in-accurately as a "lapse": for him it had to be out of character and of short duration. Yet, even with this pejorative characterization, Boyd thought he "could make out a very strong case indeed, supported by many evidences, that if Jefferson ever suffered a lapse it was in the late 1790s when he re-turned to Virginia, bruised deeply and determined never again to occupy public office." Firmly believing that no "lapse" had occurred, Boyd was nevertheless willing to concede, "I could certainly present a mass of plau-sible evidence to show that, if he ever did [engage in sex with Sally Hem-ings], this was the time and that habits of character in the face of power-ful temptations might have been overridden." Even the Jefferson establishment was not as monolithic as sometimes portrayed on the ques-tion of an attraction between Jefferson and Hemings.[42]

Sex between whites and blacks created, in Douglass Adair's words, "a tangled web of love and hatred, of pride and guilt, of passion and shame." Erotic activity brought whites and blacks close together, blurred the dis-tinctions between them, and broke down barriers; but by threatening to close the gap between the free and the enslaved, and producing a group of people whose position was deeply ambiguous, it was also potentially ex-plosive. It often arose in brutal and violent demonstrations of power, with white men asserting their sexual mastery and exerting their control over the bodies of black women. Some sexual encounters were marked by tenderness, esteem, and a sense of responsibility, but most were ex-ploitative and unspeakably cruel—nothing more than rapes by white men of black women—a testament to the ugliness of human relations when people are treated as objects. Love and cruelty, affection and callousness, composure and frenzy—such were the contradictory strands that bound whites and blacks together sexually. This twisted emotional knot may well explain Jefferson's explosive condemnation of slavery, especially his description of the "whole commerce between master and slave" as the "perpetual exercise of the most boisterous passions."[43]

A contextual reading of interracial sex in the British Atlantic world has also emphasized that a tradition of interracialism often ran in families. Thus, the entangled history of the Hemingses, Wayleses, and Jeffersons was not unusual. Once an interracial union occurred, the progeny tended to follow the path of the parents. An English sea captain and an African woman gave birth to Betty Hemings; she in turn had six children with

John Wayles; and those six in their turn tended to gravitate to white part-ners. In interracial families, "mulattoes" who found partners of a different complexion typically married or mated with whites rather than dark-skinned blacks. A progressive whitening occurred. Given the ways of a racist society, such a strategy is hardly surprising.[44]

Furthermore, well-positioned slave women who crossed racial lines of-ten did so to improve their children's chances of survival. Phibbah was one such slave in Jamaica, and Lettice aimed to be another. Sally Hemings had six known children, the first when she was twenty-two, the last when she was thirty-five. Apparently, she had enough influence over Jefferson to gain the freedom of all her children, the only case of an entire enslaved Monticello family achieving freedom. Sally Hemings had many of the at-tributes potential slave mistresses needed: she was beautiful, white in ap-pearance, and worked as a domestic. Furthermore, like many another prime mover in an interracial family, she named her children after Jeffer-son's relatives and close friends. In addition, one of her sons, Eston Hem-ings, would later changed his name to Eston Hemings Jefferson, presum-ably to indicate his belief in his paternity.[45] Those who have questioned Jefferson's relationship with Sally Hemings because of the significant gap in their ages need look no further than some of the relationships dis-cussed in this essay. John Custis, Thomas Thistlewood, William Prest-wood, and most spectacularly Thomas Cramphin prove that early mod-ern slaveowners had sex and children well into their sixties, seventies, even eighties. That Jefferson apparently fathered Sally's children from age fifty-two to sixty-five is well within the bounds of feasibility. Bachelors such as Cramphin, the early Calvert, and Thistlewood were no doubt most tempted by the possibilities of sexual exploitation, but widowers, as the examples of Custis and Page indicate, were also prone to resort to black women, although there is always the example of Wythe to suggest otherwise.[46]

Finally, although interracial sex in the early national Chesapeake was occasionally open, it more often involved covert and concealed intima-cies—certainly much more so than in Jamaica or the Carolinas. In the Chesapeake community ideals seem often at odds with some individuals' practice. Jefferson may have had his own reasons for reticence, but he was hardly unusual for his place and times. He makes just one direct reference to Sally Hemings in all his massive correspondence: he merely notes that

she had given birth. For this reason, the existence of interracial relationships is often difficult to prove. In an earlier work, I accepted too readily
the conventional wisdom that one of the Carr nephews fathered Sally's
children. I have tried to rectify my own lack of care by subjecting the
myth of Wythe's interracial liaison to close scrutiny. And demonstration
of this myth needs to be recalled as Jefferson's culpability is pondered. Ultimately, the DNA evidence, as E. A. Foster notes, "neither definitely ex-
cludes nor solely implicates" Jefferson in the paternity of Sally Hemings's
children. The weight of evidence now tilts heavily in his direction and the
burden of proof has dramatically shifted. The circumstantial evidence, as
Winthrop Jordan, Fawn Brodie, Lucia Stanton, and Annette Gordon-Reed
have previously noted—in some cases long ago—points its inexorable finger at him, but the mystery of the precise relationship and what it means
for an understanding of the man and his legacy still remain.[47]

NOTES

I am extremely grateful for the expert assistance of Kevin Butterfield, a colleague at the
Omohundro Institute of Early American Institute of Early American History and Culture,
who tracked down many of the references in this paper and who readily offered views on
its subject matter. For specific information, I also thank Holly Brewer, Thomas E. Buckley,
S.J., Melvin Ely, Kevin Kelly, Debra Meyers, Sue Peabody, Julie Richter, Charles Royster,
Jean Russo, Jim Sidbury, Kirt van Daake, Lorena Walsh, and especially Michael Nicholls.

1. [Fairfax Harrison], "Notes to Virginia Council Journals, 1726–1753," *Virginia Magazine
of History and Biography*, 32 (1924), 44 (I owe this reference to Charles Royster).

2. Petition of John Custis, 18 April 1744, in H. R. McIlwaine, ed., *Executive Journals, Council of Colonial Virginia*, 6 vols. (Richmond, 1925–1926), 5: 141; Jo Zuppan, ed., "Father to Son:
Letters from John Custis IV to Daniel Parke Custis," *Virginia Magazine of History and Biography*, 98 (1990), 99–100; deed of manumission, 3 Feb. 1748, York County Deeds and Bonds 5,
236–37, and deed of manumission, 15 Feb. 1748, York County Judgments and Orders, 1, 63
(Kevin Kelly generously supplied all the York County material).

3. Deed of land, stock, and slaves, 6 Feb. 1748, York County Deeds and Bonds, 5, 237–38;
Bond, 6 Feb. 1748, York County Deeds and Bonds, 5, 238–39.

4. Indentures between John Custis, Matthew Moody, Negro John (called Jack), and
George Kendall, 18 and 23 Jan. 1749, York County Deeds and Bonds, 5, 272–74, 274–78 and
also 21 Feb. 1749, York County Judgments and Orders, 1, 169; will of John Custis, 14 Nov.
1749, Custis Papers, Virginia Historical Society, Richmond.

5. Lyon G. Tyler, ed., "Diary of John Blair," 9 Sept. 1751, *William and Mary Quarterly*, 1st
ser., 7 (1898–1899), 152; John Doe, lessee of George Kendall vs. Daniel Parke Custis, 18 May
1752, York County Judgments and Orders, 2, 26–27; deed of land, 1 Jan. 1753, York County
Deeds and Bonds, 5, 515–19.

6. George Washington Parke Custis, *Recollections and Private Memoirs of Washington*
(New York, 1860), 20; a good sketch of Custis is in Josephine Zuppan, "The John Custis

Letterbook, 1724 to 1734" (master's thesis, College of William and Mary, 1978); Julie Richter kindly supplied the information on the Moodys and a map of York County land ownership 1735–1755; will of Matthew Ashby, 25 Nov. 1769, York County Wills and Inventories, 22, 25–26; will of Daniel Parke, 28 Sept. 1687, York County Deeds and Wills, 8, 239; Natalie A. Zacek, "Sex, Sexuality, and Social Control in the Eighteenth-Century Leeward Islands," in Merril D. Smith, ed., *Sex and Sexuality in Early America* (New York, 1998), 197–200. For previous studies that have not got the Custis story wholly right, see Mechal Sobel, *The World They Made Together: Black and White in Eighteenth-Century Virginia* (Princeton, 1987), 150–52, and Kathleen M. Brown, *Good Wives, Nasty Wenches, and Anxious Patriarchs: Gender, Race, and Power in Colonial Virginia* (Chapel Hill, 1996), 355.

    7. For an interesting case, the truth of which is murky, see Graham Russell Hodges, "The Pastor and the Prostitute: Sexual Power among African Americans and Germans in Colonial New York," in Martha Hodes, ed., *Sex, Love, Race: Crossing Boundaries in North American History* (New York, 1999), 60–71.

    8. Wythe witnessed Custis's indentures dated 18 and 23 Jan. 1749 (see note 4). Many historians accept without question Wythe's interracial relationship. Fawn Brodie made the charge in *Thomas Jefferson: An Intimate History* (New York, 1974), 92, 390–91; John Chester Miller, *The Wolf by the Ears: Thomas Jefferson and Slavery* (New York, 1977), 43, states categorically, but without attribution, that Wythe "succumbed to the sexual attractions of a slave woman"; Sobel, *The World They Made Together*, 152, declares that Wythe had a mulatto child but that the woman responsible for his upbringing was Lydia Broadnax; Annette Gordon-Reed is more cautious but supportive, saying that Thomas Jefferson's (hereafter TJ's) venerated law teacher "was said to have had a son by a black mistress," *Thomas Jefferson and Sally Hemings: An American Controversy* (Charlottesville, 1997), 136 and 267, n. 43; and Joseph J. Ellis exaggerates the number of children involved, when he says that "Wythe's mulatto housekeeper was his mistress and mother of two of his children," *American Sphinx: The Character of Thomas Jefferson* (New York, 1997), 327 n. 32. For a contrary view, see Imogene E. Brown, *American Aristides: A Biography of George Wythe* (Rutherford, N.J., 1981), 298–305.

    9. Most of these quotes are from Julian P. Boyd and W. Edwin Hemphill, *The Murder of George Wythe: Two Essays* (Williamsburg, 1955), 5–7; see also William Brown to Joseph Prentis, 24 Sept. 1804, cited in Brown, *American Aristides*, 283; George W. Corner, ed., *The Autobiography of Benjamin Rush* (Princeton, 1948), 151; "Glimpses of Old College Life," *William and Mary Quarterly*, 1st ser., 8 (1899–1900), 154; William Munford to John Coalter, 12 June 1791, Brown-Coalter-Tucker Papers, College of William and Mary, Williamsburg. For other of TJ's testimonials to Wythe, see TJ to Richard Price, 7 August 1785, in Julian P. Boyd et al. eds., *The Papers of Thomas Jefferson*, 27 vols. to date (Princeton, 1950–), 8:356–57.

    10. Manumission of Lydia, 15 Sept. 1787, York County Deed Book 6, 351; Alonzo Thomas Dill, *George Wythe: Teacher of Liberty* (Williamsburg, 1979), 71; Boyd and Hemphill, *The Murder of George Wythe*, 20; Dr. John Dove's memorandum concerning the death of George Wythe, 16 Sept. 1856, Thomas Hicks Wynne Correspondence and Documents 1848–1860, folder 4, Box 133, Brock Collection, Huntington Library, San Marino.

    11. Mrs. Elizabeth Wythe died on 18 August 1787. That Lydia lived elsewhere in Richmond, see Richmond City Tax Records, 1797, cited in Robert Bevier Kirtland, "George Wythe: Lawyer, Revolutionary, Judge" (Ph.D. diss., 1983), 163, and for hiring, see Brown, *American Aristides*, 299. For the suggestion that Lydia and Ben were married, I am indebted to Cathy Helier, "George Wythe's Slaves in Williamsburg," 1987 memorandum, Colonial Williamsburg Foundation. For more on Wythe's slaveholding, see also Kevin Kelly, "George Wythe's Slaves in Elizabeth City County," 1991 memorandum, Colonial Williams-

burg Foundation. Boyd and Hemphill, *The Murder of George Wythe*, 10–11, 13; Henry Clay to Benjamin Minor, "Memoirs of the Author," 95; for Dove family details, see Kirtland, "George Wythe: Lawyer, Revolutionary, Judge," 162.

12. Boyd and Hemphill, *The Murder of George Wythe*, 35, 44–52; newspaper accounts include *Richmond Enquirer*, 10, 13, 16, 17, and 24 June, 8 July, 9 Sept. 1806, *Virginia Argus* (Richmond), 10 and 17 June, 17 Sept. 1806, *Virginia Gazette and General Advertiser* (Richmond), 8 June-8 July 1806, *National Intelligencer and Washington Advertizer*, 15 Dec. 1806, *Impartial Observer* (Richmond), 8 June-8 July 1806; Brodie, *Thomas Jefferson*, 391; W. Asbury Christian, *Richmond: Her Past and Present* (Richmond, 1912), 62; John P. Kennedy, *Memoirs of the Life of William Wirt* (Philadelphia, 1851), 141. For further evidence on how Wythe was viewed, see John Page to St. George Tucker, 29 June 1806, Tucker-Coleman Papers, Colonial Williamsburg (hereafter CW).

13. Charles F. Hobson et al., eds., *The Papers of John Marshall* (Chapel Hill, 1987), 5:542, 548–49; "George Wythe's Gift" to Richard Taliafero, 20 August 1787, *William and Mary Quarterly*, 1st ser., 12 (1903), 125–26; manumission of slaves Polly, 20 Feb. 1788, and Charles, 13 August 1788, York County Order Book 6, 371, 390–91; William Munford to John Coalter, 22 July 1791, Brown-Coalter-Tucker Papers; George Wythe to Elizabeth Call, 14 Sept. 1793, Richmond Hustings Court Deed Book 11, f. 116, Virginia State Library, Richmond (hereafter VSL); George Wythe's deed of manumissions to Ben and James, 1797, Henrico County Deed Book 5, 201–2 (information kindly supplied by Michael Nicholls); Kennedy, *Memoirs of the Life of William Wirt*, 142 (wife of Judge Cabell).

14. Michael Nicholls generously provided information on the free blacks named Brown in Richmond: Dr. Robert Brown's deed of manumission to Sally and Billy, 1784, Henrico County Deed Book 1, 199; petition of Sally Brown, 14 Dec. 1802, Richmond City Legislative Petitions, 1798–1803; William DuVal's deed of manumission to three children of Nancy Brown, 1800, Richmond Hustings Deed Book 3, 1799–1803, 133; deed of sale to Ann Brown, 1797, Henrico County Deed Book 5, 1796–1800, 199–200; Boyd and Hemphill, *The Murder of George Wythe*, 17, 24.

15. James A. Bear, Jr., and Lucia C. Stanton, eds., *Jefferson's Memorandum Books: Accounts, with Legal Records and Miscellany, 1767–1826*, 2 vols. (Princeton, 1997), 1:460; Boyd and Hemphill, *The Murder of George Wythe*, 24; Charles Coleman Sellers, *Portraits and Miniatures by Charles Willson Peale*, Transactions of the American Philosophical Society, new ser., 42, part 1 (Philadelphia, 1952), 254; will of Lydia Broadnax, 25 Sept. 1820, Richmond City Hustings Court Wills 4, 361, VSL. Wythe had close ties to the Jewish community in Richmond and he took weekly lessons in Hebrew; in his will Isaac Judah, a bachelor, successful merchant, and first minister of Beth Shalome synagogue in Richmond, freed two female slaves (Maria and Betsy), one of whom was rumored to be his unofficial wife, and gave special bequests to Philip Norbonne Wythe and Benjamin Wythe, free mulatto boys whom he had raised and were thought to be his sons: see will of Isaac H. Judah, 16 April 1827, Richmond Hustings Court, Will Book 4, 313, Myron Berman, *Richmond's Jewry, 1769–1976: Shabbat in Shockoe* (Charlottesville, 1979), 39, 164. See also Andrew Nunn McKnight, "Lydia Broadnax, Slave, and Free Woman of Color," *Southern Studies*, 5 (1994), 17–30.

16. Brown, *Good Wives, Nasty Wenches*, 126, 189, 195–201, 205, 234, 237; Martha Hodes, *White Women, Black Men: Illicit Sex in the Nineteenth-century South* (New Haven, 1997), 19–38; Eric Papenfuse, "From Recompense to Revolution: *Mahoney v. Ashton* and the Transfiguration of Maryland Culture, 1791–1802," *Slavery and Abolition*, 15 (1994), 38–62; Robert Carter Daybook, 18 Jan. 1775, XIII, 65–66, Duke University, Durham; for more on Howell, see Cumberland County Order Book, 1762–1764, 494, *Virginia Gazette* (Purdie & Dixon), May 2,

Oct. 27, 1766; Turk McCleskey, "The Radical Challenge of Edward Tarr: The Free Black as Freeholder on Virginia's Colonial Frontier" (paper delivered at Southern Historical Association Meeting, Atlanta, 1992); McCleskey is writing a book on Tarr, entitled "Black Ned: A Life on the Colonial Frontiers."

17. *Anne Batson v. John Fitchet and wife Mary,* Northampton County Loose Papers, 1731, as cited in Douglas Deal, "A Constricted World: Free Blacks on Virginia's Eastern Shore, 1680–1750," in Lois Green Carr, Philip D. Morgan, and Jean B. Russo, eds., *Colonial Chesapeake Society* (Chapel Hill, 1988), 279–80; J. Douglas Deal, *Race and Class in Colonial Virginia: Indians, Englishmen, and Africans on the Eastern Shore during the Seventeenth Century* (New York, 1993), 180; McCleskey, "The Radical Challenge of Edward Tarr"; Bolling Stark to George MacMurdo, 15 Dec. 1764, Maxwell, MacMurdo, and Newhall Family Papers, box 3, National Library of Scotland, Edinburgh; Walter Skinner, *Maryland Gazette,* 12 Oct. 1769; Hartwood Baptist Church, 25 June 1785, Virginia Baptist Historical Society, Richmond; William Faris diary, 31 Dec. 1795 and 23 July 1796, Maryland Historical Society, Baltimore (references kindly supplied by Jean Russo, who is preparing an edition of the diary). In 1792 Lydia Whitaker married William Rummells, who seems to have been white, but there was a black Rummels family nearby and perhaps this confusion accounted for the on-off-on-again marriage of West and Whitaker. Nancy Quynn cannot be traced; her father was undoubtedly Allen Quynn, a local notable, who had a son named Allen who indeed lived in Frederick County. Quynn had four known daughters, but none of them was a Nancy. Perhaps the family suppressed all mention of her because of her disgrace. I owe all this information to Jean Russo. For the law on interracial sex, see A. Leon Higginbotham, Jr., and Barbara K. Kopytoff, "Racial Purity and Interracial Sex in the Law of Colonial and Antebellum Virginia," *Georgetown Law Journal,* 77 (1989), 1967–2029, and for more on sexual slander, see Kirsten Fischer, "'False, Feigned, and Scandalous Words': Sexual Slander and Racial Ideology among Whites in Colonial North Carolina," in Catherine Clinton and Michele Gillespie, eds., *The Devil's Lane: Sex and Race in the Early South* (New York, 1997), 139–53.

18. I am indebted to Melvin Ely, my colleague, for the information on the Fearses and Dungeys in Prince Edward County. The material is from "Israel on the Appomattox: A Southern Experiment in Black Freedom, 1796–1870," his forthcoming book on Israel Hill, a community of landowning manumitted blacks. For other cases of white women married to blacks—but black slaves—see Allan Kulikoff, *Tobacco and Slaves: The Development of Southern Cultures in the Chesapeake, 1680–1800* (Chapel Hill, 1986), 387; journal of Robert Ayres, 9 April 1788, microfilm, Duke University.

19. Joshua D. Rothman, "'To Be Freed from Thate Curs and Let at Liberty': Interracial Adultery and Divorce in Antebellum Virginia," *Virginia Magazine of History and Biography,* 106 (1998): 443–81, esp. 461n.; Thomas E. Buckley, S.J., *"The Great Catastrophe of My Life": Divorce in the Old South"* (book manuscript). I am grateful for Mr. Buckley's willingness to share with me his chapter, "'Acts of the Greatest Lewdness': Crossing the Color Line."

20. Legislative Petitions, Lancaster County, 1697, as cited in Philip Alexander Bruce, *Economic History of Virginia in the Seventeenth Century: An Inquiry into the Material Conditions of the People,* 2 vols. (New York, 1896), 2:110; Letterbook of Stephen Loyde, 3 July 1709, 15 August 1710, Virginia Historical Society; Richard Godbeer, "William Byrd's 'Flourish': The Sexual Cosmos of a Southern Planter," in Smith, ed., *Sex and Sexuality,* 145; John Hartwell Cocke Journal, 26 Jan. 1853 and 23 April 1859, University of Virginia, as cited in Lucia C. Stanton, "The Hemings-Jefferson Controversy: A Review of the Documentary Evidence" (Thomas Jefferson Memorial Foundation, Dec. 1998), 4.

21. Hunter Dickinson Farish, ed., *Journal and Letters of Philip Vickers Fithian, 1773–1774: A*

Plantation Tutor of the Old Dominion (Williamsburg, 1957), 115, 241–43, 246, 248; Judith Sheppard to Philip Sheppard, 6 May 1793, correspondence of Philip Sheppard, 1791, 1793, and undated, Sheppard Family Papers, Meadow Farm Museum, Henrico County (I owe this reference to Jim Sidbury).

22. Charles Carroll of Carrollton to Charles Carroll of Annapolis, 30 Oct. 1769, Carroll Papers, MS 206, Maryland Historical Society; Ronald H. Hoffman, *Princes of Ireland, Planters of Maryland: A Carroll Saga, 1500–1782* (Chapel Hill, N.C., 2000). Carroll removed the slave woman from the quarter to his house in Annapolis, although he thereby split the slave family—her husband and sons stayed at the plantation, while a daughter moved with her.

23. Thomas E. Buckley, S.J., "Unfixing Race: Class, Power, and Identity in an Interracial Family," *Virginia Magazine of History and Biography,* 102 (1994), 349–80, reprinted in Hodes, ed., *Sex, Love, Race,* 164–90.

24. This amazing family saga is documented in Margaret Law Callcott, ed., *Mistress of Riversdale: The Plantation Letters of Rosalie Stier Calvert, 1795–1821* (Baltimore, 1991), 378–84; for Calvert's reaction to Rosalie's death, see 366, 367, 371.

25. Kirt van Daake, "Race, Family, and Community in Jefferson's Albemarle" (unpublished paper, 1998), 5–6. This valuable paper documents other late eighteenth-century interracial relationships.

26. Lucia Stanton, "'Those Who Labor for My Happiness': Thomas Jefferson and His Slaves," in Peter S. Onuf, ed., *Jeffersonian Legacies* (Charlottesville, 1993), 151, 152 (quote), 173; Lucia Stanton, "Monticello to Main Street: The Hemings Family and Charlottesville," *The Magazine of Albemarle County History,* 55 (1997): 95–126. Von Daacke's paper explores the relationship of Thomas West, a wealthy planter, and his former slave Priscilla, who had at least two children: James Henry West, born probably in the 1770s and freed in 1785, and Nancy West, born in 1782 a free child. James Henry West would eventually pass as white, marrying a white woman in 1794 and inheriting his father's plantation two years later. Nancy West would later live openly with David Isaacs, a Jewish merchant in Charlottesville, with whom she had seven children. She also ran her own business.

27. Complaint against Rev. Patrick Lunan, Fulham Palace Papers, miscellaneous typescripts, CW; Ferdinand-M. Bayard, *Travels of a Frenchman in Maryland and Virginia,* ed. and trans. Ben C. McCrary (Williamsburg, 1950), 20; Robert Sutcliffe, *Travels in Some Parts of North America* (New York, 1811), 53; Sarah Mifflin Bordley to Mrs. Jenny Shippen, 22 March 1784, Bordley-Calvert Papers, Box 2, 1753–1785 and undated, ms. 82, Maryland Historical Society (reference kindly supplied by Jean Russo); the man referred to as "the Chief" who inspired these rumors has been identified as William Paca in Gregory A. Stiverson and Phebe R. Jacobsen, *William Paca: A Biography* (Baltimore, 1976), 66–68, but Jean Russo has persuaded me that this attribution is tenuous; *Norfolk Herald,* 14 April 1803 and Grand Jury Presentment, Nov. 1804, Petersburg City Hustings Court Minute Book, 1800–1804, 267 (both these last pieces of information generously supplied by Michael Nicholls). For the scandalous effects—the ruining of reputation—of rumors about an alleged affair between an older married man and a younger unmarried woman, both white, see Anya Jabour, *Marriage in the Early Republic: Elizabeth and William Wirt and the Companionate Ideal* (Baltimore, 1998), 92–93. For white wives' expressions of shame and disgust at their husbands' transgressions across the color line in the nineteenth century, see Rothman, "'To Be Freed from Thate Curs,'" 469.

28. Thomas Gerard Will, 1672, Wills 1, 567, and will of Timothy Goodridge, 1682, Wills 4:134, Maryland Hall of Records, Annapolis (information kindly supplied by Debra Meyers); will of Thomas Jarvis, 2 Feb. 1781, York County Wills and Inventories, 23, 537–38 and

York County Register of Free Negroes and Mulattoes 1798–1831 (information kindly supplied by Julie Richter).

29. Michael Nicholls has compiled this information on urban manumissions and I am grateful to him for sharing it with me; will of Joseph Ashlin, 16 July 1807, Richmond City Hustings Deeds no. 5, 1807–1810, 117, and R. Demoiter's deed of manumission, 29 April 1806, Norfolk City Deed Book 10, 159. Until manumission laws were liberalized after the revolution, few fathers attempted formal legal provisions for their slave children because manumission then entailed removing the freed slaves from the colony. For another will noting paternity, see that of Richard Cocke Jr., 4 Oct. 1800, Cocke Family Papers, U. Va. (information kindly supplied by Lorena Walsh).

30. Edward Long, *The History of Jamaica* 3 vols. (London, 1774), 2:328; John Hook to Charles Hook, 1 Nov. 1779, Business Records, John Hook Letterbooks, 1763–1784, VSL (my thanks to Minor Weisiger for securing a photostat of this letter).

31. Thomas Thistlewood diary, 27 April, 11 June 1750, in possession of Lord and Lady Monson, Lincoln County Record Office, (my thanks for permission to quote); Richard Price and Sally Price, eds., *Stedman's Suriname: Life in an Eighteenth-Century Slave Society* (Baltimore, 1988), 242.

32. These patterns are part of my analysis of the diary. There are other interesting patterns: by month (fall, not spring and early summer, as in England, were the high peaks of sexual activity); the increasing propensity for sexual activity to be "stans" (standing), often "backward"; the number of times sex occurred with heavily pregnant women; and the correlation of sex and health (particularly the cycles of venereal disease). All his sexual acts are recorded in pig Latin. For another analysis, see Trevor Burnard, "The Sexual Life of an Eighteenth-Century Jamaican Slave Overseer," in Smith, ed., *Sex and Sexuality*, 163–89.

33. Diary, 19 August 1750, 28 July 1755 (public); 12 March 1755 (gang rape), (sailor); 20 Feb. 1753 (burning). See also 8 Jan. 1751, 2–5 May 1756, 19 Feb. 1758 (reports of attempted rapes and rapes by others). For beatings, see 21–22 Nov. 1775, 31 July 1778, 8 Oct. 1781, 25 August 1782.

34. Diary, 13, 23, 26 Feb., 15 Oct. 1755, 24, 26 Feb., 15 March, 25 Sept. 1756 (bookkeeper); 1 Oct. 1768 (Coobah, who was Phibbah's daughter, must have been in her early twenties when she composed her poem; she was a house slave, and apparently literate; she had just returned from a year in England). Coobah, like Phibbah, sought to be a mistress of a white man.

35. Diary of John Thistlewood, 3 Feb. 1765 (John does not mention Lettice again); diary, 31 Dec. 1765.

36. For payments, see diary, 28 Sept. 1751, 24 Sept., 8, 22 Oct. 1752, and once Thistlewood became an independent proprietor, he almost always paid for sex, expenditures running usually at 2 bits (1s 3d), sometimes 4 bits (2s 6d) (except sex with Phibbah, who shared his bed, and with whom most sexual encounters were at night); in 1760 Egypt Susannah and Mazarine made 17–18 bits apiece; on Phibbah's possessions, see 29 Feb., 3 and 5 Sept. 1756, 27 May 1758, 5 April 1760, 22 March, 24 July 1765, 27 Sept., 16 Nov. 1767, 17 May 1772; John was born 29 April 1760, manumitted in 1762 (Manumissions 1B/11/6/7/119, Jamaica Archives, Spanish Town), and died 7 Sept. 1780.

37. Diary, 28 July, 21–26 August 1755 (sweetheart); 25 Feb. 1753, 17 April, 25 July, 4 Oct., 19 Nov. 1754, 2 and 7 Feb., 6 July, 26 August 1755, 13, 17, and 31 August 1759 (tiffs); 4 and 10 May 1752, 3 Oct., 15 Nov., 22 Dec. 1754, 28 July, 5 August 1755 (her affairs); 7 July 1754 (Billingsgate); June-Dec. 1757 (new job). Thistlewood freed Phibbah postmortem (she became free in 1792) and had land bought for her, see will, 25 Nov. 1786, proved 31 Jan. 1787, Island Record Office, Spanish Town, and Manumissions 1B/11/6/7/170. For more on Thistlewood and

Phibbah, see Douglas Hall, *In Miserable Slavery: Thistlewood in Jamaica, 1750–86* (London, 1989), and "Above all Others: Phibbah," *Jamaica Journal*, 22/1 (1989), 57–64.

38. Ferdinand-M. Bayard, *Travels of a Frenchman*, 20; Mark Antony De Wolfe Howe, ed., "Journal of Josiah Quincy, Junior, 1773," Mass. Hist. Soc. *Proceedings*, 49 (1915–1916), 463; G. Moulton to [?], 23 Jan. 1773, Add. mss. 22677, 75, British Library, London.

39. Nathaniel Clenroy Browder, "The William Thomas Prestwood Enciphered Diary 1808–1859" (typescript, 1984), 21–30, 53, 72, North Carolina State University Library, Raleigh. I am grateful to Holly Brewer for bringing this diary to my attention and for providing me with a copy of Browder's entire deciphered diary and selected pages of the original diary.

40. Prestwood's vocabulary is raunchy and explicit. The three New World plantation diaries known to me that mention sexual activity—those of Byrd, Thistlewood, and Prestwood—are all encoded, to some degree.

41. Gordon-Reed, *Thomas Jefferson and Sally Hemings*, 61, 245–46, 252; Page Smith, *John Adams, 1784–1826*, 2 vols. (Garden City, 1962), 2:1094; Samuel Johnson, *A Dictionary of the English Language* (London, 1755), entry for concubine; Douglas R. Egerton, "Thomas Jefferson and the Hemings Family: A Matter of Blood," *The Historian*, 59 (1997), 327–45.

42. Julian P. Boyd to Douglass Adair, 12 Oct. 1960, *William and Mary Quarterly* files. Of course, if TJ fathered all Sally's known children, he began somewhat earlier than Boyd was prepared to allow, i.e., 1795; and, if the conception of a child in Paris is believed, even earlier—to 1790. For another concession—by Dumas Malone—see Scot A. French and Edward L. Ayers, "The Strange Career of Thomas Jefferson: Race and Slavery in American Memory, 1943–1993," in Onuf, ed., *Jeffersonian Legacies*, 444.

43. Douglass Adair, *Fame and the Founding Fathers: Essays by Douglas Adair*, ed. Trevor Colbourn (New York, 1974), 191; Philip D. Morgan, *Slave Counterpoint: Black Culture in the Eighteenth- Century Chesapeake and Lowcountry* (Chapel Hill, 1998), 404, 411–12.

44. Melvin Ely has cautioned me that it is easy to pay insufficient attention to mulatto-black unions, in part because the partners are not considered a "mixed" couple.

45. Gordon-Reed, *Thomas Jefferson and Sally Hemings*, 52, 66, 160, 164–65, 196–201; Stanton, "The Hemings-Jefferson Controversy: A Review of the Documentary Evidence," 3. I am skeptical about the claim that Sally Hemings struck a bargain in Paris and returned to Virginia in return for the freedom of her family. From 1787 to 1789, when Sally was in Paris, the issue of freedom was still contested, racism was mounting, and master-initiated manumissions outnumbered petitions for freedom. Sally would have had to find a lawyer, go to court, have her case successfully argued, and find a new employer—all this in a foreign tongue and without access to a local support network. Further, by challenging her freedom in court after 1777, when the *Police des Noirs* was in effect, Sally risked being confiscated and transported to the living hell of Saint Domingue, not back to her family and friends in Virginia. I am indebted to Sue Peabody for her advice on these matters, and see her *"There Are No Slaves in France": The Political Culture of Race and Slavery in the Ancien Regime* (New York, 1996), 106–40.

46. TJ was fifty-two when Harriet was born and sixty-five when Eston was born; he would have been forty-seven when Tom Woodson was born.

47. Morgan, *Slave Counterpoint*, 404; E. A. Foster, "The Thomas Jefferson Paternity Case," *Nature*, 197 (7 Jan. 1999), 32; Winthrop D. Jordan, *White over Black: American Attitudes toward the Negro, 1550–1812* (Chapel Hill, 1968), 464–69; Brodie, *Thomas Jefferson*, 32–33, passim; Stanton, "'Those Who Labor for My Happiness,'" in Onuf, ed., *Jeffersonian Legacies*, 152, 174; Gordon-Reed, *Thomas Jefferson and Sally Hemings*, xvii–xviii, passim, and 178 (direct reference).

PART II

Stories and Lies, Remembering and Forgetting

CHAPTER 4

James Callender and Social Knowledge of Interracial Sex in Antebellum Virginia

Joshua D. Rothman

*There is not an individual in the neighbourhood of Charlottesville
who does not believe the story and not a few who know it.*
—Richmond Recorder, Sept. 1802[1]

Thomas Jefferson was particularly ill-equipped to conceal his sexual relationship with Sally Hemings. In private correspondence, Jefferson was extremely cautious about what he revealed of himself, and his personal elusiveness remains notorious among historians. At the same time, however, Jefferson was characteristically gregarious. It was his wont throughout his life to entertain large numbers of guests, and a constant stream of visitors made its way to Albemarle County to call whenever he was at Monticello. As early as 1796, a number of French visitors noted evidence of sex across the color line on Jefferson's resident plantation. The Duc de La Rochefoucauld-Liancourt mentioned "particularly at Mr. Jefferson's" slaves who had "neither in their color nor features a single trace of their origin, but they are sons of slave mothers and consequently slaves." The Comte de Volney, also traveling during the summer of 1796, similarly noted slaves at Monticello "as white as I am."[2] Since Sally Hemings's first child, presumably conceived with Jefferson in France in 1789, had probably already died by 1796, and her second, a girl named Harriet born in 1795 (who would die in 1797), was just an infant when these men made their observations, they could not have been describing her children.[3] Yet the evidence of racial mixing at Monticello must have been quite obvious, and no matter how discreet he was, Jefferson could not have hidden it from guests. The children of his relationship with Sally Hemings also would be visible to visitors. As a member of the Virginia gentry, Jefferson knew of similar affairs carried out in supposed secrecy and likely understood that he could never hide every clue or quash every rumor. Still, he never anticipated *Richmond Recorder* editor James Callender, and in 1802 Thomas Jefferson's relationship with Sally Hemings became a rumor far more widespread and far more public than he ever could have foreseen.

Callender's reasons for making the Jefferson-Hemings connection public deserve reassessment, for they illustrate perfectly why and when awareness of sexual affairs across the color line went from being common knowledge in particular communities to public knowledge available to anyone. Any student of interracial sexual relationships in the early republic and antebellum periods quickly realizes not only their ubiquity and variety, but also their notoriety. Such matters were rarely secrets. Most people in the small communities that composed much of Virginia's landscape knew precisely who was engaged in such illicit sexual conduct, and they gossiped among themselves accordingly. Despite legal and cultural sanctions against such connections, however, whites almost never exposed them to open public or legal discussion, except when useful as a means of gaining personal advantage. Especially when financial interests were at stake, evidence of interracial sex was a strategic weapon sometimes utilized to undermine one's opposition. A public accusation of an interracial sexual affair frequently had its foundation in a larger set of calculations, part of a battle between conflicting white parties over other issues. So too in the dispute between Thomas Jefferson and James Callender. Callender used the partisan newspaper as his sword, but the thrust against Jefferson was purely personal.

James Callender was an angry, bitter, and cynical man who made a career by specializing in invective and character assassination. He ruthlessly, viciously, and often crudely ravaged anyone unfortunate enough to be caught in his journalistic sights, and contemporaries and historians alike have found him an easy target for attacks on both his personal and professional practices. As a result, Callender's reports of the relationship be-

tween Thomas Jefferson and Sally Hemings have been casually and cate-
gorically dismissed as unreliable—the libelous rants of a scandal-mongering, drunken, and disgruntled office-seeker. Historian John Chester
Miller, for example, wrote that "Callender made his charges against Jefferson without fear and without research. . . . He never made the slightest
effort to verify the 'facts' he so stridently proclaimed. It was 'journalism'
at its most reckless, wildly irresponsible, and scurrilous. Callender was
not an investigative journalist; he never bothered to investigate anything."[4]

Since most historians, as we now know, have been wrong about the
truth of James Callender's reportage, the journalist's reports on Jefferson
and Hemings require reconsideration. Although some of what he presented as true now appears false, considering that he pieced together his
stories from gossip and rumor, what stands out is not that he made some
mistakes but that for the most part Callender's reports were essentially accurate. It is obvious not only that he researched the matter but also that
he talked to numerous people, primarily from Jefferson's own county and
class, who had reliable information, even if they did not necessarily know
every detail about life at Monticello. To brand Callender reckless in his
journalistic style regarding Jefferson and Hemings, then, is to overstate
the case. He was purposefully sensationalistic, to be sure. But with respect to the facts he presented, his tone was more cautious and variable.
He used strong and definitive language when he believed in the reliability
of his sources, but he also occasionally corrected incorrect information
he had first reported as fact, and when he printed stories he considered
dubious he noted that they were merely rumors. James Callender was a
lot of things, but he was not usually a liar. When he ran the Jefferson-
Hemings story in 1802, he believed it to be the most damaging information he had on the president, and he hoped it would ruin Jefferson's political career. He knew Jefferson's supporters would deny it, but he wanted
to be certain they could not refute it, and he repeatedly dared them to do
so. They never did.

Significantly, it didn't make any difference. Callender's attacks were by
and large true, yet they had almost no impact upon Jefferson's political
fortunes. Nationally, voters bolstered Republican congressional majorities
in 1802, and Jefferson won reelection to the presidency in a landslide in
1804.[5] Especially in Virginia, Callender's accusations missed their mark

not so much because people refused to believe them, but because he over-estimated the injury revelations of interracial sex would do to Jefferson's political standing. The editor fundamentally misread the sentiments of white Virginians toward sexual affairs between masters and enslaved women. As far as most white Virginians were concerned, Jefferson acted with propriety in his liaison with Sally Hemings, and when Callender published his information and directly challenged Jefferson before the nation, he violated an unwritten cultural rule by bringing the story out of the realm of gossip. If people were at all shocked by Callender's reports, the fact that the story appeared in the newspaper was probably at least as significant as the story itself.

❧

James Callender emigrated to the United States from his native Scotland in 1793, fleeing British authorities he feared would charge him with treason for his 1792 publication of *The Political Progress of Britain,* a pamphlet in which he attacked British political institutions and advocated Scottish independence. Callender was a radical egalitarian who detested the pretension and condescension he saw in wealthy and powerful men. Once in the United States he was drawn to Jeffersonian Republican politics for their antielitist, anticorruption, and anti-English overtones, and he began working for the *Philadelphia Gazette* reporting the proceedings of Congress. Most Republican Party leaders were ambivalent about Callender from the outset of his American career. They found his journalistic style unpalatable, and moderates feared the extremism of his advocacy. But the Republicans of the 1790s were a party struggling desperately to get into power, and, in the words of his biographer, Callender "could be guaranteed to diminish the public stature of his opponents."[6] Thus, even after the editor of the *Gazette* fired him in 1796, party officials continued to feed Callender information for his anti-Federalist attacks. Callender struck his sharpest blow in 1797, when his *History of the United States for 1796* forced Alexander Hamilton to reveal an adulterous affair in order to counter allegations of his complicity in an illegal speculation scheme. Callender was thrilled with his own efforts, writing to Jefferson in September 1797 that Hamilton's embarrassing written reply to the *History of 1796* was "worth all that fifty of the best pens in America could have said against him."[7]

Jefferson and Callender probably first met in June or July 1797 at the

Philadelphia printing office of Snowden and McCorkle, where Jefferson, then the vice president, gave Callender $15.14 for copies of his *History of 1796*.[8] Callender thereafter repeatedly turned to Jefferson for financial support. Jefferson responded by giving Callender over two hundred dollars—more money than he gave to any other Republican journalist—from his personal accounts during the nearly four years following their first meeting, and he solicited others to subscribe to Callender's publications.[9] Jefferson rarely wrote to Callender personally, but when he did he encouraged Callender to continue his publishing work and indicated that he appreciated the journalist's efforts. In October 1799, for example, after seeing some pages of Callender's soon-to-be-published *The Prospect before Us*, a relentless political and personal attack on John Adams, Jefferson sent his congratulations and his assurance that "such papers cannot fail to produce the best effect. They inform the thinking part of the nation."[10]

Callender became increasingly hostile to most Republicans in 1798 and 1799. He perceived—quite accurately, in fact—that they looked down their noses at him, using him when he served their interests and leaving him to face Federalist anger and threats of physical assault alone when his work got him into trouble. In 1798 Callender fled Philadelphia, eventually ending up in Richmond, fearing arrest under the Alien and Sedition Acts. He wrote to Jefferson in September 1798 that he was "entirely sick even of the Republicans, for some of them have used me so dishonestly . . . that I have the strongest inclination, as well as the best reason, for wishing to shift the scene."[11] As Callender's anger toward the party grew, he became increasingly attached to Jefferson, the one man who seemed to offer the support and respect that he felt he deserved. In letters to Jefferson during 1799 and 1800, Callender began to use the pronouns *us, we,* and *our* when discussing Jefferson's chances at winning the presidential election of 1800.[12]

In June 1800 James Callender's fears came to pass as he was tried under the Sedition Act, primarily for his excoriation of John Adams in *The Prospect before Us*. He was found guilty, fined two hundred dollars, and sentenced to nine months in Richmond's dark, damp, and insalubrious jail. Republicans turned Callender into a political martyr, publishing the minutes of his trial as a campaign document for Jefferson, and Callender continued to write both political pamphlets and letters to Jefferson from jail. Having to pay his fine for sedition mostly out of his own pocket forced Callender nearly into bankruptcy, but Jefferson won the election of 1800, a victory in which Callender, not unfairly, believed he had played an important role. By the time he got out of jail in March 1801, he had already made entreaties to Jefferson about a remission of his fine and about a job as a postmaster in the new administration.[13]

Thomas Jefferson never wrote to Callender in prison and by the time Callender had served his sentence, Jefferson no longer needed him.[14] Callender's antagonistic and purposefully provocative style was highly effective for an opposition party, but for a party in power, it might prove more a liability than an asset. In addition, there was always the risk that Callender's extremism would turn him into a critic rather than a supporter of the party, most of whose members he distrusted anyhow. In prison, Callender had already begun to sense that Jefferson might be freezing him out.[15] In October he implored Jefferson to write him "a few lines, at first or second hand." Ostensibly Callender wanted acknowledgment that Jefferson was receiving the political materials he had sent, but more importantly he wanted some sign from Jefferson that he still remembered Callender and valued his support.[16]

On assuming the presidency, Jefferson pardoned all Republican journalists, including Callender, who had served time in jail under the Sedition Act, and he promised to remit all fines paid as a consequence of the convictions. Remitting Callender's fine, however, would prove particularly complicated, because it had been collected by federal marshal David Meade Randolph, who, though a distant relative of Jefferson's, hated the president and had lost his job as a consequence of the election. Randolph took his time returning Callender's fine, and Callender, desperately in need of money, still suffering from the illness he contracted in the Richmond jail, and hearing nothing from Jefferson, quickly became impatient. He wrote a hostile letter to Jefferson in April 1801, expressing his disgust that Jefferson had failed to help him retrieve his fine or give him any reward upon taking office, both of which he took as personal slights. He claimed that he had done the party's journalistic dirty work when most Republicans felt too principled to do it themselves, and that now that the party was victorious they wished "to bury the memory of offensive obligations." Callender had always known that few people in either party liked him, but now he regretted ever having devoted himself to any single cause. He told Jefferson this would be the last letter he would write to him. By supporting the Republicans, Callender wrote, "I have lost five years of labor; gained five thousand personal enemies; got my name inserted in five hundred libels. . . . In a word, I have been equally calumniated, pillaged, and betrayed by all parties. I have only the consolation of reflecting that I had acted from principle, and that with a few individual exceptions, I have never affected to trust either the one or the other."[17]

By the end of April 1801, Callender had still not heard a word from Jefferson. Sensing that in writing to the president he "might as well have addressed a letter to Lot's wife," Callender appealed instead to James Madison, the secretary of state and Jefferson's closest political ally. Subtlety, never Callender's strong point, had now left his writing entirely. He failed to understand how Jefferson, who "repeatedly said that my services were considerable" could cast him out after winning the presidency. Callender berated himself as much as Jefferson when he explained that he had always suspected that Jefferson might turn on him. While he claimed to respect and admire the president, Callender wrote that "he has on various occasions treated me with such ostentatious coolness and indifference, that I could hardly say that I was able to love or trust him." Callender also threatened the president in his missive to Madison. Writing that "I now begin to know what Ingratitude is," he warned Madison that he would reveal to the Federalists what he believed to be Jefferson's duplicity respecting the fine, and hinted that he had items of even greater significance to bring to light. "I am not the man," he suggested, "who is either to be oppressed or plundered with impunity."[18]

Madison met with Callender in Washington in mid-May and informed the journalist politely but clearly (and by Callender's account, condescendingly) that there would be neither a postmastership nor any other federal job for him forthcoming.[19] Jefferson had tired of Callender's constant harassment, but he did not want to bring the matter of repayment of the journalist's fine before Congress, as the publicity would only gratify both Callender and the Federalists. Surely, the president had heard about Callender's threats from Madison, and Jefferson knew that Callender relished tearing apart public figures in the press. The president would not submit to his threats, but neither did Jefferson wish to antagonize the man further. Under these circumstances, the wisest strategy for dealing with Callender was probably to give him some immediate satisfaction in the hopes it would contain his temper.

Accordingly, Jefferson sent his personal secretary, Meriwether Lewis, to call on Callender in Washington and give him fifty dollars to tide him over until the rest of the fine could be recovered. Callender replied to Lewis's offer with an even more overt attempt to blackmail Jefferson than that contained in his letter to Madison. According to Jefferson, who described the encounter between Callender and Lewis to his friend and Virginia governor James Monroe, Callender "intimated that he was in possession of things which he could and would make use of in a certain case: that he received the 50. D. not as a charity but a due, in fact as hush money; that I knew what he expected, viz. a certain office, and more to this effect." Jefferson, insulted and appalled at Callender's temerity, canceled all financial assistance he had authorized for Callender and assured Monroe that Callender "knows nothing of me which I am not willing to declare to the world myself."[20]

Jefferson clearly anticipated that Callender would carry out his threats, and he therefore made a preemptive effort to shape the perception of his prior relationship with Callender by including in his letter to Monroe the somewhat disingenuous explanation that he had long wished Callender would end his activities as a political writer. Furthermore, he added that any money he had given the journalist was strictly as charity.[21] Whether Jefferson suspected that Callender's threats entailed revealing his relationship with Sally Hemings is uncertain, but with such an unequivocal rejection of Callender's blackmail he effectively chose to let whatever materials Callender might possess appear in the newspapers.

Considering what he published in the fall of 1802, Callender himself probably alluded to the liaison when he told Meriwether Lewis he had damaging "things" to write about Jefferson. Callender almost certainly had heard hints of the relationship between the president and Sally Hemings by the spring of 1801. Although Callender would be the first editor to put any specifics of the story in print, he was not the proximate source of the information, which had been bandied about by Virginians and others for a number of years before Callender published it. Jefferson's political enemies alluded to the affair even before the election of 1800. In June of that year, William Rind, editor of the *Virginia Federalist,* claimed that he had "damning proofs" of Jefferson's "depravity." Presumably, Rind had heard the gossip from others, and he probably told others the details, in this way serving as a conduit for the rumor.[22] Vulgar poems intimating Jefferson's sexual involvement with black women appeared in newspapers months before Callender ever directly linked the president to any particular woman.[23] Shortly after Callender published his report of the story, the *Gazette of the United States* announced that it would not print the story without greater corroboration from its own sources, but acknowledged it had "heard the same subject freely spoken of in Virginia, and by Virginia Gentlemen."[24] Although the Jefferson-Hemings story can hardly be said to have been common knowledge nationally by the time Callender got hold of it, some people, especially in Virginia, clearly had already ground it in their gossip mill.

Callender detested African Americans and found the notion of sex across the color line repulsive. He frequently lambasted Richmond's gentry for their illicit interracial sexual encounters, even going so far as to publish the names of white men caught at "dances" where blacks and whites mixed. Once he reported the Jefferson-Hemings story, he described Hemings herself in the most racist terms, calling her a "wench" and "a slut as common as the pavement," accusing her of having "fifteen, or thirty" different lovers "*of all colours,*" and referring to her children as a "yellow litter."[25] When he had held Jefferson in esteem, Callender discounted the Hemings rumor, later writing, for example, that he believed the hints emanating from Rind's *Federalist* to be "absolute calumn[ies]." In prison, however, feeling himself falling out of Jefferson's favor, he began to turn against the man he had once admired. After his release he made inquiries of his own, some of which confirmed what he once refused to accept about his patron. Now he had ammunition.[26]

Although David Meade Randolph finally repaid Callender's fine in June 1801, it was too late to restore Callender's good opinion of the president. By this time Callender had been run out of one city and had served nine months in jail in another. All his work in the United States had been as a Jefferson supporter and once Jefferson made it clear that the relationship would not be reciprocal, Callender wanted revenge. He began writing for the *Richmond Recorder,* a nominally Federalist newspaper, in February 1802, but he used the paper less to support Federalist policies than to voice his own hostility toward the Republicans, who taunted him mercilessly in their papers for his misfortunes.

By May 1802 a full-scale newspaper war was underway between Callender at the *Recorder* and his former employer, Meriwether Jones of the

Richmond Examiner. Jones accused Callender of apostasy, relentlessly an-
tagonized him, and baited him to reveal whatever damaging information
he claimed to have on Jefferson.[27] For his part, Callender hurled epithets
and accusations of his own at Jones, including the claim that Jones entertained a black mistress in his home whenever his wife was away.[28] The personal salvos flew back and forth and escalated in the degree of their vitri-
ol. Editors of newspapers in other major cities got involved. On 25 August
1802, William Duane, editor of the *Philadelphia Aurora*, accused Callender
of infecting his wife with venereal disease and of getting drunk in the
next room while she languished and died and while his children went
hungry. This charge was too cruel even for Callender. In the next issue of
the *Recorder*, under the heading "The President Again," he wrote that it
was "well known that the man, *whom it delighteth the people to honor*, keeps,
and for many years past has kept, as his concubine, one of his own slaves.
Her name is SALLY."[29] In the early republic vicious personal enmity was
frequently integral to and inseparable from partisan politics. It is only fitting that James Callender thought releasing a story about the president's
personal life would inflict maximum damage to Thomas Jefferson's political career.

❧

    In early national and antebellum Virginia, standing sexual affairs be-
tween white men and African American women were nearly always open
secrets. Divorce petitions in Virginia involving accusations of interracial
adultery, for example, amply demonstrate that neighbors, friends, and relatives—although rarely saying anything publicly until called on by the pe-
titioner to provide testimony in court—always knew, sometimes for many
years, about the illicit sexual conduct of both men and women in their
families and communities. Other legal cases from the late eighteenth century to the Civil War in which sex across the color line became an issue,
such as in disputes over wills or executions of estates, also show that in
Virginia, where racial definition fundamentally helped order society, sexual conduct that blurred the color line made for piquant and prurient local
chatter.[30] Interracial sex became scandalous, however, only when it was
made public, meaning that whites involved in such liaisons had to rely on
others to adhere to a cultural code of public silence. Such reliance, in
turn, made exposure the ultimate weapon for anyone with an ax to grind
against a white participant in interracial sex.

That a personal grudge motivated James Callender is not surprising, for personal antagonisms, especially those involving conflicting financial interests, often help explain why and when interracial sexual relationships became matters of public record. Take, for example, a case in Jefferson's own backyard, that of David Isaacs and Nancy West. Isaacs, a Jewish merchant, and West, a free woman of color and a baker, had their first child in Charlottesville in 1796. By 1819, the couple had seven children. Only in 1822, however, did the Albemarle County Court bring West and Isaacs into court on a charge of fornication. A careful reading of the documentary record indicates that two elements of their relationship changed around 1820, provoking one or more of their neighbors into asking the court to bring the charge. West and Isaacs only began living in the same house in 1820. By acting as if their relationship were legitimate, they surely aroused some hostility. More importantly, Nancy West began accumulating valuable property in 1820, and Isaacs began divesting himself of some of his assets and selling them to West. Because the couple could not legally marry, this arrangement freed West from the laws of coverture, enabling her to retain ownership of her own property. Particularly in the event of deep debt or insolvency—risks that merchants such as Isaacs always faced—West and Isaacs both had greater economic stability than most businesspeople ever could. For West and Isaacs simply to have sex and bear children did not pose any particular threat, but when they attempted to use their peculiar, and illegal, situation for economic advantage, other Charlottesville residents (most probably other merchants) chose that moment to complain publicly. The penalty for fornication was a small fine and could hardly have affected West, Isaacs, or their relationship. The point of their antagonists was to harass and embarrass the couple by making their private lives matters of public scrutiny. Similarly, humiliating Jefferson was an important goal of Callender's even as he had a broader vision of catastrophic consequences for Jefferson's political career.[31]

What, though, did Callender really know about Thomas Jefferson and Sally Hemings? The crux of the matter, as Callender originally reported it 1 September 1802, was that Thomas Jefferson and his house servant Sally were involved in a sexual relationship; that Sally had gone with Jefferson to France, where he was serving as the American minister, along with his two daughters; that the two had "several" children together, including a

ten- or twelve-year-old son named Tom; and that "President Tom," as
Callender sarcastically called this boy, closely resembled Jefferson. Two
weeks later, Callender brought specificity to the number of Sally's offspring, writing that the couple had exactly five children.[32] By presenting so
many details of the relationship, Callender tried to establish from the outset that his charges, far from being concocted, were grounded in verifiable
fact. He challenged Jefferson's supporters to refute them, writing that "if
the friends of Mr. Jefferson are convinced of *his* innocence, *they* will make
an appeal. . . . If they rest in silence, or if they content themselves with
resting upon a *general denial,* they cannot hope for credit. . . . We should
be glad to hear of its refutation. We give it to the world under the firmest
belief that such a refutation *never can be made.*"[33]

Callender got most, if not all, of the information for his first round of
articles directly from individuals who lived in Albemarle County, and he
may even have made a special trip there after being released from prison,
as suggested by a toast made in his honor at Richard Price's Albemarle
tavern just over a month after he got out of jail.[34] Callender certainly implied that people in Jefferson's county were his sources when he claimed
there was "not an individual in the neighbourhood of Charlottesville who
does not believe the story; and not a few who know it."[35] Callender correctly reported not only the story's outline, but he also knew some significant details. He correctly identified Hemings by her first name, and he
knew both that she had been in France with Jefferson and that she worked
at Monticello as a house servant. That Hemings had had exactly five children was also true in 1802. After having the two children mentioned earlier, she had given birth to a son named Beverley in 1798, to an unnamed
daughter who was born and died in 1799, and to another girl named Harriet in 1801.[36] The accuracy of this information strongly suggests that
some of Callender's informants had, or knew people who had, extensive
familiarity with domestic life at Monticello over the course of at least a
dozen years.

The original source of the information easily could have been the enslaved population of Albemarle County. Everywhere in the South, enslaved African Americans had kin and community networks that extended across vast distances. Slaves at Monticello knew of the association
between Hemings and Jefferson and had greater access to details of their
relationship than nearly anyone else. Edmund Bacon, Jefferson's overseer

between 1806 and 1823, described the entire Hemings family as "old family servants, and great favorites," and Jefferson's grandson, Thomas Jefferson Randolph, reported that other slaves envied the special treatment af-
forded the Hemingses and suspected ulterior motives, "account[ing] for it
with other reasons than the true one," which he claimed lay in their trustworthiness and intelligence.[37] Israel Jefferson, meanwhile, a Monticello
slave who worked as a postilion, scullion, and waiter, confirmed late in his
life and after gaining his freedom that Jefferson and Hemings were sexually involved based on his "intimacy with both parties."[38]

Given Callender's disgust for African Americans, it is unlikely that he
spoke directly to any Albemarle slaves. He claimed in print to have collected evidence from a large number of people, even asserting in December 1802, in response to repeated denials of the Hemings affair by Republican journalists, that he would happily meet Jefferson in any court and
"prove, by a dozen witnesses, the family conviction, as to the black wench
and her mulatto litter."[39] If he was serious about this challenge, his witnesses would have to have been white. He would have acquired his information from the most likely places to hear local gossip in Albemarle, as in
any Virginia county—taverns, markets, the steps of the courthouse, and
other social gatherings. He probably relied especially on members of the
Virginia gentry from Albemarle and counties nearby for what he believed
to be his most accurate evidence. These men—and they were almost certainly men, given the significant breach of etiquette it would have been
for a woman to discuss sexual matters with a man not her husband—
might have overheard their slaves discussing the Hemings story. They also
would have been the whites most likely to have visited Jefferson at Monticello, to have been inside the house (and to have seen Sally Hemings and
perhaps her children), and to have heard the prevalent gossip about Jefferson and Hemings in elite circles. Callender may well have received some
reports from other whites who might only have been at Monticello briefly
if at all but could see Jefferson or his slaves when they came down from
the mountain to town. Some sources were more reliable than others, but
anyone who lived near Jefferson was a possible source of material. As
Henry Randall, an early biographer of Jefferson, wrote in private correspondence in 1856, Callender "was helped by some of Mr. Jefferson's
neighbors."[40]

For five weeks after the middle of September, Callender added no new information to the Jefferson-Hemings story. The story was an evolving one, however, and once it appeared for the first time in print, new sources—possibly but not necessarily from Albemarle—came to Callender in Richmond to feed him new information or to correct errors he had originally published. That Callender changed the number of Sally Hemings's children from "several" to "five" in the two weeks between September 1 and September 15 is likely an example of just such a dynamic. Similarly, on October 20, Callender wrote that a few days after the original article ran, "a gentleman" came into the district court in Richmond and offered to bet anyone present a suit of clothing or any amount of money that the story was true, except for one small detail, namely that Sally Hemings had not actually gone to France with Jefferson, but had joined him later (Jefferson originally left for France in 1784, but Sally Hemings did not arrive until 1787 as a travel escort for Jefferson's daughter Mary).[41] Callender corrected this mistake but used the correction as an opportunity to reassert how reliable his information was, writing, "if we had been mad enough to publish a tale of such enormous, of such inexpressible ignominy, without a solid foundation, the *Recorder,* and its editors must have been ruined." Callender did not identify the man in the district court, but noted that no one would take the bet, since the man was known both to be wealthy and "to have the best access to family information."[42] Whether or not the courtroom drama actually took place, there is little reason to doubt Callender's description of his source, for the correction the man called for was not only accurate but was such a tiny detail that only someone unusually familiar with the Jefferson family—after all, the events in question had taken place almost two decades earlier—could have known it.

In the first few months after Callender published his original story, people started to bring him just as much misinformation and innuendo as fact, some of which he printed. On November 10 Callender wrote that Jefferson had freed Sally Hemings's brother, who had an "infirmity" in one of his arms and had been seen selling fruit in Richmond. Callender also added that "it is said, but we do not give it as gospel" that one of Sally Hemings's daughters, presumably fathered by someone other than Jefferson, was a house servant currently working somewhere in Richmond.[43] Jefferson had indeed freed Sally Hemings's older brother James, who had also been with the president in Paris, but there is no corroborating evidence verifying that James either sold fruit in Richmond or that one of his arms functioned improperly.[44] The story about the purported daughter of Sally Hemings was patently false, since no such person ever existed. That Callender printed the latter story at all indicates that despite all he did know, there were some important things about Sally Hemings he did not, including her age. In 1802, Sally Hemings was twenty-nine years old, making the possibility of her having a daughter old enough to be a house servant unlikely.

Callender did not catch every error he made in reporting the Jefferson-Hemings story, but he was a journalist very familiar with dealing with personal gossip about public figures, and he had a good sense of when a story might be inaccurate. Consequently, he noted that the story of Hemings's daughter was only a rumor. It may be no coincidence that although he continued to hammer away at Jefferson for his relationship with Hemings for another month or two, Callender printed no new information about Jefferson and Hemings after November 10. Most importantly, the midterm elections had passed by then, limiting the utility of continuing to develop the story. But it is also possible that his sources dried up. There was, after all, probably little anyone could have added to what Callender had already published. Similarly, by November Callender may have suspected the rumor mill had begun to spin wildly and the stories he now heard contained more falsehoods than truths. Before September 1, the story circulated mostly in private among people relatively close to the original sources of information. After September 1, so many people in so many places had heard the story that it became impossible to tell where the various pieces of gossip originated anymore. Callender was concerned with accuracy, and when he ran out of useful material, he stopped publishing additions to the story.

It is not surprising that Callender's reports contained some inaccuracies. White informants with the most intimate knowledge based their suppositions not on anything Jefferson told them directly, but at best on deductions and inferences from what they had seen at Monticello or in Charlottesville. Even Israel Jefferson, who lived at Monticello and saw both Jefferson and Hemings frequently, acknowledged that he could not "positively know" of Jefferson and Hemings's relationship but that he was certain of it "from circumstances."[45] Most people who knew the story had probably heard it secondhand, at best. Callender's information came to him through at least one other person and more likely through two,

three, or four. The more people the story passed through before it got to
Callender, the less likely that all the facts would be correct. People who
knew about Sally Hemings's children, for example, might not have heard
that three of the five had already died by 1802. The detail that Hemings
and Jefferson went to France in two different ships a few years apart could
easily have been collapsed into a single ocean voyage or, alternatively, Sally could have been confused with her brother James, who had in fact been
on the same ship as Jefferson when he first left America. The inaccurate
material about James Hemings might simply have been embellishments
grafted onto the most important element of that aspect of the Jefferson-
Hemings story, namely that Jefferson had freed James.

Callender's most significant and most persistent error was his insistence that Jefferson's and Hemings's oldest child was a boy named Tom,
who resembled Jefferson and was living at Monticello in 1802. Thomas Jefferson recorded nothing in his Farm Book pointing to the birth of any
child to Sally Hemings around 1790 and there is no record of an enslaved
boy born in 1790 named Tom at Monticello. The same DNA study that
linked Jefferson to Hemings cast significant doubt on the possibility, suggested by generations of oral history, that "President Tom" grew up to
become a man named Thomas Woodson.[46] It is always possible that no
such child ever existed. According to Madison Hemings's recollection of
his mother's story, however, by the time Thomas Jefferson and Sally Hemings returned to Monticello in December 1789, she was already pregnant
with her owner's child. Hemings herself claimed this child died shortly after being born. It seems unlikely that Sally Hemings lied about this aspect
of her story to Madison, when so many other details can be verified. Pre-
suming that Hemings had, in fact, given birth to a child in 1790, her explanation of that child's disappearance appears most logical.[47]

Callender probably never corrected this mistake because no one told
him that he was in error. To the contrary, even Jefferson's supporters never denied there was a "President Tom" (although they obviously claimed
Jefferson was not his father), and Callender's informants clearly believed
that there was such a child living at Monticello.[48] Obviously, these informants could not have seen a child around twelve years old born to Jefferson
and Hemings, and it remains a mystery why they insisted they had. Hemings's children were well known to look just like Jefferson. Perhaps Callender's sources conflated four-year-old Beverley Hemings with some

older light-skinned enslaved boy at Monticello, thus creating "President Tom."[49] To those who did not claim to have seen the boy purported to be Sally Hemings's oldest child, however, that there was such a person would have seemed very plausible. Would not the story have more credence if Sally Hemings's first child was still alive, looked like Jefferson, and bore his father's name? How many people had enough access to Monticello to confirm or deny that particular element of the story? Not knowing which of Sally Hemings's children had died, most people would presume that her first child was still alive, and not hearing he had disappeared or been sent away, where else would he be if not at Monticello? We are all aware of rumors with grains of truth that get embellished to the point that they nearly lose their truthfulness altogether. Especially regarding a story of this nature, the possibilities for exaggeration to become hyperbole as the Jefferson-Hemings story passed from person to person and then to Callender were enormous. That Callender got so much of the story right is a remarkable testimony to the extent and transmission of social knowledge about private interracial sexual affairs in Virginia communities.

Not everyone in Albemarle had information for Callender because not everyone had heard the story, but we should not doubt Callender's assertion that nearly everyone in the county he mentioned it to believed it. Given what Virginians already knew about sex and slavery in their society in general, they did not need to have heard the details of Jefferson's relationship with Sally Hemings to believe he might be sexually involved with her. Even Meriwether Jones, who tried to defend Jefferson in the pages of the *Examiner* against Callender's charges, conceded that "in gentleman's houses every where, we know that the virtue of unfortunate slaves is assailed with impunity."[50] Of course, not every slaveowner conducted himself in this fashion, but enough did that the allegations about Jefferson would not have been implausible. Jefferson's particular actions and associations also gave residents of Albemarle County reason to believe the Hemings story. First, there was the significant presence of "white slaves" at Monticello, commented on since at least the 1790s. Second, Jefferson's thrice-widowed father-in-law, John Wayles, was also Sally Hemings's father, having had a long-term sexual liaison with Betty Hemings, Sally's mother.[51] The Hemings family still filled the most prominent roles in Jefferson's household in 1802, and Jefferson had already freed Sally Hemings's brother. Third, Jefferson may have had other close relatives who engaged in interracial sexual conduct. Jefferson's granddaughter, Ellen Randolph Coolidge, picking up on a family story told by Thomas Jefferson Randolph, blamed Jefferson's nephew Samuel Carr for the paternity of Sally Hemings's children in an 1858 letter, accusing him of being a "master of a black seraglio kept at other men's expense."[52] Although the recent DNA test has ruled out both Samuel and his brother Peter Carr as the father of Sally Hemings's last son, they nonetheless might have been selected as the scapegoats because they were known to participate in sex across the color line. Finally, and perhaps most tellingly, Jefferson was already known by 1802 to have facilitated the interracial sexual relationship of one of Betty Hemings's daughters. In 1792 Jefferson had sold Sally Hemings's oldest sister Mary, at Mary's request, to a white man named Thomas Bell, and the couple lived together on Main Street in Charlottesville's downtown, across from David Isaacs and part of a burgeoning interracial community.[53] Many people who lived in Jefferson's neighborhood believed the Hemings story because Virginia's slaveowners and Jefferson himself had prepared them to believe it.

By the turn of 1803 the newspapers in Virginia for the most part ceased discussing Jefferson's relationship with Sally Hemings, and the Jefferson-Hemings story was little more than a footnote in the 1804 national presidential campaign.[54] For numerous reasons, even in Virginia Callender's articles failed to have the impact he had hoped. For some people in Virginia the Jefferson-Hemings story was as much as twelve years old by 1802, and Callender's claims were unlikely to change whatever opinions they already held. Other Virginians were unlikely to believe anything written by James Callender, given his motives and his usual methods of operation, or to accept that Thomas Jefferson might have sex with a slave. Those who strongly admired Jefferson might very well have felt, as did Jefferson's granddaughter (and the vast majority of subsequent historians), that there were "such things, after all, as moral impossibilities."[55] In addition, in July 1803 James Callender, stumbling drunk through the streets of Richmond, fell into the James River and drowned. Other newspapers had picked up on the Jefferson-Hemings story, but their editors had neither the network of informants nor the desire for personal vengeance that animated Callender. When Callender died, a significant portion of the energy behind the story died with him.

Finally, and perhaps most importantly, Callender misunderstood white attitudes toward interracial sex in Virginia and thus failed to foresee that although his allegations might embarrass Jefferson and his white family, they were unlikely to provoke any larger consequences for his career or standing. To be sure, few white men would publicly voice their approval of sex across the color line. Children of mixed race confused the ideally bifurcated racial order and, as Jefferson himself noted, sex with black women was thought to degrade whites morally. As Callender observed, "it is only doing justice to the character of Virginia to say that this negro connection has not a single defender, or apologist, in Richmond, as any man, that even looks through a spyglass at the hope of a decent character, would think himself irretrievably blasted, if he had lisped a syllable in defence of the president's mahogany coloured propagation."[56]

Callender misread the silence among white male Richmonders. It did not necessarily mean that they were outraged or disgusted by the suggestion of interracial sex. Most white men, especially slaveowning whites, understood that the systematic sexual abuse of enslaved women helped bolster slavery by reminding all slaves that their masters held power over their bodies. Moreover, since slaves followed the condition of their mothers, all the children produced by liaisons between white masters and slave women, even if consensual, would still be slaves and hence far less potentially destabilizing to the social order than free people of color. Finally, what a man chose to do with his slave property was for the most part his business. With Virginians being of at least two minds about interracial sex, a story about a white man—no matter who he was—having sex with his female slave could hardly be expected to elicit universal outrage.[57]

No great tumult was likely to occur when it came to Thomas Jefferson, not only because of who he was but also because of how he conducted himself in his relationship with Sally Hemings. In the slave South, ethical norms governed even activities not generally perceived to be intrinsically ethical, such as interracial sex. If a white man engaged in a sexual relationship of any duration with one of his slaves, he could never prevent people in his community from gossiping. No one in his community, however, was likely to say anything to him directly provided that he kept his affairs discreet, which entailed never acknowledging any rumors about his sexual behavior and never demonstrating that he cared for his enslaved sex partner or treated any mixed-race offspring as legitimate blood relations.[58] From 1789 until the day he died, Jefferson never directly addressed the rumor of his relationship with Sally Hemings. Whatever the nature of the relationship, Jefferson acted with sufficient discretion that, according to his grandson, not "a motion, or a look, or a circumstance" would lead anyone "to suspect for an instant that there was a particle more of familiarity between Mr. Jefferson and Sally Henings [*sic*] than between him and the most repulsive servant in the establishment."[59] Jefferson rarely showed affection toward his children with Sally Hemings and apparently never in front of others. As Madison Hemings recalled, his father "was not in the habit of showing partiality or fatherly affection to us children."[60] If there ever was such a thing in white eyes as the ethical amalgamator, Thomas Jefferson was the prototype.

Just as he failed to appraise accurately how most Virginians were likely to respond to his revelations about Jefferson, Callender never understood that in Virginia and in other parts of the South there were honorable and dishonorable ways of sharing information about the interracial sexual affairs of elite men. Consequently, he never foresaw that even people who believed Jefferson's sexual behavior was less than admirable might very well feel that Callender's own behavior in publishing the story was at least distasteful. The *Frederick-town Herald* from nearby Maryland, for example, believed Callender's reports and thought the entire affair to be a subject of great hilarity. But its editors also called Callender a "sad fellow" and claimed they would not pursue the story. "Modesty," the paper argued, "orders us to drop the curtain. . . . We therefore assign it over to less scrupulous hands, confessing at the same time, that there is a merriment in the subject, which we should be graceless enough to pursue at the President's expence, were it less offensive to serious and decent contemplation."[61]

Virginians may have found Jefferson's sexual behavior wonderful material for gossip. Some even fed Callender information knowing he would print it, but no one, not even Callender's informants, would ever say anything to Jefferson directly about it. To do so not only would have been extraordinarily insulting but would also have been a challenge to Jefferson's honor as a gentleman. As one hostile letter writer to the *Recorder* castigating Callender asserted, "He has no character, no honor, no sensibility."[62] By moving the rumor of Jefferson's interracial sexual affairs from private gossip to public discourse, Callender touched off whole new rounds of discussions about the president all over the country, but he also succeeded in cementing his own reputation as a scoundrel, a judgment that has lasted two hundred years.

The story of Sally Hemings and Thomas Jefferson remained in the memories of many African Americans, especially those descended from the Hemings family, who have never doubted the oral history passed down to them over the past two centuries.[63] At least some white Americans also continued to believe the story's basic truth even after Jefferson died in 1826. British traveler and author Frances Trollope, for example, writing of a visit to America shortly after Jefferson's death, reported that Jefferson's interracial sexual affairs were openly spoken of in the United States. The Americans from whom she heard the story claimed that Jefferson had children with numerous enslaved women, that he took great pleasure in having those children serve at his dinner parties, and that he allowed his enslaved children to run off the plantation if they were white enough to pass unsuspected in white society.[64] In Trollope's account, as in Callender's, we can see fact and fiction mixing, as a liaison with a single enslaved woman had become sexual relations with many. As Jefferson's children with Hemings grew older, they acted as house servants when their father had guests, but Trollope's storytellers gave this truth a perverse spin, foreshadowing the abolitionists later in the antebellum period who leapt onto the story, sometimes making up facts and frequently exaggerating the truth to make their case against the peculiar institution.[65] Jefferson did allow both Beverley and Harriet Hemings to leave Monticello after they turned twenty-one, making notations in his Farm Book that they were runaways. Both also were able to marry into white families and pass as whites in the Maryland and Washington, D.C., areas. But there is no evidence that he allowed them to leave specifically because they could pass, or that Jefferson ever made a policy of allowing any other "white slaves" to run away as a means of covertly emancipating them, a claim later made by his granddaughter.[66]

Whites in Albemarle County kept the story in their minds too at least until the Civil War. John Hartwell Cocke owned a large plantation, served as a general in the War of 1812, and held an original membership on the University of Virginia's Board of Visitors. Cocke was also a close friend of Jefferson's. In his journal in 1853, he commented on the prevalence of sex across the color line, particularly the practice of married white men having children with enslaved women. Cocke observed that such cases were hardly exceptional. "I can enumerate a score of such cases in our beloved Ant. Dominion that have come my way thro' life, without seeking for them," Cocke wrote. "Were they enumerated with the statistics of the State they would be found by hundreds. Nor is it to be wondered at when Mr. Jefferson's notorious example is considered."[67]

During the lifetimes of Jefferson and his contemporaries, the statesman's relationship with Sally Hemings was notorious, simultaneously well known and infamous. As historians took control of the story, they almost universally accepted the denials of the Jefferson family and crafted fictions about the social worlds of the antebellum South. Henry Randall, writing in 1868, explained that Jefferson's supporters never attributed paternity of Sally Hemings's children to the Carr brothers because "nobody could have furnished a hint of explanation outside the family. The secrets of an old Virginia Manor house were like the secrets of an Old Norman Castle." Randall claimed that "an awe and veneration was felt for Mr. Jefferson among his neighbors which in their view rendered it shameful to even talk about his name in such a connexion."[68] Randall, trapped by his own awe and veneration, helped create a myth. Virginia plantations were not fortresses. Slaveowners were not kings and lords. Local communities, free and slave, were not medieval fiefdoms where peasants spoke only in hushed and reverent tones about their superiors. Antebellum Virginians paid close attention to the lives of their neighbors and shared all sorts of information about them. James Callender understood this reality all too well, even if he never understood that salacious gossip did not necessarily provide the makings of political scandal.

NOTES

The author wishes to thank the editors, as well as Philip Morgan and Cinder Stanton, for their helpful comments and suggestions. The research for this essay was made possible in part by a fellowship from the Center for Children, Family, and the Law at the University of Virginia.

1. Full text can be found in Appendix B.

2. Both quoted in Lucia Stanton, "'Those Who Labor for My Happiness': Thomas Jefferson and His Slaves," in Peter S. Onuf, ed., *Jeffersonian Legacies* (Charlottesville, 1993), 152 (La Rochefoucauld-Liancourt) and 173, n. 18 (Volney).

3. Jefferson's (hereafter TJ's) guests could have been referring in part to Sally Hemings herself, who would have been visible in the house. One of Hemings's grandmothers was African, but her other grandmother and both grandfathers were of European descent. Thomas Jefferson Randolph (hereafter TJR) claimed that Hemings was "light colored,"

while Isaac Jefferson, a former Monticello slave, remembered she was "mighty near white" and that she had "long straight hair down her back." TJR, quoted in letter from Henry Randall to James Parton, 1 June 1868, reprinted in Fawn M. Brodie, *Thomas Jefferson: An Intimate History* (New York, 1974), 495; *Memoirs of a Monticello Slave* [Charlottesville, 1951], 13).

4. John Chester Miller, *The Wolf by the Ears: Thomas Jefferson and Slavery* (New York, 1977), 154. The best source on James Callender's (hereafter JTC's) life and career is Michael Durey's biography, *"With the Hammer of Truth": James Thomson Callender and America's Early National Heroes* (Charlottesville, 1990). Also on JTC, see Charles A. Jellison, "That Scoundrel Callender," *Virginia Magazine of History and Biography*, 67 (1959), 295–306.

5. Robert M. S. McDonald assesses the national impact of JTC's TJ-Hemings articles in "Race, Sex, and Reputation: Thomas Jefferson and the Sally Hemings Story," *Southern Cultures*, 4 (1998), 46–63.

6. Durey, *"With the Hammer of Truth,"* chs. 1–5; quote on 91.

7. On JTC's role in the Hamilton scandal particularly, see Durey, *"With the Hammer of Truth,"* 97–102, and Jellison, "That Scoundrel Callender," 297– 298. Quote from JTC in letter from JTC to TJ, 28 Sept. 1797, *Thomas Jefferson and James Thomson Callender, 1798–1802*, Worthington Chauncey Ford, ed. (Brooklyn, N.Y., 1897), 8 (hereafter cited as *TJ and JTC*).

8. *Richmond Recorder*, 3 Nov. 1802; James A. Bear, Jr., and Lucia C. Stanton, eds., *Jefferson's Memorandum Books: Accounts, with Legal Records and Miscellany, 1767–1826*, 2 vols.(Princeton, 1997), 2:963.

9. For additional payments from TJ to JTC, see Bear and Stanton, *Jefferson's Memorandum Books*, 2:971, 975, 979, 980, 984, 986, 990, 1005, 1018, 1028, and 1042.

10. TJ to JTC, 6 Oct. 1799, *TJ and JTC*, 19. Also see TJ to JTC, 6 Sept. 1799, ibid., 16–17.

11. JTC to TJ, 22 Sept. 1798, ibid., 10.

12. JTC to TJ, 10 August and 26 Sept. 1799, 14 March and 27 April 1800, ibid., 15–16, 17–18, 20–21, 21–22.

13. See JTC's letters to TJ from prison, ibid., 25–33.

14. TJ did send JTC fifty dollars in jail (*Jefferson's Memorandum Books*, Vol. 2, 1028 n. 53).

15. Durey suggests that the Republican political strategy changed around JTC while he remained in jail, and that James Madison suggested to TJ that he assume a low profile during the election campaign, advice that TJ took (Durey, *"With the Hammer of Truth,"* 139–140).

16. JTC to TJ, 11 Oct. 1800, *TJ and JTC*, 28–29 (quote on 28). Later in the same letter, JTC repeated his entreaty, writing, "I by no means wish to take up time devoted to purposes so much more important, but just a few lines, if not improper, would be very welcome" (28–29).

17. JTC to TJ, 12 April 1801, *TJ and JTC*, 33–34 (quotes all from 34). On the delay in remitting JTC's fine, his overtures for a patronage position, and his subsequent fury toward TJ, see Durey, *"With the Hammer of Truth,"* 143–148.

18. JTC to Madison, 27 April 1801, *TJ and JTC*, 35–37 (quotes on 35, 36).

19. Jellison, "That Scoundrel Callender," 301–02.

20. TJ to Monroe, 26 and 29 May 1801, *TJ and JTC*, 38–39.

21. TJ to Monroe, ibid. TJ wrote to Monroe that he gave JTC "from time to time such aids as I could afford, merely as a man of genius suffering under persecution, and not as a writer in our politics. It is long since I wished he would cease writing on them, as doing more harm than good" (TJ to Monroe, 29 May 1801, ibid., 39). Nearly a year later, TJ reiterated a similar and lengthier explanation of his association with JTC in another letter to Monroe, dated 15 June 1802, ibid., 39–40). TJ's strategy of trying to convince his political al-

lies that he had never been a supporter of JTC was prescient. In the wake of the Hemings revelations, TJ's defenders claimed the president had never approved of JTC's work, prompting JTC at one point to print the letters TJ had sent him indicating otherwise.

22. *Richmond Recorder,* 1 Sept. 1802 (Appendix B); Brodie, *Thomas Jefferson,* 323.

23. One such poem appeared in July 1802 in the *Port Folio,* a Federalist newspaper in Philadelphia, and JTC reprinted the poem when he publicly revealed the TJ-Hemings story in the *Recorder* on 1 Sept. 1802. The verse, written in dialect as if by one of TJ's slaves, included the following:

> And why should one hab de white wife,
>> And me hab only Quangeroo?
> Me no see reason for me life!
>> No! Quashee hab de white wife too.
>> Huzza, &c.
> "For make all like, let blackee nab
>> De white womans . . . dat be de track!
> Den Quashee de white wife will hab,
>> And massa *Jefferson* shall hab de black.

24. Cited in *Richmond Recorder,* 22 Sept. 1802.

25. *Richmond Examiner,* 11 April 1800; *Richmond Recorder,* 1, 15, 22 Sept., 15 Dec. 1802.

26. *Richmond Recorder,* 1 Sept. 1802 (Appendix B); Brodie, *Thomas Jefferson,* 323.

27. See, for example, *Richmond Examiner,* 9 June, 11 August 1802.

28. *Richmond Recorder,* 26 May 1802.

29. *Aurora,* 25 August 1802; *Richmond Recorder,* 1 Sept. 1802 (Appendix B). Later, JTC explained that he had intended to wait until the election campaign of 1804 to reveal the Hemings story, hoping to cause maximum political damage for TJ. When the Republican papers brought JTC's dead wife (she had died in 1798 shortly before JTC left Philadelphia, too poor at the time even to bring his four sons with him) into their personal conflict, he decided to run the report early. Writing to Duane at the end of October 1802 in the pages of the *Recorder,* JTC asserted "if you had not violated the sanctuary of the grave, SALLY, and her son TOM would still, perhaps, have slumbered in the tomb of oblivion. To charge a man as a *thief,* and an *adulterer,* is, of itself, bad enough. But when you charge him with an action that is much more execrable than *an ordinary murder* . . . is the party injured not to repel such baseness, with ten thousand fold vengeance upon the miscreant that invented it?" (*Richmond Recorder,* 22 Sept., 27 Oct. 1802).

30. Joshua D. Rothman, "'To be freed from thate curs and let at liberty': Interracial Adultery and Divorce in Antebellum Virginia," *Virginia Magazine of History and Biography,* 106 (1998), 443–81; Martha Hodes, *White Women, Black Men: Illicit Sex in the Nineteenth-Century South* (New Haven, 1997), chap. 4.

31. The charge against West and Isaacs eventually reached the General Court of Virginia in 1826, where they were found not guilty of fornication. See *Commonwealth* v. *David Isaacs and Nancy West,* 5 Rand. 634 (Va.). On the West-Isaacs family, see Lucia Stanton, "Monticello to Main Street: The Hemings Family and Charlottesville," *Magazine of Albemarle County History,* 55 (1997), 105–08; Joshua D. Rothman, "'Notorious in the Neighborhood': Nancy West, David Isaacs, and Free Blacks in the Antebellum South," paper presented at the "Telling About the South Conference," University of Virginia, March 1996; Carol Ely, Jeffrey Hantman, and Phyllis Leffler, *To Seek the Peace of the City: Jewish Life in Charlottesville* (Charlottesville, 1994), 3–5.

32. *Richmond Recorder,* 1 Sept. 1802, Appendix B in this volume, and 15 Sept. 1802.

33. *Richmond Recorder,* 1 Sept. 1802 (Appendix B).

34. Durey, *"With the Hammer of Truth,"* 142.

35. *Richmond Recorder,* 1 Sept. 1802 (Appendix B).

36. That Sally Hemings had an unnamed daughter in 1799 is strongly suggested by a let-ter TJ wrote to John Wayles Eppes, in December 1799 noting that "Maria's maid" had had a child and that both mother and daughter were fine. TJ's daughter Mary, who also went by Maria, had already married Eppes in 1797 and left Monticello, but there is no indication anyone other than Sally Hemings had ever served as her maid (TJ to Eppes, 21 Dec. 1799, Jefferson Papers, Alderman Library, University of Virginia).

37. Hamilton W. Pierson, *Jefferson at Monticello: The Private Life of Thomas Jefferson* (New York, 1862), 106–07; TJR, quoted in Stanton, "Those Who Labor," 151–52. On the Hemings family, also see Stanton, "Those Who Labor," 147–80, and James A. Bear, Jr., "The Hem-ings Family of Monticello," *Virginia Cavalcade,* 29 (1979), 78–87.

38. "Life among the Lowly, No. 3," *Pike County (Ohio) Republican,* 25 Dec. 1873. Israel Jef-ferson claimed in his interview that he had been TJ's personal attendant for fourteen years, which was not true. He probably overestimated his "intimacy" with both TJ and Sally Hemings. Nonetheless he, like other Monticello slaves, believed TJ and Hemings had a sex-ual relationship.

39. *Richmond Recorder,* 8 Dec. 1802.

40. Henry Randall to Hugh Grigsby, 15 Feb. 1856, *The Correspondence between Henry Stephens Randall and Hugh Blair Grigsby, 1856–1861,* Frank I. Klingberg and Frank W. Kling-berg, eds. (Berkeley, 1952), 29–30.

41. Brodie, *Thomas Jefferson,* 216–17.

42. *Richmond Recorder,* 20 Oct. 1802, Appendix B in this volume. The *Richmond Examiner* had pointed out the error in the timing of Sally Hemings's presence in France nearly a month before JTC printed his retraction. JTC, though, certainly trusted his sources more than Jeffersonian editors, and while the *Examiner* notice may have prompted him to investi-gate the matter, he probably waited to confirm the error himself before taking any action in print (*Richmond Examiner,* 25 Sept. 1802).

43. *Richmond Recorder,* 10 Nov. 1802.

44. TJ promised James Hemings his freedom in writing in 1793 and emancipated him in 1796. Edwin Morris Betts, ed., *Thomas Jefferson's Farm Book* (1953; Charlottesville, 1987), 15–16.

45. "Life among the Lowly, No. 3."

46. Eugene A. Foster et al., "Jefferson Fathered Slave's Last Child," *Nature,* 196 (5 Nov. 1998), 27–28.

47. "Life among the Lowly, No. 1," *Pike County (Ohio) Republican,* 13 March 1873, Appen-dix A in this volume.

48. On 3 Nov., for example, JTC refuted a Lynchburg *Gazette* article asserting that Tom had accompanied Sally Hemings to France, arguing that his "correspondent" had seen the boy and denied he could possibly have been as old as the *Gazette* claimed (*Richmond Recorder,* 3 Nov. 1802).

49. As TJR would later say, perhaps revealing more than he intended, Sally Hemings's children "resembled Mr. Jefferson so closely that it was plain that they had his blood in their veins," while Thomas Turner, a Virginian commenting on TJ's relationship with Hemings for a Boston paper in 1805, claimed that Beverley Hemings was "well known to many" though he was still a child. TJR, in Randall to Parton, 1 June 1868, reprinted in Brodie, *Thomas Jefferson,* 494; Boston *Repertory,* 31 May 1805.

50. *Richmond Examiner,* 25 Sept. 1802.

51. Historians have generally accepted that Wayles and Betty Hemings had as many as six children together. Madison Hemings claimed that his grandmother "was taken by the widower Wales as his concubine." Isaac Jefferson, also formerly enslaved at Monticello, said of Betty Hemings's children that "folks said that these Hemings'es was old Mr. Wayles' children." Thomas Turner reported in 1805 that Sally was "the natural daughter of Mr. Wales, who was the father of the actual Mrs. Jefferson." "Life among the Lowly, No. 1" [Appendix A]; *Memoirs of a Monticello Slave,* 13; Turner, in Boston *Repertory,* 31 May 1805.

52. Ellen Randolph Coolidge to Joseph Coolidge, 24 Oct. 1858, reprinted in Annette Gordon-Reed, *Thomas Jefferson and Sally Hemings: An American Controversy,* (Charlottesville, 1997), 260.

53. TJ to Nicholas Lewis, 12 April 1792, in Julian P. Boyd et al., eds., *The Papers of Thomas Jefferson,* 27 vols. to date (Princeton, 1950–), 23:408.

54. McDonald, "Race, Sex, and Reputation." Although this essay focuses on regionally specific reasons why the story failed to damage TJ's political stature in Virginia, McDonald makes the broader observation that so long as TJ acted legally and responsibly as president, few Americans cared much about his personal affairs.

55. Coolidge to Coolidge, 24 Oct. 1858, reprinted in Gordon-Reed, *Thomas Jefferson and Sally Hemings: An American Controversy,* 259.

56. *Richmond Recorder,* 29 Sept. 1802.

57. On how interracial rape and sexual relations between masters and slaves generally helped bolster slavery, see, for example, Darlene Clark Hine, "Rape and the Inner Lives of Southern Black Women: Thoughts on the Culture of Dissemblance," in Virginia Bernhard, Betty Brandon, Elizabeth Fox-Genovese, and Theda Perdue, eds., *Southern Women: Histories and Identities* (Columbia, Mo., 1992), 177–89; Catherine Clinton, "Southern Dishonor: Flesh, Blood, Race, and Bondage," in Carol Bleser, ed., *In Joy and in Sorrow: Women, Family, and Marriage in the Victorian South, 1830–1900* (New York, 1991), 52–68, and "Caught in the Web of the Big House: Women and Slavery," in Walter J. Fraser, Jr., R. Frank Saunders, Jr., and Jon L. Wakelyn, eds., *The Web of Southern Social Relations: Women, Family, & Education* (Athens, Ga., 1985), 19–34; Thelma Jennings, "'Us Colored Women Had to Go through a Plenty': Sexual Exploitation of African-American Slave Women," *Journal of Women's History,* 1 (1990), 45–74; Karen A. Getman, "Sexual Control in the Slaveholding South: The Implementation and Maintenance of a Racial Caste System," *Harvard Women's Law Journal,* 7 (1984), 115–52; and Eugene Genovese, *Roll, Jordan, Roll: The World the Slaves Made* (New York, 1976), 413–31.

58. On the ethics of sex across the color line among Southern elites, see Bertram Wyatt-Brown, *Southern Honor: Ethics and Behavior in the Old South* (New York, 1982), chap. 12, esp. 307–10. Wyatt-Brown, who doubted the truth of the TJ-Hemings story, adds that ethical behavior also demanded that a man's enslaved partner was seen as sexually attractive to white men, which usually meant that she had light skin, and that a man's sexual practices were not part of a larger pattern of alcoholism or other dissoluteness. TJ's relationship with Sally Hemings fit these patterns, with TJR describing Sally Hemings as "decidedly good looking." TJR, in Randall to Parton, 1 June 1868, reprinted in Brodie, *Thomas Jefferson,* 495.

59. TJR, in Randall to Parton, 1 June 1868, reprinted in Brodie, *Thomas Jefferson,* 495.

60. "Life among the Lowly, No. 1" (Appendix A).

61. The restraint shown by the editors of the *Herald* wore off within a few months. By December they were running stories on TJ and Hemings based on information received

from their own informants, justifying their change of heart by claiming that "although the subject is indeed a delicate one, we cannot see why we are to affect any great squeamishness against speaking plainly of what we consider as an undoubted matter of fact interesting to the public." Frederick-town *Herald,* quoted in *Richmond Recorder,* 29 Sept. and 8 Dec. 1802.

62. *Richmond Recorder,* 12 Jan. 1803.

63. See, for example, Judith P. Justus, *Down from the Mountain: The Oral History of the Hemings Family* (Perrysburg, Ohio, 1990).

64. Frances Trollope, *Domestic Manners of the Americans,* 2 vols. (London, 1832), 1:98–99.

65. TJR reported that at least one man having dinner with TJ "looked so startled as he raised his eyes . . . to the servant behind him, that the discovery of the resemblance was perfectly obvious to all." TJR, in Randall to Parton, 1 June 1868, reprinted in Brodie, *Thomas Jefferson,* 494.

66. *Thomas Jefferson's Farm Book,* 130; "Life among the Lowly, No. 1" (Appendix A); Coolidge to Coolidge, 24 Oct. 1858, reprinted in Gordon-Reed, *Jefferson and Hemings,* 258.

67. Journal of John Hartwell Cocke, 26 Jan. 1853, in John Hartwell Cocke Papers, Box 188, Alderman Library, University of Virginia. Also see Cocke's journal entry dated 23 April 1859, in which Cocke argued that "in Virginia this damnable practice [of having sexual relationships with one's slaves] prevails as much as any where and probably more, as Mr. Jefferson's example can be pleaded for its defence."

68. Randall to Parton, 1 June 1868, reprinted in Brodie, *Thomas Jefferson,* 497.

CHAPTER 5

Monticello Stories Old and New

Rhys Isaac

To be a person is to have a story. To not be allowed a story is to be marked for obscurity and oppression. African Americans and women certainly know this, having so lately prevailed in a proud insistence that history must include their stories. Stories are the great means of effective knowledge of human life. Knowing them, and being able to follow them or even anticipate their unfolding, is an essential prerequisite to engaging in social action. Historians therefore recognize that carefully attending to the stories past people told and enacted is one powerful way to gain understanding of those past people.

Before Monticello there were stories from the birthplace, Shadwell, and then the Randolph place, Tuckahoe. . . .

The old man could first remember himself as a three-year-old boy on a cushion on horseback supported by the strong black arms of the enslaved man who was taking him on his first long journey—from Shadwell to Tuckahoe.[1]

This was the very earliest memory that the aging Thomas Jefferson could summon up to tell his grandchildren. It was a simple little story, and yet it told so much—more, no doubt, than the teller consciously knew. It was a story recalling the start of a lifetime of intimacy with and dependence upon the care of members of the African American communities among which the third president of the United States had been born and had lived for the greater part of all those years.

Thomas Jefferson—like all boys of his race and class—learned early to outwardly distance and despise those who once had nurtured him; in the years of the prime of his manhood he strenuously denied any stories about warm closeness between the races. In *Notes on the State of Virginia,* written as he approached forty, Jefferson denied the warm intimacies of the African American nurturing he had received. The story he told of the relationship of the races that lived so close together is both shockingly true and sadly incomplete: "The *whole* commerce between master and slave is a perpetual exercise of the most boisterous passions, the most un- remitting despotism on the one part, and degrading submissions on the other. Our children see this, and learn to imitate it."[2]

Monticello was already a place of stories, before ever its owner had set- tled on a name for it or begun to build his dream house on his chosen hill. Stories, however, are always preceded by earlier stories. What were the fantasies shared by the two young men, Thomas Jefferson and Dabney Carr, when they took to rambling on that hillside and swore to arrange to be buried under their favorite oak near the summit? Jefferson kept that promise to his friend when he died in 1773. But by then he had already chosen the name "Monticello" and begun the house whose building and rebuilding was part of his life's work. He had already started the massive mythologization of the mountaintop whose legend grew as did his own.

So now, on the threshold of the twenty-first century, the stories en- shrouding Monticello are a part of national history. Or rather, they are part of global history, because most of the planet's inhabitants still yearn for the fulfillment of the promises of equality and freedom that Thomas Jefferson so boldly penned at the outbreak of the great democratic revolu- tion that is still at work in the world.

And now the DNA tests give a new story that also pertains to the worldwide meaning of Monticello. Or, rather, the tests bring into sudden prominence, with the great authority of "science," a set of stories long told by families that have always known Monticello as an origin place— the stories of Sally Hemings and the children she bore to Thomas Jeffer- son on that little mountain top.

❧

For a long time I have been a collector of the stories that the young Thomas Jefferson told and reenacted for himself and others as he set out in life and moved toward the first Monticello. I was born at the Cape of Good Hope, an old slave-supported colony at the southern end of Africa; I have lived in Australia, another colonized place, most of my adult life. Finding the repressed and denied stories, and bringing into history those to whom they belong seems to me a needed part of decolonization; it is part of the work of carrying forward the freedom and equality that Jefferson proclaimed in his revolutionary Declaration of Independence. So now I am drawn into a quest for the stories of the second Monticello, starting with questions about Sally Hemings's stories, and about the new stories of the place arising from their relationship.

❧

What stories did Thomas Jefferson "write" in his location and design of this amazing house?

Insufficient attention has been paid, I feel, to the story that the young Jefferson told in his extraordinary and unprecedented decision to build on an uninhabited—almost uninhabitable—eminence. (In the age of the internal combustion engine, we forget the vast impracticality—and costliness—of that decision when it was made.) The possible meanings of this story told not in words but in landscape design and the masonry of bricks and mortar deserve much more searching out than they have as yet received.

These are the stories that I have sensed to be enacted in the designing of the first version of this legendary house.

Jefferson, the young landscape designer, severed his dream house as much as possible from the corn and tobacco culture that paid for its building and its continuing support. He took his house up out of its fields onto a wild, wooded mountain top. So Monticello was initially built in denial and division—even though it could not help incorporating some of what it denied.

That kind of separation of estate house and estate was not only unprecedented but ran against the fundamental conception of such a house in the teachings of Andrea Palladio, the sixteenth-century Italian architect whom Jefferson revered above all others. Nobody before Jefferson had thought to build an estate house on a deserted eminence; Palladio had designed his country villas to be organic body metaphors of the estates into which they were integrated.[3]

There was surely an impulse toward romantic stories in Jefferson's ascent to the heights. In his desire for removal out of the settled valley, the young man was led by the inspiration he found in the wild Celtic landscapes that so stirred his soul in the epics of the newly discovered Gaelic bard, Ossian.[4] But the withdrawal from envelopment by the larger estate with its African American communities was unmistakable. Nor can we suppose that the choice, and the denial and division it entailed, was accidental or unintended. He was cutting himself off symbolically—and, as much as possible, physically—from the surrounding presence and the sounds of laughter, song, and dance of the villages of laborers whose women had nurtured him in infancy, and whose youngsters had been his companions.

Jefferson, the architect, reinforced that severance. Palladio's estate houses conceived of the service areas as the lesser parts of the body of the whole; they flanked the center that they thereby elevated to greater eminence. Their extension displayed magnificence, as had the retinue of servants traditionally attending a great man. In Jefferson's design for Monticello, the service buildings, instead of being displayed as an expression of the great-estate household, were suppressed into an arc of basement.

There was also another profound innovation for a great house of this type. At the same time the young Thomas Jefferson withdrew the house onto its little mountain, he began to mythologize it as a temple of married love, a sacred place for himself and Martha as they retired from the world into the conjugality for which Jefferson continually expressed a yearning.[5]

And yet there had been another story that the young builder of Monticello projected in his dreams of how he would live in the married state. It was a story that ran counter to the manifest one in subtle ways. Ardent in his youthful friendships, the young Jefferson made at least four proposals that his favorite companions should upon marriage make joint establishments. They and their wives would live in adjacent households. (Among the small proportion of Jefferson's letters to survive the 1770 fire at Shadwell, this plan is found articulated three times; there was a fourth expression of it through an invitation for Jefferson's brother-in-law to bring his bride to live on the mountaintop at Monticello beside her sister, Jefferson's fiancée, Martha.) This fantasy, too, was against fundamental rules. Such an arrangement had been taboo in Western Europe for centuries. There it had become the rule since 1500 or earlier that there could only be one married couple in a properly constituted household. So I am impelled to ask: where could Jefferson have experienced and been drawn to such an arrangement? My answer: surely it was at the quarters that had surrounded him in infancy—the quarters from which his other impulses were separating him as much as possible. The close coresidence of married pairs was commonplace in the quarters of large plantations.[6]

This African American dream, however, could not be an immediate reality for a young Virginia gentleman becoming a householder in the 1770s. Later, as a widower living in the second Monticello, Jefferson created a different kind of extended family by bringing his elder married daughter, Martha, and her children to live with him—her husband in the offing. Still hankering for this kind of drawing together, the master of Monticello even tried unsuccessfully to cajole his less biddable younger married daughter, Maria, and her husband into a similar arrangement.[7]

❧

The second Monticello seemed in some ways to "tell" the stories of division and denial in even more marked form than had the first. The house atop its still suppressed service "wings" was redesigned into an apparently one-story pavilion house. This certainly intensified the turning away from Palladian traditional expressions of estate lordship and its reliance on the toils of its bound laborers.

But the changed character of his household led Jefferson to enact new stories that made the second Monticello different in important ways.

Monticello was no longer a house to enshrine a married couple, although it was, perhaps, in part memorial to that lived ideal. In reality it was now the house where a widower would rear his surviving daughters, and where he would practice the refined sociability and conversation for which he had acquired such a taste in France. The second Monticello also came to be more encroached upon by agriculture—especially by the wheat crop that Jefferson and his peers hoped would make a more wholesome Virginia, freer of the usurious grip of London and Glasgow merchants. In the quest for means of solvency, the great house came to be more and more surrounded by industrial manufactories.

The second Monticello was enacted differently in a profound though hidden way. Stories have long told or hinted at a new sexual relationship that haunted the house, where it was not permitted to be proclaimed. Now the results of DNA tests dramatize that sexual relationship to the world.

It must have been common knowledge on the mountaintop that there was a beaten path between the master's great chamber and Sally Hemings's lodging. The collector of the stories of Monticello has now to include a cumulating story—as the relationship endured—of a custom-of-the-place marriage.

Marriage? That is a bold assertion, apparently without documentation. But Annette Gordon-Reed's book *Thomas Jefferson and Sally Hemings* reminds us that just because some event or state of affairs is not in the record, it does not mean that it did not happen or exist.[8]

A lot of evidence tells us—DNA now clinching it—that Sally Hemings faithfully bore Thomas Jefferson's children and *his* children *only*. She loved him probably, and he her. We cannot really know, although we do know that some of her grandchildren told it as part of their own story. Probably, for the relationship to have been so longlasting in the face of the world's mocking prurience, he loved her. For that to be in any way plausible now, twentieth-century persons with a strong sense of the requirements of equality in love relationships have to remind themselves that it would at best have been for Sally and for Thomas as it has been for most marriage partners through the ages: a kind of love and affection within a framework of profound inequalities as to power and freedom. (We have to recognize that gender relations in past times and other cultures make "love," as we are inclined to idealize it, extremely problematic.) Sally Hemings's situation as Jefferson's slave was at an extreme, but it was not so different from the common lot of women. We have to recognize that gendered property allocations have made and often still make women ready to enter lasting sexual relations with men who are attracted to them, if those men will "support" them and the children resulting from the union. "Love" in such matches—if it is present—has then to arise already accommodated to the coercion of the unequal circumstances.

The long fidelity of an attractive, fertile woman, such as Sally, living in a crowded, sexually alive community, indicates that she regarded herself as Jefferson's woman, and was so regarded by all the relevant males in the community. She was his "plantation wife," although not his acknowledged legal wife to bear him children who would be heirs at law; neither was she his acknowledged parlor-and-dining-room wife to share in the entertaining of his many guests. These exclusions surely enabled Jefferson's daughters and grandchildren to both "have" this inescapable knowledge and to strenuously deny and repress it.

Wise counselors have protested my use of the terms *marriage* and *wife* (even *secret marriage* or *secret wife*) for this enduring, known, enforced, and observed relationship. I respect their objections, but I am not persuaded, for instance, to prefer the term *concubine*. (That is the word James Callender applied in derision in 1802; it reappears in the newspaper report of the story told by Sally's son, Madison Hemings, that was published in Ohio in 1873.) The term *mistress* has usually been applied to a second woman kept away from a gentleman's residence. The word *wife* historically has a broad scope—in the Teutonic languages it connotes "woman" and by extension, female of the species; in the King James Bible it is the word used to describe the handmaiden Hagar, whom Abram took to bed.[9]

According to Madison Hemings's account, our most reliable source, Sally Hemings not only agreed to come and live at Monticello with special privileges, but she had a verbal contract—a promise that her children would be freed when they came of age. This was a promise honored in every way it can be checked in the record throughout the thirty-six-and-a-half years of coresidence that followed. Among Jefferson's last acts was a codicil freeing his and Sally's youngest sons; they would have been sold as slaves after his death had he not provided for their freedom.[10]

What *were* the stories that began to haunt the second Monticello, the Monticello that was publicly segregated but intimately joined by a secret relationship that had to be known by everyone there?

Perhaps there were surviving African stories, and surely there were emerging African American stories that encompassed this situation, but we can only speculate about them.

We can also only speculate how African American repertoires of stories might have been modified, extended, or displaced in Sally's own repertoire. She had, after all, a year-and-a-half's residence in Paris during the time of her sexual maturation. Paris was already Paris, and Robert Darnton's studies have revealed the active currency of *livres philosophiques* in this prerevolutionary time.[11] These forbidden but widely circulating books were often very explicit about sexual pleasure and a new "natural" morality endorsing its enjoyment. (It was with the *philosophes* after all that Jefferson's public life had much connection.) Perhaps Sally learned stories and forms of action to go with them. We simply do not know, although we do know that the Thomas Jefferson of these years seemed to enter into "Parisian" *"philosophique"* stories when he paid exuberant court to the married lady Maria Cosway, with whom he was highly infatuated.

After Paris, Sally Hemings spent her mature "married" life almost entirely at Monticello. Unsurprisingly, her story of the second Monticello comes not in erotic form at all; it is a story of herself as a determined mother-to-be, who secured a contract, if not for a secret marriage, then for a lifelong special relationship, from the man, her master, who had already gotten her pregnant. And so the story that she—by then a convincingly sober matron—told to her maturing second-youngest son was the story of that contract. By it she had lived decently, and by its covenant she could promise to Madison and his younger brother, as a birthright, the same freedom that their two older siblings already enjoyed. (As is pointed out by Dianne Swann-Wright elsewhere in this volume, *this* Sally thus told a modest but convincing story of herself as "liberator"; perhaps she already hoped that, if she lived so long, she could end her days in a household that a free-man son could form, as indeed she did.)[12]

And Thomas Jefferson? What were the stories that he, the widower returned from France, told himself as he settled into an enduring mated-pair relationship that was secretly reconstituting the second Monticello? What modifications, overturnings, or supplantings was he making of the stories that he had built into the design and the mythologizing of the first Monticello? In the design of that house, the house for his public marriage, he had made a maximum separation from the supporting African American communities. As he constructed the second Monticello, how did he now tell and enact to himself and to Sally (and inevitably to the plantation community at large) the story of the union in his bed of that once-separated great house and quarter?

We can only speculate on the stories Thomas Jefferson might have been telling himself, but the wealth of written records from this man of the pen who could also build enduring, highly visible structures threatens to overbalance the other's stories. Jefferson's written and built "volubility" could easily drown out whatever insecure speculations we might engage in about African American stories of master and Sally told in the quarter, and even the richer recorded oral history that the Hemings family derive from their founding mother. I shall therefore confine speculation on Jefferson's possible stories to a brief set of queries.

Was it for Thomas Jefferson a story of conquest? We know he dwelt upon that theme in his first published contribution to the political crisis from which grew the revolution.[13]

Was it biblical? We know he searched the Bible for accounts of marriage that could be used to resolve a 1770 lawsuit. He could not have missed the story of Abram being given a "wife," Hagar, to remedy Sarai's barrenness, nor the outcast status of Ishmael, the issue of that union.[14]

Was it a lyrical passage about secret love from MacPherson's *Ossian*? That passage, a poetic paean to the moon, is the longest that Jefferson had transcribed in youth from this, his dearest work in all literature.[15]

Was it the sensuality of "philosophic" literature and art? Jefferson had already expressed admiration for erotic stories set in Paris, long before he went there; in 1771 he recommended Sterne's *Sentimental Journey* as a lesson book of natural morality. While they stop short of consummated sex, many of the incidents in Sterne's narrative of travels to Paris and on through the South are highly charged with erotic anticipation.[16] We know that Jefferson threw himself into an erotically charged relationship with Maria Cosway. One of his letters to her ends up sharing some discreetly bawdy mirth from the section of Laurence Sterne's *Tristram Shandy* about the celebration of the coming to Strasbourg of the gigantic, unmistakably phallic "nose" that all the women longed to touch![17] That same letter had already reported Jefferson's excitement in Dusseldorff over a highly sexualized painting of a young slave woman, by the early eighteenth-century Dutch painter, Adriaen van der Werff. The evidently amorous Jefferson described the scene of "Sarah delivering Agar to Abraham" as "delicious"; he had desired to be transformed into Abraham—as shown about to lie with the young woman in the bed on which they are already seated—"though the consequence would have been that I should [now] have been dead five or six thousand years." He thought himself little of a "connoisseur," but rather "a son of nature, loving what I see and feel."[18]

Was it a Frenchman's story of Suliman and his chosen wife from his seraglio? Jefferson had also placed Marmontel's *Moral Tales* high on his

1771 recommended reading list of contemporary works. The story of Suliman, the Magnificent, the Ottoman emperor, and his seraglio, is prominent in that collection. Suliman kept five hundred slaves "for his pleasure." The salaciousness of this narrative is pronounced, and we know that Jefferson read it as coming from a highly admired author. Whether it could have had for him any application, even in fantasy, to his seemingly (although secretly) uxorious relationship with one slave—Sally—is something we shall probably never know.[19]

The leads for these and many other stories of virile prowess and patriarchal assertion that could be both erotic fantasies and forms of social display, are plentiful. They could elicit elaborations that would not be appropriate in this essay. In the end with Thomas, as with Sally, we come back to a single much more sober story. It is a story—in his case enacted not told—of a "marriage vow" taken (or minimally a contract made) and obligations promised *and fulfilled* over the long years of the joint lives that followed.[20]

We know furthermore that Sally and Thomas's descendants believed that these two loved each other but understood that disparity of status made a marriage impossible, as indeed it did. The Hemings descendants have asserted that since blood is thicker than water, the great ancestor made due provision for his children. They have honored Jefferson as a white man who—unlike most white men in their bitter collective experience—kept his word to a black woman, and kept his promise for the children that she bore him.[21]

❧

Despite the respect shown by the Hemings family members, the distance that Thomas Jefferson kept from his secret family confronts us with a deep problem of comprehension. Some are impelled to exclaim: "Why then he *was* a monster to be so cool and to provide so little!" (This view is supported by knowledge of other similarly placed slave masters of that time who tried to do more.) But here we should perhaps hold back from anachronistic twentieth-century expectations of love between equals and of a norm of familial closeness. Historians will recognize that the same theory and practice of inequality that made it utterly impossible for Thomas to marry or even acknowledge Sally in any public way made it impossible for him to see her children—although also his own—as anything other than lower class. Even if the proportions of their ancestry enabled those children to be taken for "white," Sally's children could not be "gentlemen" or "ladies." Thomas Jefferson's sense of categories was very strong and, even for his time, remarkably inflexible.[22] A training as artisans (with a gift of access to music, if they proved apt) was the most that Jefferson, seeing the world as he did, could feel that he should give them. And that he did give them.

❧

In the end we look at perplexities as to the stories that entered into, were enacted in, and were passed on from the second Monticello.

At the start I stressed the intimacy with black folk that Thomas Jefferson—like so many others, even in the North—was sustained by from birth throughout his life. His mature years, again like those of all his peers, had to be lived in a scornful denial of that intimacy. But as I review the open and secret stories of the second Monticello, I find myself asking: was there for Thomas a secret joining of what had once been severed, brought about by his relationship with Sally? This could have been for him a stitching up of a rent in his life, while for us, because of its shame-clad secrecy, it appears repellent.

❧

In this time, on the threshold of the twenty-first century, we are now engaged in telling more openly than at any time since the abolition movement a story of the harsh injustices and the perpetual atrocities of the system of race slavery. Now is therefore a time when we both face up to the bitter legacies and take pride in the steps already made toward redressing them with provisions for interracial equality and freedom. So we are led to try to make histories for ourselves out of the stories that we find told in the words, actions, and built environments of the enslaved and their masters. We are impelled to find in the relationship of Sally Hemings and Thomas Jefferson both an appalling story of the systematic inequalities and the systematic tyrannies of the world of the makers of the American Revolution, and an inspiring story for us to enact through an honoring of the now more fully proven African American descendants of Thomas Jefferson. Thereby the great family of the United States of America—and indeed of a multiracial world that yearns to enter into the promise of the democratic revolution—may find in the new story of Monticello some increased sense of being one family.

I shall end this engagement with the Hemings-Jefferson history by telling a story that I hope will carry a message of encouragement.

Colonial Williamsburg is currently engaged in a valiant effort to tell the conflicted history of the races in America. It has, for this purpose, enlisted a superb team of actor-historians, women and men, black and white, who study the documentary record in order to vividly enact scenes from the troubled past. They enact their histories rather than write them into articles and books.

Bill Barker is a tall, white man who enacts with great distinction the part of Thomas Jefferson. Harvey Bakari is a tall, African American man who plays with equal distinction a number of roles, including that of William Moses, the free black preacher.

This is what I was told about the Monday after that Halloween weekend, when the DNA "revelations" received such enormous nationwide publicity. Harvey thought to himself, Bill may be disturbed by this, so I should find something appropriate to say when we meet. Harvey need not have worried. They met, not in the workroom, but approaching each other from different directions on Williamsburg's Duke of Gloucester Street. Harvey was still searching for something to say, but before he had come up with anything, he saw Bill's hand raised in greeting: "How y'-goin', Cuz'?" were the words that sounded down the street.

NOTES

The author wishes to acknowledge the support of the James Pinckney Harrison bequest through the history department of the College of William and Mary during the time of the preparation of this essay. The following individuals have given sharp critical assistance: Cindy Hahamovitch, Colleen Isaac, Peter S. Onuf, and Fredrika Teute. I thank them, while taking full responsibility for the views expressed here.

1. Henry S. Randall, *The Life of Thomas Jefferson* (New York, 1858), I, 11.

2. Thomas Jefferson (hereafter TJ), *Notes on the State of Virginia*, ed. William Peden (Chapel Hill, 1955), Query XVIII ("Manners"), 162, emphasis added (Appendix E in this volume).

3. Isaac Ware, trans., *The Four Books of Andrea Palladio's Architecture* (London, 1738), i.

4. On TJ's passion for Ossian—and for the stories/dreams planned into Monticello treated in more detail—see Rhys Isaac, "The First Monticello," in Peter S. Onuf, ed., *Jeffersonian Legacies* (Charlottesville, 1993), 77–108.

5. Ibid.

6. These proposals are discussed in ibid., 87–88.

7. Jan Ellen Lewis, "The White Jeffersons," chapter 6 in this volume.

8. Annette Gordon-Reed, *Thomas Jefferson and Sally Hemings: An American Controversy* (Charlottesville, 1997).

9. Genesis, xvi:3.

10. Gordon-Reed, *Thomas Jefferson and Sally Hemings*, 38–46.

11. The subject of Sally Hemings's education in cosmopolitan outlook and manners—and, indeed, of her awakening to sexuality toward her master in a Parisian context—is thoughtfully and persuasively dealt with by Gordon-Reed, *Thomas Jefferson and Sally Hemings*, 164, 188–91. For the philosophe moralization of erotic love, see Robert Darnton, *The Forbidden Bestsellers of Pre-Revolutionary France* (New York, 1995). On TJ and Maria Cosway, see note 17 below.

12. Gordon-Reed, *Thomas Jefferson and Sally Hemings;* Lucia Stanton and Dianne Swann-Wright, "Bonds of Memory: Identity and the Hemings Family," chapter 7 in this volume.

13. See Isaac, "First Monticello," 94.

14. Genesis, xvi:1–16; Frank L. Dewey, "Thomas Jefferson and a Williamsburg Scandal: The Case of *Blair v. Blair,*" *Virginia Magazine of History and Biography,* 89 (1981), 44–64, esp. 48, n.13.

15. For TJ's passion for Ossian, see Isaac, "First Monticello," 77–78, 83–85.

16. See TJ to Robert Skipwith, with a List of Books for a Private Library, in Julian Boyd et al. eds., *The Papers of Thomas Jefferson,* 27 vols. to date (Princeton, 1950–), 1:78; and Laurence Sterne, *A Sentimental Journey through France & Italy by Mr. Yoricke,* vols. I & II (London, 1768), passim, and esp. vol. II, chap. 32.

17. TJ to Maria Cosway, 24 April 1788, in Boyd et al., eds., *The Papers of Thomas Jefferson,* 13:103–04; Laurence Sterne, *The Life and Opinions of Tristram Shandy, Gentleman* (1760–1767; New York, 1950), vol. 3, chaps. 31–42; vol. 4. It may be important to the understanding of the sexual history of TJ in Paris that, whereas he wrote to Maria of prodigious phallic prowess and of ravishment anticipated, she ignored the topic of ravishment and either did not understand the phallic metaphor or affected not to; see Maria Cosway to TJ, 29 April 1788 in Boyd et al., eds., *The Papers of Thomas Jefferson,* 13:114–16. See also the discussion in the next note.

18. TJ to Cosway, 24 April 1788, in Boyd et al., eds., *The Papers of Thomas Jefferson,* 13:103–04. TJ's taste for the art of van der Werff is noted in William Howard Adams, ed., *The Eye of Thomas Jefferson* (Washington, D.C., 1976), 193; but the painting chosen to illustrate the style is a bland scene of "Jacob blessing the Sons of Joseph"; nor do the notes make any mention of the "delicious" scene in that other van der Werff painting that so aroused TJ. (Readers can conveniently find a rich color reproduction of this important painting in E. M. Halliday, "An overlooked rationale for the Jefferson-Hemings connection," *New Yorker,* 16 Nov. 1998, 34–36. I am indebted to Phillip Morgan for this reference.) The omission of this image in *The Eye of Thomas Jefferson* is reminiscent of the conspiracy to conceal TJ's documented sexuality that Gordon-Reed discusses in *Thomas Jefferson and Sally Hemings,* passim.

19. For TJ's admiration of Marmontel, see TJ to Robert Skipwith, with a List of Books for a Private Library, 3 August 1771, in Boyd et al., eds., *The Papers of Thomas Jefferson,* 1:78. The story of Suliman is told in the second tale of this famous collection. TJ sold his edition of the *Contes moraux de Marmontel,* 3 vols. (Paris, 1766), to the Library of Congress in 1815.

20. Gordon-Reed, *Thomas Jefferson and Sally Hemings,* 22–46, 218–21.

21. Gordon-Reed, *Thomas Jefferson and Sally Hemings;* Stanton and Swann-Wright, "Bonds of Memory."

22. Gordon-Reed, *Thomas Jefferson and Sally Hemings.*

CHAPTER 6

The White Jeffersons

Jan Ellen Lewis

This is what we now know. A man and a woman have children. The woman is the half-sister of his now-departed wife; she is the aunt, then, of his two grown daughters. She is also his slave. By law, their children are also his slaves. The children grow up on his plantation, and, like their mother, they work there, but their work is always light. They all seem to know that one day they will be free. Then, in the year 1802, a newspaper publishes a story that says that this man is the father of this woman's children. He does not deny this story explicitly, but instead he says that his enemies have spread a number of untruths. Everyone, including his family, takes the evasion as a denial, a refusal to honor an ugly story with a direct comment.

A man and a woman have children. He already has children. This woman is those children's aunt, the half-sister of the man's now-deceased wife. The man has two families, then, a first family and a second. Because this woman, the mother of his second family, is his slave, their children are also slaves. His first family does not know about his second family, even though they all live together on a plantation at the top of a mountain in Virginia. Or perhaps they know, in the way that children and grandchildren know these things but cannot acknowledge.

❦

Four children are born on a plantation at the top of a mountain in Virginia. Their mother is the half-sister of their father's wife, a woman who died ten years before the youngest of them was born. They have two older half-sisters, the children of the aunt they never knew, the woman their mother has replaced. And they have nieces and nephews, their sisters' children; they grow up with these children, on top of the mountain, but their nieces and nephews do not seem to know that they are all related, that the man some of them call Grandpapa, the others know is their father.

❦

Two daughters are born on a plantation at the top of a mountain in Virginia. Their mother dies when they are quite young. Their father becomes mother and father both to them. Sometime later, when they themselves are young mothers, a story is printed in a newspaper that says that their father has kept one of his slaves as a mistress and that together they have had children, that one of the children looks just like him. What do these daughters say? What do they tell their children? What do their children say? They love their father more than anything.

❦

Thomas Jefferson was the third president of the United States. After bearing him six children in ten years, his wife died, leaving him only two surviving daughters, Patsy and Polly. Twenty years after her death, in the second year of his first term as president, a newspaper published a story accusing him of fathering children by a slave mistress. He never honored the rumor with a direct response, but he clearly implied that it was a lie, fomented by his political enemies. To his dying day, Jefferson was troubled by the scurrilous stories that his political rivals spread, and they bothered the daughter who outlived him and they bothered her children, too. Abolitionists kept the rumor about the slave mistress and slave children alive, and after the Civil War, one of those children published an interview in which he claimed to be the son of Thomas Jefferson. For almost two centuries, most historians discredited the rumor, seeing in it only scandal and in the ex-slave's story only a longing to belong to something greater than himself. Still, the rumor stayed alive, and people continued to debate its merits. Then, in 1997, a scientist decided to perform a DNA test that might help resolve the dispute.

❧

These are the stories of families, of parents and children, of a white family and a black family, of a national family of blacks and whites. These are the stories of Thomas Jefferson and Sally Hemings, of white Jeffersons and black, of Americans black and white. They are the stories of a family and of a nation.

❧

All families have secrets. The family itself rests upon the terrible secret that mothers and fathers share: that their children were conceived in passion in the dark of night. This a truth that the child is at once driven to discover and terrified to behold. And this truth, its hiddenness, its compulsion to be discovered, is a metaphor for family life itself. The child perceive her parents as through a veil; there are always mysteries she cannot fathom, even in the happiest of families, even in those that are seemingly the most banal.

The white Jeffersons thought of themselves and told each other that they were a happy family. Less than half a year before he died, Thomas Jefferson counted his blessings and they were many, but "above all, a family which has blessed me by their affections, and never by their conduct given me a moment's pain."[1] Families are not by their nature happy. Making a family happy requires work, and sometimes it is work of imagination pure and plain: We imagine ourselves to be a happy family; we tell ourselves that we are; we suppress those murmuring suspicions that we are not. As a young widower in the 1780s, Thomas Jefferson worked very hard to make his small family—two surviving daughters and, later, their children—into a model of happiness. When they were young, he wrote his daughters deeply affectionate—and patently manipulative—letters. "I have placed my happiness on seeing you good and accomplished, and no distress which this world can now bring on me could equal that of your disappointing my hopes," he wrote Patsy when she was only twelve, placing a huge burden upon the motherless girl, but one that she happily shouldered.[2] In years to come, she would entertain her friends by showing them her father's letters, the ones in which he told her how well she had succeeded in making him happy.

In August of 1809—and this would have been a little more than a year after Sally Hemings's last child, Eston, was born—Margaret Bayard Smith visited Jefferson and his family at Monticello. One morning Patsy, by now a married woman with eight children of her own, was indisposed. Mrs. Smith visited her in her room, where "the conversation turned chiefly on her father." Patsy showed her friend some of her father's letters. Mrs. Smith copied certain passages into her journal, ones that contrasted the pleasures of family life with the miseries of politics. "When I look to the ineffable pleasures of my family society," Jefferson had written his daughter, "I become more and more disgusted with the jealousies, the hatred, the rancorous and malignant passions of this scene, and lament my having been drawn into public view." Mrs. Smith copied another passage in which Jefferson contrasted the miseries of governmental service to family life: "Worn down here with pursuits in which I take no delight, surrounded by enemies and spies, catching and perverting every word which falls from my lips, or flows from my pen, and inventing where facts fail them, I pant for that society, where all is peace and harmony, where we love and are beloved by every object we see . . . these are the only times existence is of any value to me."[3]

As everyone who has read Jefferson's *Family Letters* knows, during the 1790s, when Jefferson served in the Washington administration and then as John Adams's vice president, he wrote both his daughters a number of letters in which he contrasted the realm of politics and the realm of the family. So familiar have these contrasting ways of describing politics and the family become that they are what literary scholars call *tropes,* rhetorical devices in which words are used to convey something other than their literal meaning. Politicians seemed like "salamanders, to consider fire as their element." Family is "the only soil on which it is worth while to bestow much culture."[4]

These tropes have become familiar to us. Many of us would agree, instinctively, with Jefferson's characterization of the nation's capital as representing "every thing which can be disgusting" and the family as "every thing which is pleasurable to me in this world."[5] But when Jefferson spoke in these terms, they were novel. Only recently had men and women begun to sentimentalize the family, to think of it in almost religious terms as a sanctuary or haven. We need think only of Shakespeare's families— the warring Montagues and Capulets, the conflict-ridden Lears, the scheming Macbeths—to realize how remarkable, how revolutionary was the notion that a family might be a source of any pleasure at all, let alone the source of *everything* pleasurable.[6]

Likewise, Jefferson's depiction of the world of politics in such starkly negative terms was also an innovation. Only a few years before, American revolutionaries had thought of public service as the highest of callings; to give oneself over to the public, to sacrifice personal interest for the public good was the measure of greatness. For complex reasons involving changing political thought and practices both, Americans began to question the moral worth of government itself. Thomas Paine had said that "government even in its best state is but a necessary evil," and many Americans came to agree. Private life, social life, all life that was outside of government was what was valuable, and the purpose of government was to protect that life, primarily from government itself. From time to time, good men would have to take their turn in public service, but the public had no right to demand this sort of sacrifice. As Jefferson wrote in a particularly bitter moment, shortly after his wife had died and his friends were trying to draw him back into government, "If we are made in some degree for others, yet in a greater degree are we made for ourselves. It were contrary to feeling & indeed ridiculous to suppose that a man had less right in himself than one of his neighbors or indeed all of them put together."[7]

When Jefferson wrote to his daughters, telling them how he hated his life in government and how he longed to be with them, he was weaving together the strands of liberal political thought, which held that the purpose of government was to protect private life. Patsy and Polly and their children were the fleshly embodiment of the abstract reason that Jefferson worked for the public good. Moreover, once Jefferson and other liberal political practitioners disparaged the political life, then they could no longer draw from it the sense of fulfillment and worth that was available to men like Washington who thought of public service as a noble calling. Jefferson turned to his family for the appreciation, the love—the validation, we would say today—that he could not get from an increasingly boisterous and democratic citizenry.[8] By telling his daughters and their children how much they meant to him, how much he needed them, he trained them to give him the love that he needed for personal and political reasons both.

As we read Jefferson's letters, we can infer his intent. It is somewhat more difficult to imagine what might have been the effect of receiving such missives. As historians and amateur psychologists, we read the letters of the dead, and we wonder. What did it mean to Jefferson's daughters to be told, in letter after letter, that their love was "the best solace remaining to me in this world"; that "my only object in life is to see yourself and sister, and those deservedly near to you, not only happy, but in no danger of becoming unhappy"; to be enjoined "to love me as I do you." What might it have meant to see every letter closed in a slightly different way—"with constant love," "in all the warmth of my love," "everlasting love," "tender and unmingled effusions of my love," "tender and unceasing love," "unspeakable tenderness," "constant and unbounded love," "unalterable and tenderest love," "tenderest and unalterable love," and "tenderness without bounds."[9]

In the case of Martha Jefferson Randolph—Patsy—we need not speculate much at all. She showed the letters to her friend, Margaret Bayard Smith. Years later, when they renewed acquaintance, when Martha Randolph was an aging widow and her father had died, she was still showing her old friend her father's letters and displaying the artifacts of family love. One day, when Martha Randolph was not feeling well, Mrs. Smith sat with her in her room. They talked about Jefferson, and Martha took "up the down cover-lit, which was over her," and explained that it "'was the one he used for 40 yrs. And this bed was his.'—The one, I imagine, on which his last hours were past, for she stopped, choked by emotion and could not restrain her tears, tho' she concealed them by drawing the bedclothes over her face." Another day, Martha Randolph showed Mrs. Smith "the last lines he ever wrote." She told the story of how her father wrote these lines during his final illness, how he gave them to her the day before he died, how she did not read them until after he was gone. He had written her a poem, telling her not to cry for him, "that his last pang would be in parting from her, but that he would carry her love and memory to the two happy spirits (her mother and sister) who were waiting to receive him."[10]

Every family constructs a narrative. It tells itself a story about itself. Jefferson's family told themselves that they were a happy family, and so deeply did they believe their family narrative that the story engraved itself on the unconscious. As a grown woman, living in Boston, Jefferson's granddaughter Ellen Coolidge found herself haunted by the ghosts of her happy childhood. "When I dream it is mostly of long past times. Night after night I have been surrounded by the friends of childhood and early youth—my grandfather, mother, brothers, sisters, those whom I dearly loved and who dearly loved me, and who I hope in God's own time to rejoin."[11]

To be able to drive away the demons that haunt us in the night, to suppress the memories of family conflicts, of loss, of terror—this is an extraordinary accomplishment. No family, of course, is without its share of anguish and grief. In the case of the Jeffersons, they had more than their share, with not only the early death of Jefferson's wife and four of their babies but also the loss of Monticello to satisfy Jefferson's debts, a calamity that befell his descendants. The white Jeffersons proved themselves more than able to add to that sum of misery that life entails upon us all.

Perhaps it is a false distinction, to differentiate between natural catastrophes and the misery we make ourselves. The premature death of a loved one, the sudden collapse of the economy—these disasters hit Jefferson, and hit him hard. He can hardly be faulted. Yet a biographer has suggested that Jefferson should have understood that his wife was frail and that repeated pregnancies—six births in ten years of marriage—put her life at risk.[12] With perhaps more justification, others have remarked that Jefferson's expensive tastes and poor judgment were more to blame for his late-life insolvency than inherited debts and the collapse of Virginia's economy. Curiously, there is no consensus about the role Jefferson's slaveholding played in his financial demise. Some have argued that Jefferson's taste for expensive wine and rich brocade made it impossible for him to live as he wished without relying upon the labors of slaves. Others have seen his refusal to liquidate his slaves to pay off his debts as a sign of his softheartedness, a tenderness at odds with the requirements of a heartless economy.[13]

How deeply is the individual implicated in those vast impersonal forces of life, death, and profit that give shape to his life? This is a hard question, one with no easy answers. Most of us are inclined to cut the individual a little slack, whether out of too much appreciation for life's complexities, or too little comprehension of those forces we cannot direct. When it comes to choices that seem purely personal, however, we are often more ready to judge. And if we are so inclined, then we might note that the Jefferson women had a tendency to marry badly. Both Patsy Jefferson and her oldest daughter, Anne, married young, even for their time and place, and their marriages, in their family's eyes, were unhappy. Each was seventeen, and each married a man from the neighborhood who had Jefferson's hearty approval. He had known Patsy's young husband, her first cousin, Thomas Mann Randolph, all his life. Four years earlier, when only seventeen himself, young Randolph had asked Jefferson for his advice about his studies, and the older man gladly complied, with a letter so long and so full of sage advice that he finally cut himself off, worrying that "by this time . . . you will think that I have sermonized enough." Perhaps that is indeed what Randolph thought; it does not appear that he ever answered his future father-in-law's letter.[14] Whatever his early promise, Randolph turned out to be a man of unstable temperament who ended his unhappy life estranged from his family. His eldest son once described him as "more ferocious than the woulf [sic] & more fell than the hyena."[15]

Patsy's daughter fared even worse. Like her mother, she had been free to choose her own mate and, like her mother, she selected someone who appeared at first as if he might be one of Jefferson's protégés. Shortly after his marriage to Jefferson's granddaughter, Charles Bankhead returned to Monticello with his young bride so that he might read law with the family patriarch, who had just retired from the presidency. Jefferson welcomed his granddaughter and her husband, inviting them to stay at Monticello as long as they wished. "I hope . . . that you will both ever consider yourselves as a part of our family until you shall feel the desire of separate establishment insuperable."[16] At the time, Sally Hemings's last child, Eston, was an infant, having been born the previous spring. Whatever Charles Bankhead's early promise, within a few years' time he had become an alcoholic who beat his wife and had bankrupted himself and his own small family. Just as the family—that is, the members of the family who thought of themselves as the family—worried about how to cope with the erratic Thomas Mann Randolph, so they struggled with the problem presented by Charles Bankhead. Anne's brother Jeff, the oldest of Jefferson's grandsons and the one who seemed to take upon himself the role of family protector, once got into a violent fight with Charles in Charlottesville's courthouse square. When it was over, Jeff had been stabbed in the hip and Charles smacked in the face with the butt of Jeff's horsewhip. Still Anne refused to leave her husband and return to the sanctuary of

Monticello. In the last letter he ever wrote Jeff, Thomas Jefferson reported the sad news that Anne had died, at her home, at the age of thirty-five. Only then was she brought home to Monticello, where her bones still rest in the family graveyard.[17]

One cannot help wondering how far into the future a seventeen-year-old girl might have seen. Is character fixed at so early an age? Might a girl have seen the signs of her husband's later erratic behavior? Might a young man have anticipated his life's trajectory as a member of a great and greatly loved man's household? Thomas Mann Randolph later described himself as a duck, "the proverbially silly bird . . . among the swans."[18] Presumably, no one chooses consciously to be the duck, but one day he realizes that the duck he has become.

Every family is two families. First there are those who are born into it, marry into it, and give birth to its children. These are the figures on the family tree, their place on it signified by the facts of the demographic record, members in name, but sometimes name only. Then there are those who think of themselves as the real family—those who write its family story. Chief among those who considered themselves the real Jeffersons, of course, was Thomas Jefferson himself, the man who created the original idea of the family as "every thing which is pleasurable" and worked all his life to make his white family conform to that ideal. And then there was his oldest surviving daughter and her children, chief among them her first son, Jeff, and her second daughter, Ellen. But there were others who were members in name only. Two of them we have already met: the estranged son-in-law, Thomas Mann Randolph, and the knife-wielding drunkard, Charles Bankhead. But there was also Jefferson's second surviving daughter, Polly, the one who was left with her aunt in Virginia while her father went off with Patsy to represent the new nation in France. At the age of nine, against her desperate pleas, Polly was put on a ship, accompanied only by the fourteen-year-old slave Sally Hemings, to join her father in Europe. Ten years later, she married her cousin John, the son of the beloved aunt from whom she had been torn. Polly received, as best we can tell, the same expressions of her father's tender love, the same entreaties to love him well. But she did not always answer his letters. "I did not write to you, my dear Poll, the last week, because I was really angry at receiving no letter. . . . I ascribed it at first to indolence, but the affection must be weak which is so long overruled by that," her father scolded. And he closed his letter with a simple "Adieu."[19] It had been nine weeks since he had heard from her; she was twelve. Once she married, she rarely returned home.

So this was the Jefferson family constellation—an inner circle, committed to and writing with its every breath the story of a happy family and returning to Monticello even in its dreams, and an outer circle, so estranged, so remote, that a son could describe his father as more lethal than the earth's wildest beast. And yet, there was another family still, one that grew up alongside the white Jeffersons: Sally Hemings and her children, the unacknowledged children of Thomas Jefferson.

Everyone said that Sally Hemings's children looked like Thomas Jefferson. That had been one of the chief items in James Callender's 1802 newspaper article, the first public assertion that Jefferson was the father of Sally Hemings's children. The fourth line of that scurrilous piece of journalism had pointed to the resemblance. Sally's son's "features are said to bear a striking resemblance to those of the president himself."[20]

The family resemblances must have been quite remarkable indeed, for even Jeff Randolph acknowledged them. Jeff said that "the resemblance" between his grandfather and one of the Hemings children was "so close, that at some distance or in the dusk, dressed in the same way, [he] might be mistaken for Mr. Jefferson." He also said that one day "a gentleman dining with Mr. Jefferson, looked so startled as he raised his eyes from the latter to the servant behind him, that his discovery of the resemblance was perfectly obvious to all."[21] That, at least, is what Henry S. Randall, an early Jefferson biographer, told the historian James Parton in 1868. The letter that Randall sent Parton, describing his conversation with Jeff Randolph about ten years earlier, constitutes part of what Fawn M. Brodie once termed "the family denial." Thirty and more years later, after Jefferson's death, his oldest surviving grandchildren, Jeff Randolph and Ellen Coolidge, each offered a semi-official refutation of the allegation that their grandfather had been the father of Sally Hemings's children. Ellen Coolidge set out her answer to the questions in a letter to her husband, written in 1858, when she was visiting Jeff and his family in Virginia. A little while earlier, Jeff Randolph had told Randall his version of the family story, which Randall recounted in a letter to Parton. Then, in late 1873 or early 1874, Jeff Randolph wrote, but apparently never sent, a letter to the editor of the *Pike County Republican,* which had published autobiographical essays by Sally Hemings's third son, Madison, and Israel Jefferson, a former Monticello slave. Jeff's letter was a direct response to Israel's essay; its main purpose seems to have been to cast doubt upon Israel's credibility, thereby to refute his contention that Madison Hemings was speaking the truth when he claimed Thomas Jefferson as his father.[22]

None of these accounts entered the public record immediately. Parton described Randall's letter in his biography of Jefferson, published in 1874, but the letter itself was not published until 1951, in a biography of Parton.[23] Ellen Coolidge's letter remained in the hands of her descendants, although a copy is in the collection of her papers at the Alderman Library of the University of Virginia. As late as the summer of 1976, two years after Fawn Brodie argued that Jefferson was the father of Sally Hemings's children and eight years after Winthrop D. Jordan had suggested the same thing,[24] the librarians' notation at the top of the letter said, "RESTRICTED absolutely."[25] Copies—either in xerox or in one's own hand—were forbidden; publication in whole or in part was banned. The restrictions placed upon Ellen Coolidge's letter only enhanced its credibility, making it seem, like a whispered family secret, more true than the published record. The family story seemed true precisely because it was secret.

Similarly, Henry Randall's letter to James Parton, which has the form of a private communication of confidential information, did not become fully public until 1951. Randolph's response to Israel Jefferson still has not been published, although it has been available to researchers. If the family had an alternate explanation for the family resemblance of Sally Hemings's children, and an answer to Callender's never-forgotten charge, they never offered it publicly or in any private communications that have made their way into the historical record. Indeed, the family kept its denial almost entirely to itself, sharing it only with a trusted biographer, whom Jeff Randolph forbade to publish it. In their penchant for privacy, Jefferson's white family followed his example. During his lifetime, Jefferson had refused to answer the accusation directly. In 1805, he acknowledged to his secretary of the Navy that "when young and single I offered love to a handsome lady"—Betsey Walker, the wife of a good friend. "I acknoledge [sic] its incorrectness. It is the only one founded in truth among all their allegations against me."[26] Implicitly, the allegation about Sally Hemings was false.

So far as we know, that is the closest Jefferson ever came to addressing directly the Sally Hemings allegation, in either public or private. We have no record of his having denied the charges to his family, although he certainly led them to believe that they were untrue. In 1806 William Burwell, Jefferson's former secretary, showed Patsy a scurrilous poem written about her father by a young Irishman, Thomas Moore. He pointed out the most offensive passages, ones that intimated that the president "dreams of freedom in his bondmaid's arms." According to Henry Randall, the "indignant pair" showed Jefferson the poem, and "Mr Jefferson broke into a hearty, clear laugh." From this distance, we might say that the laugh was on Patsy and Burwell, and through them and Randall, on posterity, although Randall interpreted Jefferson's laugh as a clear denial. "There was more than argument—there was conviction in that laugh."[27] As was his habit, Jefferson had implied the denial without stating it directly, and for those who wanted to believe him, the implication was as good as his word.

When children confront their parents, they do not necessarily want to be told the truth. Sometimes they want only for order to be restored to their world, their suspicions laid to rest. When Patsy and the ever-loyal William Burwell burst in upon Jefferson, waving Moore's scurrilous poem, they wanted a denial, not a tear-filled confession. So also when Patsy and Polly asked their father why they no longer visited John Walker's, "knowing [how] intimate they were before he went to F[rance]." There was, in fact, a very good reason: In 1768, when he was unmarried, Jefferson made some improper advances to his good friend's wife, Betsey, when her husband was away from home for several months. As John Walker later told the story, after its outlines had been revealed in 1805 by the partisan press, Jefferson continued pushing himself on Betsey for more than a decade, long after he had married, once stuffing a sort of love letter up the sleeve of her dress and several times accosting her when one or the other of them was in a state of partial undress. Most Jefferson biographers have been willing to concede only what Jefferson himself conceded, that he had propositioned Betsey Walker only once, when he was young and unmarried. Dumas Malone concluded that "our knowledge of Jefferson's temperament and personality" make it hard to believe that Jefferson would have approached Betsey repeatedly and grossly, as her husband charged. But since these are the same historians who rejected the Sally

Hemings story because of their supposed knowledge of Jefferson's temperament and personality, perhaps we should not be so quick to accept Jefferson's account and reject John Walker's.[28]

According to Walker, his wife did not tell him about Jefferson's unwanted attentions until Jefferson left the country in 1784. Whether that is exactly what happened or not, when Jefferson returned to Virginia, he was no longer welcome at his old friend's house. His children seemed to sense that something was wrong. Rather than telling them just what that something was, "to quiet them [Jefferson] said some difference had arisen about money matters." This account, by the way, comes from William Burwell, who seems to have been present during the only two recorded times that Jefferson's daughters confronted him with questions about his private affairs. In this instance, his daughters had guessed right; there had been a rupture with the Walkers. Although it was about love, Jefferson told them it was about money.

It is not clear why Jefferson thought that this lie about his break with Walker would quiet his daughters. He had told them, after all, that one of his oldest and dearest friends had—and this was the way Burwell put it—tried "to defraud him in some money transactions."[29] Someone their father had loved and trusted had tried to cheat him, and he was too honorable, too decent, to denounce his old friend; no one would have known had not his daughters pressed him. It should not be surprising that Patsy and Polly talked; if their father would not denounce Walker, they would. And in this way, Jefferson's lie about his old friend made its way out into the public, as family secrets sometimes will.

Jefferson's daughters told David Meade Randolph, whose brother-in-law was Patsy's husband Thomas Mann Randolph. It was still a family lie, an extended family lie, we might say. As sometimes happens, however, families have fallings out. Jefferson sued David Meade Randolph in a complex lawsuit over Jefferson's father-in-law's estate. Then, a few years later, Jefferson fired Randolph from his post as United States marshal; shortly after that, Randolph was telling people that Jefferson had slurred John Walker's reputation. The newspapers had gotten hold of the Betsey Walker story at just the time that Callender was publishing his allegations about the Sally Hemings liaison, so Randolph was able to contribute his own mite: Not only had Jefferson attempted to seduce Walker's wife, he had also "fabricated a falsehood to explain the cause of their rupture."

Burwell, ever the Jefferson loyalist, was scandalized by Randolph's behavior. Jefferson had meant no harm, but once his daughters "incautiously" told their kinsman, then "an explanation intended to preserve the happiness & tranquility of his daughters, & *never* given elsewhere was made the basis of that charge against him & handled and attributed to the iniquity of his heart."[30]

The lie Jefferson told his daughters to protect his good name, by this logic, was less wicked than that same lie repeated in public. Perhaps that is the way Jefferson saw it as well. He tried to erect a wall between his family and the wider world, but that wall—even at its strongest—was but a thin membrane, the skin of a bubble, shimmering in the light. The story he made up to "quiet" his daughters made its way out into the public, just as his confession to a single act of "incorrectness" must have made its way back into his family. We do not know what Patsy and Polly thought if they read in the newspapers the story about their father and Betsey Walker. Perhaps they believed just what most historians have believed ever since: that Jefferson had an embarrassing lapse when he was young and that his embarrassment and subsequent efforts to hide it from his family are proof of his character.

Parents, as a rule, do not confess their sins to their children, although they vary in the means that they use to protect their children, that is, to protect themselves. In Jefferson's case, when his daughters confronted him about some embarrassing matter, he either evaded the question (the "hearty laugh" when shown Thomas Moore's poem) or lied (blaming the rupture with John Walker on his old friend). As for the accusations made by his enemies, so far as we know, Jefferson never acknowledged to his family that any of them were truthful. Instead, he told them that his enemies had lied about him and that the lies hurt. He was always the person done to, never the one who was *doing*. His chief defense within the family was to point out that he was the victim of vicious attacks. In 1803, for example, he wrote out his religious creed so that "my family, by possessing this, should be enabled to estimate the libels published against me on this, as on every other possible subject"[31]—as if proving that he was not an infidel would answer also the charges about fathering Sally Hemings's children. Even on his deathbed, Jefferson was still brooding about these allegations. "In speaking about the calumnies which his enemies had uttered against his public and private character with such unmitigated and untiring bitterness," Jeff Randolph reported that his grandfather said "that he had not considered them as abusing him; they had never known *him*. They had created an imaginary being clothed with odious attributes, to whom they had given his name."[32] Jefferson's family knew the real *him*— and that person could not have engaged in a liaison with Sally Hemings. The proof against the accusation was Jefferson's character as a family man, that is, the kind of person he was in his family.

Of course, these too are familiar tropes: the outer self that the world sees and the better, purer inner self—the self as it "really" is. In this sense, Jefferson was one of the first moderns, feeling himself misunderstood by and at odds with the world. And as we now know, Jefferson was almost certainly lying about his relationship with Sally Hemings—to his political allies, to his daughter, and to her son. And the form his lie took was particularly insidious, for it gave as its proof not a fact or something that had the appearance of a fact, but instead, a seductive and contingent offer of love. To believe Jefferson innocent of the slurs against him was to know the real *him;* to accept the slanders was not, he said, to know him at all. No child could resist this invitation into her father's naked heart. The thrill of the invitation, and the relief at the sight. It is as if Ham had lifted the flap of his father's tent—only to find him fully clothed and sleeping like a lamb.

When Jefferson implied that he was innocent of the Sally Hemings charges, perhaps he believed that he was telling the truth, or at least that he was not lying. Perhaps he thought that some part of Callender's charge was untrue, and hence he could implicitly deny the whole thing. Perhaps he did not think of Sally Hemings as his "concubine."[33] He might have thought of her as something more, a true love, a second wife. Or he might have thought of her as something less, an occasional sexual partner at best. Or perhaps he knew that the slave known as Tom and reputed to be his son by Sally Hemings was some other man's child. The DNA evidence strongly suggests that Jefferson was not this slave's father.

But whatever Jefferson thought, we now know, almost for a certainty, that he was the father of Sally Hemings's son Eston, and probably Beverley, Harriet, and Madison, as well. And, unless he was delusional—and whatever has been said about Jefferson, no one has ever made this charge—he must have known why the Hemings children looked like him. He must have known that all the defenses put up by his political friends and allies were in part or in whole untrue. So far as we know—and when we have only a written record and not a spoken one, that phrase covers much uncertainty—Jefferson's defenders were the first to mount what might be called a derivative family defense. That is, they said the stories could not be true because Jefferson was a good family man; they derived the defense from Jefferson's status and character, rather than from (asserted) personal knowledge about life within his family. The *Richmond Examiner,* for example, noted that in the twenty years since the death of his wife, Jefferson had "reared with parental attention, two unblemished, accomplished and amiable women, who are married to two estimable citizens. In the education of his daughters, this same Thomas Jefferson, supplied the place of a *mother*—his tenderness and delicacy were proverbial— not a spot tarnished his widowed character."[34]

The charge against Jefferson, then, was a moral one, about his character as a family man and a father. His family and his defenders asked the rhetorical question, how could the man who signed his letters to his daughters with every possible permutation and combination of tenderness and affection have fathered another family by one of his slaves? "There are such things, after all," his granddaughter Ellen Coolidge later told her husband, "as moral impossibilities."[35]

Yet to say that it was morally impossible for a tender father to betray his children by fathering another set of children was to define the issue in wholly private terms; such behavior would have been a crime against the family—the white family that is. From our vantage point, almost two hundred years later, it may be difficult for us to see it as any crime at all. Of course, we can only speculate about the nature of Jefferson's relationship with Sally Hemings. Some assume that it was necessarily coerced. Others guess that it might have been consensual. We have two reports— one from Jefferson's overseer Edmund Bacon and the other from Israel Jefferson, a former slave on the plantation—that Jefferson promised his wife on her deathbed that he would not remarry and bring in a stepmother "over" her children.[36] If that was the case, then Jefferson's liaison with Sally Hemings might be seen—and perhaps Jefferson himself saw it this way—as a fulfillment of his commitment to his departed wife and their daughters, rather than a betrayal. It is also possible, considering the length of Jefferson's relationship with Sally Hemings and his apparent honoring of a commitment to her to free their children, that their relationship might have had elements of love. If we were so inclined, we might even say that, within the constraints imposed by the mores of his time and its peculiar institution of slavery, Jefferson behaved rather honorably, fulfilling his promises to his wife, his children, and his mistress. Our problem, as historians, is that we cannot know, with the evidence available to us today. We can tell you what the normal pattern was—the institution of slavery placed enormous power in the hands of masters—but we cannot tell you whether Jefferson was the exception or the rule.

Yet even to engage the issue in this way, as if it were only and wholly a family matter, is to accept the way that it was framed by Callender and his opponents: as one about individual character. Individual character was measured by private behavior, within the family. At the time, the issue was only secondarily one of race—the added outrage of fathering children by a mulatto woman—and even less one of slavery. If the charges had been true—and let us not forget that indeed they were—then the affront would have been to Jefferson's family, and not to society, much less its members who were black or enslaved.

Of course we cannot help wondering whether his allies' responses to Callender's charge made Jefferson feel guilty or only more secretive. It is hard to imagine that it had not occurred to him that his liaison with Sally Hemings would be perceived as an affront to his white family, but he certainly could not help knowing it now, once it had become a topic of public discussion. Once he entered into the relationship, Jefferson had no real alternatives, however, than to keep the relationship secret. It is unthinkable that he would have acknowledged Sally Hemings and her children, but then again, that is not the issue here; rather, the question is the anatomy of the lie and its consequent costs.

To say simply that those were different times—the slavery, the racism, he could never have acknowledged it—is, finally, too simple. It is to obscure the other facts, that slavery itself, at least in a land that extols freedom, is a kind of lie, for it denies that one person is another's equal; and racism is another kind of lie, the kind that follows in the first lie's train, by attempting to explain and legitimate that inequality. Neither slavery nor racism is a natural fact; rather, both are contingent historical conditions, created by human beings to serve particular ends. So to say that Thomas Jefferson could not have acknowledged his relationship with Sally Hemings, whatever it was, because of race and slavery is only to say that some lies beget other lies, something we would do well to remember.

The derivative family defense, then, set the terms for the actual family defense, which was mounted decades later. Its primary element was Jefferson's status as a family man. Its primary mechanism (or methodology) was the privileged information about Jefferson's character vouchsafed to his children. Who, after all, would dare argue with the child who had claimed to have lifted the flap of her father's tent? And its primary problem was to explain the uncanny resemblance of the Hemings children to Thomas Jefferson, master of Monticello.

If not Jefferson, then who? Given the striking familial resemblance, the family defense of necessity had to be a family accusation. Jeff Randolph accused his mother's cousin—Jefferson's nephew—Peter Carr. In fact, Jeff Randolph told Henry Randall that Peter Carr had confessed to him. At about the same time, Jeff's sister Ellen was placing the blame on Peter Carr's brother Sam. This is the story that Jeff told Randall: One day, a visitor to Monticello just happened to drop a newspaper that contained an article with "some very insulting remarks about Mr. Jefferson's Mulatto Children." Jeff was so "provoked" that he confronted the Carr brothers, who just happened to be at Monticello that day, lazing beneath a tree. When shown the article, Peter and Sam both burst into tears, and "Peter exclaimed, 'arnt you and I a couple of ——— pretty fellows to bring this disgrace on poor old uncle who has always fed us! We ought to be ——— by ———!'" Jeff told Randall that Sally Hemings was Peter's mistress and her sister, Sam's. Ellen told a similar, but not identical story. She said Jeff had told her that he and a Mr. Southall had heard Peter Carr "say with a laugh, that 'the old gentleman had to bear the blame of his and Sam's . . . misdeeds.'" There was "a general impression" that Sally Hemings's four children were "*all* the children of [Sam] Carr, the most notorious good-natured Turk that ever was master of a black seraglio kept at other men's expense."[37]

Of course, if we were inclined to believe these stories we would point to their inconsistencies as proof of their authenticity. It could have been Peter; it could have been Sam. They were emotional, so they could have laughed or they could have cried. Both were of bad character, and did it really make any difference which was consorting with Sally and which with her sister? Both had repaid their grandfather's generosity by bringing a scandal upon his name. But now we know that these stories were lies. If the DNA evidence proves anything, it was that Eston Hemings was not a

Carr; he was not the son of Sam, and he was not the son of Peter, either. Hence, when Ellen said that the "general impression" was that all four of Sally Hemings's children were Sam's, she was putting forth a falsehood. Jeff may have told her that, and she might simply have been repeating it. Maybe it even was a general impression, but if so, everyone was generally wrong. Maybe Jefferson was made to bear the blame for some number of Sam and Peter's misdeeds, but fathering Sally Hemings's children was not one of them.

Jeff, too, had Peter confessing, even more explicitly, and perhaps more sympathetically. Now that we know that neither Jeff's nor Ellen's story was true, that Peter neither confessed himself nor pinned the blame on Sam, the details of their fictions become rather intriguing. Ellen had Peter laughing, while Jeff had him crying in shame, which may tell us something about Ellen and Jeff and how they thought a man who had fathered children by a slave might feel. Curiously, it was Jeff, the male, who imagined remorse. The operative word, however, is *imagine*, for we must remember that no one, not Sam or Peter and certainly not Thomas Jefferson, acknowledged fathering Sally Hemings's children, and hence, his grandchildren's stories, fascinating as they are, were fabrications. Lies may be simple, or they may be elaborate, and, in this case, with the details that Ellen and Jeff added in—Jeff's Edenic scene with the Carr brothers lounging beneath a tree, and Ellen's more sinister one, with Peter cast as a sort of devil—the lies are elaborate.

In our attempts to plumb their complex depths, we should not forget that as lies, they are also stunning. Of course we cannot help sympathizing with the child who wishes her father an innocent, the grandchild who wants to protect the family name. But to shift the blame to a relative, to put words into his mouth: this is a shocking thing. One imagines that Jeff Randolph knew that blaming his cousin was wrong. In his apparently unsent letter to the *Pike County Republican,* the only one of the three documents in the family denial addressed to the public, he claimed that "to my own knowledge and that of others 60 years ago the paternity of these parties were admitted by others."[38] Here, Jeff Randolph was not willing to name names. To put it another way, for most of a century, the family denial was virtually a within-the-family denial. Jeff Randolph told Henry Randall about the Carrs; Ellen Coolidge told her husband, but instructed him that this part of her letter was "in confidence."[39] Randall told Parton, but when Parton published his biography, he did not mention the Carrs. One would have to imagine that Jeff, Ellen, her husband, Randall, and Parton told a few others, but whatever the whispers might have been, these documents did not enter the public record until the middle of the twentieth century. It would appear then that the chief audience for the lie about the Carrs was the white Jeffersons themselves.

All that they were willing to tell the public was that Jefferson was too good a family man, that the rumors were just part of the partisan political fights of the age, and one other story, which may not have been a lie, but only a misrepresentation. According to what Jeff Randolph told Henry Randall, his mother "took the Dusky Sally stories much to heart." And let us note, in passing, that the woman Jeff dubbed "Dusky Sally" was almost certainly his grandmother's half-sister, his mother's aunt. The story among the slaves—and we should also note that the oral testimony among the slaves is turning out to be rather accurate—was that Sally Hemings was the child of John Wayles, Martha Wayles Jefferson's father, and his mulatto slave Betty Hemings. There is no evidence, however, that Martha Jefferson ever acknowledged this blood tie. On her deathbed, legend has it, she gave Sally a small bell, but that is as close as we get.[40] As for her daughter Patsy, according to Jeff, "she never spoke to her sons but once on the subject. Not long before her death"—in 1836, a decade after Jefferson's death—she took Jeff and his brother George Wythe aside. She asked Jeff if he could remember when "'Henings (the slave who most resembled Mr. Jefferson) was born.'" Jeff said he would look it up in one of Jefferson's farm books; he confirmed that this one of the Hemings family ("the slave") was born just when his mother had supposed. Then she told her sons that her father and Sally Hemings had not been near each other for fifteen months prior to that Hemings child's birth. "She bade her sons to remember this fact, and always to defend the character of their grandfather." In repeating the story that Jeff had told him, Randall added that some time later he himself was looking at one of Jefferson's account books when "I came *pop* on the original entry of this slaves birth: and I was then able from well known circumstances to prove the fifteen months separation."[41] We now know, from the careful work of Winthrop Jordan and others, that Jeff, his mother, and Randall were all wrong; Thomas Jefferson and Sally Hemings were both at Monticello nine months before the birth of each of her children.[42]

Sometimes we lie to others; sometimes we lie to ourselves. Sometimes we wish something to be true so badly that we can convince ourselves. If Jeff Randolph was telling the truth, and the stories about her father and Sally Hemings deeply troubled his mother, then surely Patsy would have wanted to know that they were impossible. She could have asked her father, but perhaps she knew from experience what his response would be—either the hearty laugh that made her feel foolish or the denial that later turned out to be false. Perhaps it was more reassuring to look among her father's papers, perform some calculations, searching desperately for the exculpatory evidence. And so badly might she have wanted that evidence that she might accidentally have miscalculated. Or perhaps Jeff Randolph made the story up, just as he made up the one about his cousins the Carrs. But then there is the question of Randall and his research methods. Like Patsy and Jeff, so badly did he want to believe Jefferson innocent that he misread the account book, or perhaps he was just lying when he told Parton about coming *"pop"* on the entry that proved that Jefferson could not have been the father of that particular Hemings child. He equivocated a bit to Parton, telling him that the details had "faded from my memory," but he had "no doubt I could recover them . . . did Mr. Jefferson's vindication in the least depend upon them."[43] But one wonders why he told Parton in the first place about Jeff's account of the exculpatory evidence and his own subsequent encounter with that strangely popping account book had he not thought that Jefferson's vindication in some measure depended upon it. The train of misreadings, misrememberings, or lies seems too significant, too much trouble, whether conscious or unconscious, were the information it transmitted not rather important.

Now that one looks at it closely, one can see also that there are one too many fortuitous occurrences in Randall's account of Jeff's defense of his grandfather. Someone just happened to drop a newspaper article on the grounds at Monticello. The story circulated first in 1802, when Jeff was all of ten years old, and then, after a few years, so far as we know, fell out of circulation for the next several decades, until abolitionists fastened on it again.[44] And at just that moment when the newspaper fell to the ground at Monticello, the Carr brothers happened to be lounging under a tree. And as if these weren't coincidences enough, one day Randall came *"pop"* upon the entry in Jefferson's account book that proved Jeff's account right.

When James Parton published his biography of Thomas Jefferson in
1874, he included Henry Randall's account of Jeff Randolph's account of
his mother's telling him that the timing was all wrong. He omitted the
part about the Carr brothers.[45] The part of the family defense that was a
family accusation stayed within the family, leaving us with something of a
puzzle. It is not fully clear why Jeff and Ellen confined their defamation of
their mother's cousins almost entirely to the family. Part of the explanation must be the unseemliness of it: It would have been a violation of
contemporary mores to discuss matters of sexuality and reproduction
publicly, let alone accuse your second cousin of being the "master of a
black seraglio." In the part of her letter to her husband that she authorized him to share, Ellen allowed that "'dusky Sally' was pretty notoriously
the mistress of a married man, a near relation of Mr. Jefferson's, and there
can be small question that her children were his." It was only in the portion of the letter marked confidential that she named Sam Carr as the cul-
prit.[46] How curious, incidentally, that both Ellen and Jeff called their aunt
"Dusky Sally" in their accounts. It suggests either that they were cooking
up their stories in concert or that they felt themselves, or wanted to place
themselves, so far distant from their aunt that they called her by the name
that was used in the newspapers.

There is another reason why the white Jeffersons would not have wanted to publish their accusation against their cousins: the possibility that it
would be refuted. Peter's and Sam's kin could have done just what Jeff
did—or said he did—and gone to the old account books to prove that Peter and Sam were not in the vicinity nine months before each of Sally
Hemings's children was born. But all that we have explained is why Ellen
and Jeff would not have bruited the Carr name in public; it does not explain why they would have spoken it among themselves.

The need to demonstrate to themselves that their beloved grandfather
was not the father of Sally Hemings's children must have been intense.
Her children were about their ages. They all grew up at Monticello, more
or less together. Perhaps one or more of those Hemings children—who
were, almost certainly, their own half-aunt and half-uncles, their mother's
half-sister and half-brothers, just as Sally Hemings had been their mother's half-sister—looked more like Thomas Jefferson than they did. How
desperately they would have wanted an explanation other than the most
obvious one.

Then there is the question of the rivalry among brothers and sisters, common enough in conventional families, something else again when a father has two sets of children, by two different women. Perhaps it seems absurd to suggest that the white Jeffersons might have thought of the Hemings children as rivals for Thomas Jefferson's affection. They were, after all, black, the children of a slave. Yet if Thomas Jefferson took Sally Hemings as his concubine in order to fulfill a promise to his dying wife, then it was precisely to make certain that no other woman assumed the position in Jefferson's household that a white wife would have, and no other children exercised a legitimate claim upon his affections or material resources. This is how race worked its powerful magic, for it was only the color of the Hemings children's skin and their status as Jefferson's property that assured that they could not become their white siblings' rivals. They were the children of Jefferson's wife's half-sister, and the children of Jefferson himself, yet because of their race, they were denied what their white sisters claimed as right. There is the true absurdity.

But inheritance in Virginia was a serious business, complicating matters of love with those of money. Jefferson's falling out with David Meade Randolph, after all, had been over the terms of a family inheritance. In a time and place where grown children depended upon their parents to set them up with a plantation and slaves or some other means of making a living, every additional child was a potential rival for the family inheritance; a second set of children, by a second wife, threatened to displace the first set altogether. That is what happened to Patsy and Thomas Mann Randolph when her widowed father-in-law remarried a much younger woman who began bearing him children. All of a sudden, the elder Randolph raised the price of the family farm that he had been planning to let Jefferson purchase as a marriage settlement for the young couple. Perhaps this is when Patsy's husband began to feel like a duck among the swans, his new father-in-law taxed to pay the freight of a young stepmother and her growing number of little Randolphs.[47]

The white Jeffersons never acknowledged that they had black Jefferson kin. The Hemings children, however, knew that they were the disfavored children of a loving and powerful man. Madison Hemings remembered that Jefferson was "not in the habit of showing partiality or fatherly affection to us children. . . . He was affectionate toward his white grandchildren, of whom he had fourteen, twelve of whom lived to manhood and womanhood." And Madison Hemings named each one of those children, his nieces and nephews, by name: "Ann, Thomas Jefferson, Ellen. . . ."[48] Madison Hemings, incidentally, named his youngest daughter Ellen Wales, after his white niece. When Jeff Randolph wrote of his aunt and uncles, they were "these parties," or—according to Randall—"the slave." For his sister Ellen, they were "the yellow children."[49] They could not even be allowed their names.

How painful it must be to be the discarded children, to know that somewhere, perhaps in your own neighborhood, are sister and brother, or niece and nephew, whom you cannot claim. Perhaps you honor those who have abandoned you nonetheless. If you are Madison Hemings, you may remember each of your thirteen nephews and nieces by name, and you may note proudly that one was "Chairman of the Democratic National Convention in Baltimore last spring" and that another was "Jeff. Davis' first Secretary of War in the late 'unpleasantness.'" Madison Hemings's son, Thomas Eston, named after his brother, lost his life in that "unpleasantness," dying at Andersonville prison.[50] Until just a few years ago, it was possible for intelligent and reputable historians to assert that Madison Hemings, or perhaps his mother Sally, was making up stories. Madison Hemings invented a Jefferson family connection, it was surmised, because he felt "cheated by life" and "entitled to the respect and consideration that had hitherto been denied him," or "to provide an otherwise undistinguished biracial carpenter with a measure of social respect," or because of "the Negroes' pathetic wish for a little pride"[51]—as if in reminiscing about his father and bragging about his nieces and nephews Madison Hemings was attempting a bit of genetic social climbing. Now we know that Madison Hemings was, almost certainly, telling the truth, while it was his niece and nephew who were making up stories. And we must wonder about people who would sooner accuse their cousins of something they believed to be unspeakable—"the thing will not bear telling," Ellen Coolidge had said—than acknowledge their beloved grandfather's other children.

Perhaps when one has called one's own father more fell than the hyena, it is not such a leap to invent a confession for one's mother's cousin. Perhaps that judgment is too harsh. It is possible that Peter Carr really had confessed to something terrible and that if Jeff Randolph's report was not the literal truth, it was not really a lie. It is unbecoming to us to be absolutists, to wash away the gray that shades the black into white and back again. As historians, we are uncomfortable making such judgments. But here we are confronted with the DNA evidence, which, while not incontrovertible, surely demonstrates beyond the kind of certainty that most historians ever have about the evidence they are called upon to interpret that the Carrs did not father all four of Sally Hemings's children.

We have to wonder why Jeff picked his cousins the Carrs. By the time he told his story to Randall, they were dead—but there were other dead Jefferson males, as well, including Jefferson's brother Randolph, who has suddenly emerged as the prime suspect for today's diehard Jefferson purity defenders.[52] Perhaps that is only to say that people will go to great lengths to protect the reputation of a man like Jefferson, who has come to function as a sort of virgin father for some portion of the nation. It might only have been convenience that made Jeff and Ellen turn to the Carr brothers. Perhaps the primary qualification for suspicion was being a male Jefferson who was not Thomas Jefferson himself. Or it might have been some quality that the brothers shared. Both Jeff and Ellen considered Sam Carr, in particular, licentious, and they seemed to think of both cousins as moochers. Ellen, who had a real way with words, called her cousin Sam "the most notorious good-natured Turk that ever was master of a black seraglio kept at other men's expense." Jeff had Peter confessing his shame at disgracing the man "who has always fed us!"

It is not unusual for the members of families to think that they are playing a zero-sum game for the finite emotional and material resources the family has at its disposal. Jeff's outburst against his father had been prompted by the fear that he was going to make a claim upon Thomas Jefferson's estate. We certainly know that the material resources of the Jefferson family were severely depleted by the time of Jefferson's death. Anyone who has read the *Family Letters* knows how anxious the white Jeffersons were about their declining fortunes. Perhaps the white Jeffersons also felt that there was not quite enough love to go around, although that is at best an educated guess; no one complained directly about not getting enough love, while there were complaints aplenty about the family's plummeting fortunes.

Then, too, there was the matter of reputation. Perhaps the Carrs's reputations were already sullied in some way, at least within the family, and adding another item to the bill of particulars against them might have seemed a small price to pay in order to secure the reputation of the family founder. Whatever scorn we now might have for the false accusation against the Carrs, we have to assume that Ellen and Jeff at least knew how to pick likely suspects. In this context, the current slurring of Jefferson's brother Randolph seems a bit bizarre, as if today's Jefferson defenders might be better situated to find an alternate candidate for father of Sally Hemings's children than those of Jefferson's kin, who had a far greater interest in pointing a convincing finger. Or perhaps one of these defenders came *pop* on incriminating information while perusing the Jefferson family tree.

But once again we wander from our point. In order to protect the reputation of the family patriarch, some of the white Jeffersons blamed some of the other white Jeffersons for fathering Sally Hemings's children. These things happen in families; for some members, the assigned role is to be the bearer of blame. But blame for what? For, as Jeff Randolph had his cousin Peter Carr say, bringing "this disgrace upon poor old uncle." For letting people think that Thomas Jefferson might have been the sort of man who would insult "the sanctity of the home by his profligacy." For letting people imagine that Thomas Jefferson might have "selected the female attendant of his own pure children to become his paramour."[53]

Perhaps it makes little difference whether Thomas Jefferson was the father of Sally Hemings's children or whether it was one of his nephews. In either case, Jefferson kept on his plantation as slaves persons who were his kin. To be sure, their tasks were light, and all of them, as Annette Gordon-Reed has shown, were permitted their freedom at about the time they turned twenty-one. But they were all disinherited. Does it make Jefferson a substantially better man if those children were his nephew's, rather than his own? Is he significantly less implicated in the institution of slavery?

Perhaps these are not even questions that we should be addressing, either as citizens or historians. As historians, we are always concerned with the matter of truth. We argue about what is knowable, about what standards should apply. Some of us may be uncomfortable with categorical statements about what is and is not true, but we know that some things are more true than others. We know that we are not allowed to make things up. We would all agree that the Holocaust, for example, happened, or the Civil War, and to deny them is to lie. We sometimes make the occasional categorical statement, risking our reputations on a claim, but it may have more to do with the significance of the question than the certainty of the evidence. Surely the details of Thomas Jefferson's private life would not compare to either of these examples, that is, something that it is morally important to assert as fact or something so incontrovertible that no one would consider denying. Historians have written some foolish things about Jefferson, no doubt thinking that the questions they addressed required some sort of answer. Like Jefferson himself, they have considered his reputation of such great importance that a strict attention to questions of veracity and verifiability was not necessary.

It is not clear, however, why questions about Jefferson's private behavior should be of concern to us as either historians or citizens. Nor is it clear why the evidence from the recent DNA tests should be of any interest to us. Until November, we had at our disposal a great deal of what the lawyers call circumstantial evidence that argued powerfully if not conclusively that Jefferson was the father of Sally Hemings's children. Now we have a small piece of DNA evidence that, while far from conclusive in itself, when added to the circumstantial evidence, makes it very close to certain. Of course, there are always other possibilities. But the DNA evidence invalidates what until November had been the only coherent alternate story. Hence we should now be certain beyond any reasonable doubt that Jefferson was the father of Eston and probably Beverley, Harriet, and Madison as well. Whether this sort of evidence would hold up in a court of law is beside the point. This is not a court of law. It is the court of history, and the standards may be somewhat different.

As historians, we might begin by asking what is the significance of knowing whether Thomas Jefferson fathered Sally Hemings's children. To some extent, we are inquiring into the most personal and intimate aspects of one man and one woman's lives. We can say, with relative certainty, that loving relationships between powerful white men and their female black slaves were atypical. The historical record leaves us relatively few examples. Moreover, many of us would recoil at the notion that love can arise in a relationship so unequal, although that is a matter of interpretation more than of fact. Yet delineating the norm tells us very little about Sally Hemings and Thomas Jefferson as individuals. Is it possible that Thomas Jefferson and Sally Hemings had a loving relationship? History is very bad at answering metaphysical questions. History cannot answer with any certainty.

But let us, for the sake of argument, or imagination, assume that Thomas Jefferson and Sally Hemings made the best out of the possibilities offered under the institution of slavery, and that even if they did not love each other, they honored their commitments to each other and their children. Sally Hemings and all her children ended their days in freedom, and very few women who began their lives as slaves could claim as much. To put it another way, let us say that they behaved as well as they could, given the circumstances, and therefore we should not judge Jefferson harshly for evading questions, denying implicitly, and complaining about his political enemies. Jefferson believed fervently in the right to privacy, and of course he deserved privacy himself. Perhaps we should conclude that whatever took place between Thomas Jefferson and Sally Hemings was private and historically atypical, a poignant story, but nothing more.

Does it make a difference if Jefferson lied? This, finally, is the question we confront: the meaning of a lie or lies told in private, by one member of a family to another, about a private matter. Jefferson certainly threw his allies and his family off the track. It also seems that he conducted his relationship with Sally Hemings with sufficient discretion that his family either did not know about it or, more likely, could avoid confronting its reality. If Jefferson did not lie about Sally Hemings, he misled, and if he misled, he did it to protect himself—that is, his reputation, and his family—that is, their reputation, as well as their notions of themselves as a family near-perfect in its happiness.

Because Jefferson's denial was not complete or coherent enough—there was that troubling matter of the family resemblance, after all—his white family had to elaborate his little lie. His daughter Patsy tried to document it, making her sons cross-check some dates. His grandson told a historian about this account-book evidence, and the historian, thinking that second-hand "documentary" record somehow inadequate, asserted that he had double-checked it, using an account book that conveniently went *pop,* as if opened by the hand of God. Patsy could have been mistaken, but probably not Jeff Randolph, and certainly not the historian Randall. We are now into the realm of demonstrable falsehood, a falsehood that became part of the historical record when Randall told it to Parton, in the middle of the nineteenth century. Once that falsehood entered the historical record, the defense of Jefferson then seemed to rest upon something more empirical than notions of his character: secondhand testimo-

ny about a verifiable documentary record. Jeff Randolph's motive was understandable; he wanted to preserve his grandfather's reputation, and he
was, after all, talking to a historian. He must have known, however, that
the account book could not have demonstrated his grandfather's innocence. He lied for history, and to history. And then history told us that Jefferson could not have been the father of Sally Hemings's children.

Yet these were not the only lies the white Jeffersons told history. When
Jeff Randolph and his sister Ellen Coolidge implicated their cousins Carr,
they were lying only among themselves. But it was a stunning lie, all the
more stunning because they told it primarily for the other white Jeffersons. Perhaps it offered the assurance they needed in order to be able to
hold their heads high when defending their beloved grandfather in more
general terms. Perhaps it assuaged old wounds, determining for once and
for all who was in the family and who was out. But these lies, even if told
first and foremost to and for the family, made their way into the historical
record. They have become part of history.

Let us assume that the relationship between Thomas Jefferson and Sally Hemings was founded and maintained, or one or the other, in love, or
commitment, or a sense of responsibility—in other words, somewhere
along the spectrum of what we would consider responsible behavior. Let
us assume, also, that the relationship was kept a secret from Jefferson's
daughters and their children, although Sally Hemings may well have told
her children while they were still living at Monticello. "We were free from
the dread of having to be slaves all our lives long," her son Madison remembered, "and were measurably happy."[54] Is it possible that the black
Jeffersons knew who their father was, while the white Jeffersons did not?

When we look at this story, or imagine it, from the perspective of Sally
Hemings or Thomas Jefferson, it is one thing. When we try to see it from
the point of view of the children, it is quite another. This is always the
case in families. If Freud was right in the slightest, then the relationship
between parent and child always embodies at least an element of conflict,
of disappointment, of unrequited love. The secrets that look so understandable, so necessary for Thomas Jefferson, look quite another thing to
his two families. How could you do this to us, his white family must have
asked. Or rather, if we wish to confine ourselves to what we know, he
could not have done this to us, they said. There are such things, after all,
as moral impossibilities, which is another way of saying that our lives can-

not make sense if such a thing is possible. If you were a white Jefferson, and your world was ordered by the knowledge that your father or grandfather loved you above all else, that you were entrusted with the knowledge of the real him, and if these things were more real to you than the features on the faces of your Hemings kin, then perhaps you would have lied, too.

And perhaps if you were Beverley Hemings or his sister Harriet, you would have gone to Washington, taking the freedom your mother had made your father give you as his only legacy, other than a face so like his that in the moonlight strangers could not tell you apart. And if you were Beverley or Harriet, you would have married whites, seizing for your children the privilege of fair skin, promised in the moonlight of a Monticello night. And you would have turned your backs on your father's family and your mother's, as well, perhaps concluding that family was a bad business, in the process trading the truth of who you knew you were—the child of Thomas Jefferson, the child of a slave—for the lie of who you now claimed to be. And perhaps if you were Madison Hemings or his brother Eston, you would care for your mother until she died, marry a black woman, raise a family, and tell your children who they were, that is, who their parents were, and their parents before them, and who you wanted them to be. And they would tell their children and their children's children after them, and even though white people would scoff and even say that you were just trying to make yourself into something you were not, one day a scientist would come asking for a sample of your DNA. And it would confirm the story your mother had told you and your father had never acknowledged, except by the ambiguous act of letting you go free.

Let us imagine a man. Let us call him Thomas Jefferson. Let us imagine that he evades the truth, or tells a lie, perhaps to save face, perhaps to spare the ones he loves. It is probably both, for the two are in some measure inextricable. He needs his family to love him, and they cannot, he fears, if he appears to them as less than the devoted father he has claimed to be. And in the moment that he evades the truth or tells the lie, if not before, he has made a decision about whose love matters most, about who will receive his tenderest love. And those white children, and their children after, are bound by his lie, or his evasion, and they have to prop it up. It will not stand of itself. There are at the very least the family resemblances of their Hemings kin, and who knows how many half-caught glances and troubling sounds, not to mention the newspapers that just happen to fall to the ground. And there may be the nagging fears that all children have, the uncertainties about the certainty of a father's love. And so the white family imagines or invents a documentary record, fortuitously confirmed in account books that go pop. And they imagine or invent a family confession, the convenient Carrs. And in protecting the reputation of one kinsman, they tar another's.

Then, a century later, that lie, like the ones before, becomes part of the public record. White cousins whose names otherwise would have been lost to history are now known as scoundrels. Black children are written out of their family, their claim upon it dismissed by history as "the Negroes' pathetic wish for a little pride." And so the lie begun in the family becomes part of the national lie of race, which is itself a kind of truth, a fiction that orders the national life much as the moral impossibility of Jefferson's interracial liaison ordered that of his white kin.

How are we to reckon the costs entailed upon the Hemings family first by their father's silence and then by his white family's lies? Perhaps we just add them to the unpaid bill of race, the interest still compounding, year after year, day after day.

And how are we to reckon the costs to the nation of an evasion compounded and elaborated until it became a thing in itself, a cornerstone of our civic culture?

❧

Monticello sits atop a mountain; its slopes are slippery indeed. A public man enters into a private relationship. He attempts to keep it private, even from his family, even, in fact, from the family that the relationship begets. He gives his white family his love, his black family their freedom. Which legacy is the greater? The white part of his family uses its legacy—the love, the knowledge of him that this love provides—to disinherit their black kin, to dismiss their black family's claim as moral impossibility. Theirs is a lie, founded in love. Half the black family uses its freedom to escape the grasp of history altogether. The other half uses it to claim its rightful inheritance, which is to say, a heritage, a connection to history itself. Subsequent generations take sides. A family quarrel becomes a national one as well. These are the things we do for love.

NOTES

I am greatly indebted to James Goodman, Annette Gordon-Reed, James Grimmel-mann, and Cinder Stanton for suggestions and conversation.

1. Thomas Jefferson (hereafter TJ) to Thomas Jefferson Randolph, 8 Feb. 1826, Edwin Morris Betts and James A. Bear, eds., *The Family Letters of Thomas Jefferson* (Columbia, Mo., 1966), 470.

2. TJ to Martha Jefferson, 28 Nov. 1783, in Betts and Bear, eds., *Family Letters*, 20.

3. Margaret Bayard Smith, *The First Forty Years of Washington Society*, ed. Gaillard Hunt (New York, 1906), 74–77. These letters are reprinted in full in Betts and Bear, eds., *Family Letters*, 146, 195. Smith's transcriptions were generally accurate, although one error, in copying a passage from a letter of 5 Feb. 1801, is telling. In the original (in Betts and Bear, eds., *Family Letters*, 196), TJ concluded with a variant of his usual loving closing: "My personal affections would fix me for ever with you. Present me affectionately to Mr. Randolph, kiss the dear little objects of our natural love, and be assured of the constancy and tenderness of mine to you." In Smith's transcription, the passage reads this way: "'my personal affections would fix me forever with you. Kiss the dear little objects of our mutual love.' etc. etc." In Smith's version, not only has Patsy's husband, Thomas Mann Randolph, been excised, but her children have incestuously become those of her father as well. At the time, husbands and wives often called their children "pledges of our mutual love" or, as Smith rendered the phrase, "objects of our mutual love."

4. TJ to Martha Jefferson Randolph, 17 May 1798; TJ to Mary Jefferson Eppes, 1 Jan. 1799, in Betts and Bear, eds., *Family Letters*, 161, 170.

5. TJ to Martha Jefferson Randolph, 31 May 1798, in Betts and Bear, eds., *Family Letters*, 164.

6. For the changing estimation of the family, see my *The Pursuit of Happiness: Family and Values in Jefferson's Virginia* (New York, 1983).

7. TJ to James Monroe, 20 May 1782, Merrill D. Peterson, ed., *Thomas Jefferson: Writings* (New York, 1984), 777–80.

8. Jan Lewis, "'The Blessings of Domestic Society': Thomas Jefferson's Family and the Transformation of American Politics," in Peter S. Onuf, ed. *Jeffersonian Legacies* (Charlottesville, 1993), 109–46.

9. TJ to Martha Jefferson Randolph, March 10, 1793; TJ to Mary Jefferson Eppes, 7 Jan. 1798; TJ to Mary Jefferson, 25 May 1797; TJ to Martha Jefferson Randolph, 10 June 1793; TJ to Mary Jefferson, 14 June 1797; TJ to Mary Jefferson Eppes, 1 April 1798; TJ to Martha Jefferson Randolph, 23 Jan. 1799; TJ to Martha Jefferson Randolph, 21 Jan. 1800; TJ to Mary Jefferson Eppes, 6 April 1800; TJ to Martha Jefferson Randolph, 22 April 1800; TJ to Martha Jefferson Randolph, 16 Jan. 1801; TJ to Martha Jefferson Randolph, 3 Dec. 1804; and TJ to Martha Jefferson Randolph, 6 May 1805, in Betts and Bear, eds., *Family Letters*, 114, 153, 145, 120, 149, 159, 172, 182, 187, 188, 192, 265, 270.

10. Smith, *The First Forty Years*, 309, 316.

11. Undated autobiographical fragment, Ellen Wayles Coolidge Correspondence, Alderman Library, University of Virginia.

12. Jack McLaughlin, *Jefferson and Monticello: The Biography of a Builder* (New York, 1988), 196.

13. For example, Paul Finkelman, "Jefferson and Slavery: 'Treason against the Hopes of the World,'" in Onuf, ed., *Jeffersonian Legacies*, 181–221, and Garry Wills, "The Aesthete," *New York Review of Books*, 40 (12 Aug. 1993), 6–10.

14. TJ to Thomas Mann Randolph, Jr., 27 Aug. 1786, in Peterson, ed., *Jefferson Writings*, 860–64; Dumas Malone, *Jefferson and the Rights of Man* (Boston, 1951), 250–51.

15. Thomas Jefferson Randolph to Dabney S. Carr, 11 July 1826, Carr-Cary Papers, Alderman Library, University of Virginia.

16. TJ to Anne Randolph Bankhead, 8 Nov. 1808, in Betts and Bear, eds., *Family Letters*, 357.

17. For accounts, see Malone, *Jefferson and His Time: The Sage of Monticello* (Boston, 1981), 159–60, 299–300, 476–77; Martha Jefferson Randolph to TJ, 20 Nov. 1816, and 7 August 1819, and TJ to Thomas Jefferson Randolph, in Betts and Bear, eds., *Family Letters*, 417, 430, 470.

18. William H. Gaines, Jr., *Thomas Mann Randolph, Thomas Jefferson's Son-in-Law* (Baton Rouge, 1966), 48.

19. TJ to Mary Jefferson, 5 Jan. 1790 [1791], in Betts and Bear, eds., *Family Letters*, 67.

20. *Richmond Recorder*, 1 Sept. 1802, Appendix B in this volume. This son, Tom, has been supposed, but not proven, to be Thomas Woodson. The DNA tests on his descendants, however, seem to have ruled out TJ as his father.

21. Henry Randall to James Parton, 1 June 1868, reprinted in Annette Gordon-Reed, *Thomas Jefferson and Sally Hemings: An American Controversy* (Charlottesville, 1997), 254.

22. [Thomas Jefferson Randolph] to Sir, [1873 or 1874], copy, courtesy of Lucia Stanton, International Center for Jefferson Studies, Charlottesville. The texts of all the other documents—Randall's letter to Parton, Ellen Coolidge's letter to her husband, and the memoirs of Israel Jefferson and Madison Jefferson, as well, can be found in Gordon-Reed, *Jefferson and Hemings*, 245–60. See also, Fawn M. Brodie, *Thomas Jefferson: An Intimate History* (New York, 1974), 471–82, 493–98.

23. Malone, *Jefferson the President: First Term, 1801–1805* (Boston, 1970), 497; see also 493–98.

24. Winthrop D. Jordan, *White over Black: American Attitudes toward the Negro, 1550–1812* (Chapel Hill, 1968).

25. Ellen Wayles Coolidge to Joseph Coolidge, 24 Oct. 1858, in Ellen Wayles Coolidge Letterbook, Ellen Wayles Coolidge Correspondence, Alderman Library, University of Virginia.

26. TJ to Robert Smith, 5 July 1805, quoted in Brodie, *Thomas Jefferson*, 375.

27. Thomas Moore, "To Thomas Hume, Esq. M.D. From the City of Washington," quoted in Werner Sollors, "Presidents, Sex, and Race," chapter 9 in this volume; Henry S. Randall, *Life of Thomas Jefferson* (Philadelphia, 1857), 118–19; Lucia Stanton, "Looking for Liberty: Thomas Jefferson and the British Lions," *Eighteenth-Century Studies* 26 (1993), 649–68.

28. Malone, *Jefferson the Virginian*, 447–51; Brodie, *Thomas Jefferson*, 73–79. Once again, Brodie is the exception among Jefferson biographers. She thought it possible that TJ and Betsey Walker had an affair, that is, that not only had TJ persisted in his advances, but that Betsey Walker might have reciprocated.

29. Dumas Malone, *Jefferson the Virginian* (Boston, 1948), 153–55, 447–51; Gerald Gawalt, "Strict Truth: The Narrative of William A. Burwell," *Virginia Magazine of History and Biography*, 101 (1993), 119–20.

30. Gawalt, "Strict Truth," 119–20; Brodie, *Thomas Jefferson*, 350–56; Gordon-Reed, *Jefferson and Hemings*, 74.

31. TJ to Martha Jefferson Randolph, 23 April 1803, in Betts and Bear, eds., *Family Letters*, 210.

32. Sarah N. Randolph, *The Domestic Life of Thomas Jefferson* (1871; reprint, Charlottesville, 1978), 369.

33. Quoted in Brodie, *Thomas Jefferson,* 349.

34. Richmond *Examiner,* 25 Sept. 1802. This claim was made only three weeks after Callender's original charge.

35. Ellen Randolph Coolidge to Joseph Coolidge, 24 Oct. 1858, reprinted in Gordon-Reed, *Jefferson and Hemings,* 259.

36. Brodie, *Thomas Jefferson,* p. 167: "Memoirs of Israel Jefferson," in Gordon-Reed, *Jefferson and Hemings,* 252.

37. Randall to Parton, and Ellen Randolph Coolidge to Joseph Coolidge, 24 Oct. 1858, in Gordon-Reed, *Jefferson and Hemings,* 254–57, 258–60.

38. [Thomas Jefferson Randolph] to Sir.

39. Coolidge to Coolidge, in Gordon-Reed, *Jefferson and Hemings,* 259.

40. Susan R. Stein, *The Worlds of Thomas Jefferson at Monticello* (New York, 1993), 16.

41. Randall to Parton, in Gordon-Reed, *Jefferson to Hemings,* 255.

42. Brodie, *Thomas Jefferson,* 296; Lucia Stanton, "'Those Who Labor for My Happiness': Thomas Jefferson and His Slaves," in Onuf, ed. *Jeffersonian Legacies,* n. 20, 174.

43. Randall to Parton in Gordon-Reed, *Jefferson and Hemings,* 255.

44. Robert M. S. MacDonald, "Race, Sex, and Reputation: Thomas Jefferson and the Sally Hemings Story," *Southern Cultures,* 4 (1998), 46–63; Sidney P. Moss and Carolyn Moss, "The Jefferson Miscegenation Legend in British Travel Books," *Journal of the Early Republic,* 7 (1987), 253–74.

45. Gordon-Reed, *Jefferson and Hemings,* 96.

46. Coolidge to Coolidge, in Gordon-Reed, *Jefferson and Hemings,* 259.

47. Dumas Malone, *Jefferson and the Rights of Man* (Boston, 1951), 320; TJ to Martha Jefferson Randolph, 17 July 1790, in Betts and Bear, eds., *Family Letters,* 60–61.

48. "Memoirs of Madison Hemings," Appendix A in this volume.

49. "Memoirs of Madison Hemings" (Appendix A); [Randolph to Sir]; Randall to Parton, and Coolidge to Coolidge, in *Jefferson and Hemings,* 255, 258.

50. "Memoirs of Madison Hemings" (Appendix A).

51. Quoted in Gordon-Reed, *Jefferson and Hemings,* 19–20, 82.

52. For example, Dennis Cauchon, "Group Flags Other Jefferson as Father," *USA Today,* 7 Jan. 1999; Woody West, "Clinton Not Boy's Father, DNA Shows," *Washington Times,* 12 Jan. 1999, *http://www.washtimes.com/news/news3.html.*

53. Coolidge to Coolidge, in *Gordon Reed,* 258–59.

54. "Memoirs of Madison Hemings" (Appendix A).

CHAPTER 7

Bonds of Memory

Identity and the Hemings Family

Lucia Stanton and Dianne Swann-Wright

Four years into our project to collect the oral histories of Monticello's African Americans, we made our first trip to New York City, arriving in Manhattan on a December morning on a bus from LaGuardia Airport. We were deposited, along with our bags of clothing, cameras, and recording equipment, on Harlem's 125th Street, to await the downtown bus. At this point in the project, we were used to sharing the same spaces but at different comfort levels, invariably determined by the fact that one of us is black and the other white.

DIANNE SWANN-WRIGHT (DSW): *The 125th Street bus stop provided a visual feast for my imagination. Small matter that over fifty years separated me from its Renaissance or that thirty years separated me from Malcolm X's physical presence on this very street. I stretched my neck looking for Claude McKay, Zora Neale Hurston, and Langston Hughes. I strained to hear the notes that just had to be coming from the uptown jazz clubs. Some of the brothers and sisters who had heard Malcolm speak must be somewhere close. They just had to be.*

In my mind's eye, I formed a bond with the folks who shared the actual present with me on this December morning. We were in Harlem, the home and center of black cultural expression. I was home.

LUCIA STANTON (LCS): *While I eyed the dark figures coming to life in the doorways and worried about the safety of our newly purchased video camera, I craned my neck to spot the bus that would take us away from Harlem and down to familiar streets with two-digit numbers.*

Conditions were reversed a few hours later, as we sat with a white family in a comfortable room, bright with Christmas presents piled on the sideboard and paintings decorating the walls. Three generations of descendants of Eston Hemings of Monticello, who 150 years earlier had moved from the black world into the white, were present to share their family history. When the collection of family photographs was brought out after the interview, we saw several arresting images on the first pages of an album dating from the turn of the century. Artfully staged and photographed in a professional studio, they showed Eston Hemings's grandson and a friend, costumed in blackface. The young men, dressed as pickaninnies, struck comical poses and, in one photograph, leered at their female companions, who wore little girls' dresses of virginal white.

DSW: *I was hopeful that the album might suggest links between the inhabitants of the house and an honored and respected black past. I stared at each image, as someone else turned the pages. The image of Eston's grandson in blackface, mocking what he was slapped me in my own face. I needed the back of my chair to brace me from the insult, the disrespect.*

LCS: *With my mind wavering precariously between two equally strange possibilities—that Sally Hemings's great-grandson was ignorant of his race or that he knew it and was hiding or ridiculing it—I took refuge in sifting historical facts. At the time of the photograph, his family had been living as white for half a century. His grandfather Eston had died before his birth, but he had been raised by Eston's wife, his grandmother, who had been born a free woman of color in Virginia. Could he have been unaware of his racial heritage, acting like other white Americans who found the donning of blackface a titillating amusement? Or was he instead painfully conscious of his own masquerade, drawn to it unwillingly by the pleas of others or by his own need to fortify his whiteness by ridiculing blackness?*

The ambiguities and absurdities of racial definitions illustrated by this photograph seemed emblematic of our discoveries since the beginning of the project. It had been started in 1993, in order to give voice to Monticello's African American families, whose lives and contributions had gone largely unrecorded. In recognition of the importance of orality in the African American community, we named it Getting Word and hoped that present-day descendants would "get word" back to us about their ancestors' experiences at Monticello and their fates after Jefferson's death. Since 1993 we have conducted fifty-five interviews with more than one hundred descendants living in a dozen states, often with the help of our consultant, Beverly Gray, whose knowledge of the African American experience in Ohio has been indispensable. While our informants represent several enslaved Monticello families, two-thirds of them are descended from three daughters of Elizabeth (Betty) Hemings. It is particularly in our interviews with the descendants of two sons of Sally Hemings that we have learned about the legacies of miscegenation, the complexities of racial identity, and the power of memory. This chapter focuses on the different experiences of the families of Madison Hemings, who always remained a member of the black community, and Eston Hemings Jefferson, who at age forty-four crossed the color line, determined to live as a white man.[1]

Freed by the terms of Jefferson's will in 1827, Madison and Eston Hemings continued to live and work within a few miles of Monticello, as Jefferson's petition to the Virginia legislature exempted them from the 1806 law requiring freed slaves to leave the state within a year. Trained in woodworking by their highly skilled uncle, John Hemings, the Monticello joiner and cabinetmaker, they pursued this trade in Charlottesville and on plantations in Albemarle County. Eston Hemings also probably began to pursue a career as a professional musician. In 1830 the brothers bought a house and lot on the road between the town and the university, and lived there with their mother.[2]

Within five years of their emancipation, both men had married, making choices that would perpetuate their mother's skin tone. Madison Hemings's wife, Mary Hughes McCoy, was the granddaughter of a white plantation owner and the slave he freed. Eston Hemings married Julia Ann Isaacs, member of a well-to-do mixed-race family in Charlottesville; her father was a Jewish merchant and her mother the daughter of a slave and a slaveowner. Both marriages ensured that, besides freedom, the children of these unions would have a passport to upper-class status within the black community and the probable option to enter the white race.[3]

After Sally Hemings's death in 1835, the brothers and their families moved to southern Ohio. Madison Hemings worked as a carpenter in Pike County, and Eston Hemings became well known in the area as a professional musician and leader of a dance band. Two Chillicothe residents, late in the nineteenth century, recalled the musician from Monticello. One described Eston Hemings as "a master of the violin, and an accomplished 'caller' of dances," who "always officiated at the 'swell' entertainments of Chillicothe." For the other, no ball in the 1880s could live up to those of the 1840s, when the Hemings band "struck up 'Money Musk' or 'Wesson's Slaughter House'" and capped the festivities with the Virginia reel. (The Scottish fiddle tune "Moneymusk" was evidently a favorite of Thomas Jefferson, too, as one of the rare musical manuscripts in his hand is a record of that tune.)[4]

Both newspaper accounts provide descriptions of Sally Hemings's youngest son, "a remarkably fine looking colored man." Tall, well-proportioned, "very erect and dignified," he had nearly straight hair with "a tint of auburn" and a "suggestion" of freckles: "Quiet, unobtrusive, polite and decidedly intelligent, he was soon very well and favorably known to all classes of our citizens, for his personal appearance and gentlemanly manners attracted everybody's attention to him." There was one drawback, however, on whatever ambitions Eston Hemings may have had: the color of his skin. He is described as "very slightly colored" and "a light bronze color." One writer stated that, "notwithstanding all his accomplishments and deserts," there would always be "a great gulf, an impassable gulf" between Hemings and whites, "even the lowest of them." The other concluded more crudely: "But a nigger was a nigger in those days and that settled it." Even the laws did not have the power to raise Eston Hemings in the eyes of his white neighbors. In both Virginia and Ohio, he and his brother were legally white, but social practice invariably invalidated the law for those who were known in a community or who had, as one of these newspapermen noted of Eston Hemings, a "visible admixture of negro blood in his veins," echoing a phrase that by then had statutory overtones. Efforts by light-skinned mulattoes to claim their rights to the vote or public education caused confusion in Ohio courts until general practice was codified in 1859, when "a distinct and visible admixture of African blood" became the legal litmus test for separating black from white.[5]

Seven years before this visible admixture law, Eston Hemings left Ohio, where he and his family were denied access to the courts, the polls, and the public schools. In 1845 a Cleveland newspaper, very possibly referring to Eston Hemings, expressed shock that, "Notwithstanding all the services and sacrifices of Jefferson in the establishment of the freedom of this country, his own son, now living in Ohio, is not allowed a vote, or an oath in a court of justice!"[6] Since racial identities could be shifted only where one was unknown, Eston Hemings and his family had to move among strangers to claim their rights as citizens. In Madison, Wisconsin, he adopted a new name as well as a new racial identity, becoming Eston H. Jefferson. His northwestwardly course, from slavery to freedom and, finally, to whiteness and its associated privileges in Wisconsin provided his children with choices and considerations he had never had.

His brother Madison Hemings remained in Ohio, living for forty years with his family on the black side of the color line and becoming a pillar of his small rural community in Ross County, south of Chillicothe. He had at first supported his family in Ohio with his woodworking skills and, when interviewed in 1873, mentioned three buildings in Waverly for which he had crafted the woodwork, two of which are still standing. In 1865 he purchased a sixty-six-acre farm, where he continued to pursue his trade while raising corn and hogs. According to Beverly Gray, descendants of white Ross County residents remember being told of Madison Hemings's reputation in the community. Known as the "junior president," his word, they recall, "was his bond." At his death in 1878, his estate was appraised at a value of almost $1,000.[7]

DSW: *Most historians can complete W. E B. Du Bois's quotation, "The problem of the twentieth century is the problem of the ———." I wonder if Du Bois realized how true his declaration would prove to be. For me, the color line is more than a division, separating those with power and privilege from those without. For me, the color line is a hard unhoeable row.*

Walls topped with broken glass surround buildings in Nairobi, Kenya. They protect serene courtyards and lush gardens from intruders who do not stay out of where they are not wanted. Anyone able to climb the wall can go over them, but few do unless they are willing to risk being cut to the core. I think that the color line in America is very much like the broken-glass-topped walls of Nairobi. They can be crossed but at a painful, bloody cost.

LCS: *Because my whiteness protected me from having to think about racial identity, my real consciousness of the color line came late. I was struck by the ab-*

surdity of racial categories in an Ohio living room in 1993, when three genera-
tions of people who looked white spoke of the indignities they had suffered be-
cause they chose to ally themselves with black family and community. A man who
had lived in a white neighborhood growing up and whose friends were white,
played on the high school baseball team but could not join his teammates at the
soda fountain afterwards. His best friend's father, a barber, would not cut his
hair.

My response reminded me of the white travelers in the nineteenth century who
realized the injustices of slavery only when they saw men and women as white as
they were being taken down the Mississippi to the New Orleans slave market for
sale. I still have difficulty visualizing the color line. It appears nebulous, shifting,
at times a barricade guarded by gun-toting white men, at times a mist, a white
mist into which people disappear.

The color line was both painful and permeable. In every generation of
Sally Hemings's descendants, from her children in the first half of the
nineteenth century to her great-grandchildren's great-grandchildren in
the mid-twentieth century, some family members vanished into that mist.
The experiences of descendants of both Madison and Eston Hemings illustrate the benefits and costs of passing for white. Madison's son William
Beverly Hemings served in a white regiment—the 73rd Ohio—in the Civil
War and died alone in a Kansas veterans hospital in 1910. His brother
James Madison Hemings disappeared and may be the source of stories
among his sisters' descendants of a mysterious and silent visitor who
looked like a white man, with white beard and blue, staring eyes. He
slipped in and out of town to visit older family members but never
formed ties with the younger generations. According to one family
chronicler, neither of these sons married, perhaps because of concerns
about revealing skin color. Several of Madison Hemings's grandsons also
passed for white, divorcing themselves from their sisters who stayed on
the other side.[8]

This pattern of brothers leaving sisters continued in the next generations. Descendants of Madison Hemings's oldest daughter Sarah Hemings Byrd have many stories of families fragmented by passing. Even
though many of those who passed remained in southern Ohio, "we never
heard from them," said one. Her cousin, conjuring up images of amputa-
tion, said: "They tended to cross over to the white community and not

Madison Hemings's granddaughter Emma Byrd Young, her husband, and their children, ca. 1915. Courtesy of Alice Mae Pettiford and Ann Pettiford Medley.

maintain any connection with the rest of the family. It was just sort of cut off." Important life passages like births, marriages, and deaths became painful reminders of family division, and only those remaining in the black community came to family reunions. One descendant related a bitter moment in his grandmother's life, when she was not notified of the death of her brother, who had passed for white and married a white woman years before. He had remained in touch, however, through cards and phone calls on certain meaningful occasions. His new family did not send word across the color line until months after he died, perhaps to ensure that no part of the black family appeared at the funeral.[9]

Passing was not always permanent. A great-grandson of Madison Hemings through Sarah Byrd became what his family calls an "ethnic person," adopting a variety of European accents along with his fictitious identities. At the end of his life, alone and in need of support, he returned to the care of a sister who had remained a person of color. According to one informant, when he came to live with her grandmother, "we didn't understand who [he] was because [he] had an Italian accent. . . . And then we found out actually he was our uncle. And that [he] had crossed over, he had been white. And he didn't have a whole lot to do with his family. . . . But at the point where he was an old man and he didn't have anywhere else to go, he ended up staying with Grandma and he stayed with her until he died." For others, intermittent passing became a strategy for securing anything from a job to a haircut. Their racial identities calibrated by the day or hour, they were white in the workplace and black at home, or borrowed a white surname to make a hairdressing appointment in a neighboring town.

There is no way to know exactly what governed the timing of Eston Hemings's decision to slip off his African American identity and move to Wisconsin, leaving his brother behind in Ohio. When Eston and Julia Hemings headed further northwest in 1852, their children were ages fourteen, sixteen, and seventeen. By crossing the color line in unison, before the children reached marriageable age, Eston Hemings's family avoided the fragmentation that had occurred in his own generation, with the departures of his siblings Harriet and Beverley. The disappearing brothers who haunted succeeding generations of Madison Hemings's descendants would not be a part of Eston Hemings's legacy, and his adoption of whiteness was successful in its probable intention—escape for his family from the economic and social subordination that prevailed under the "black laws" of Ohio. His daughter Anna married and lived as a white woman. Her brothers were both officers in white regiments in the Union army. Beverly F. Jefferson, who married a white woman, became a prosperous and respected hotel and transfer company owner, while John Wayles Jefferson moved to the South and became a wealthy cotton broker. His articles were published in Wisconsin and Tennessee newspapers, and he corresponded with President Benjamin Harrison about conditions in the postwar South. Eston H. Jefferson's grandsons even exceeded the success of his sons, becoming lawyers and physicians, as well as prosperous businessmen.[10]

By contrast, the children and grandchildren of Madison Hemings who remained in Ohio were bound by the restricted opportunities for blacks at the time. They were, for the most part, small farmers, storekeepers, laborers, domestic servants, or caterers. While their descendants speak above all of families of love and strength, there are stories of the breaking of the human spirit rather than its triumph, when racial prejudice blighted career expectations and dreams for children. Some lives, as we have also heard in other families descended from the Monticello enslaved community, were tinged with alcohol and anger.

A move to the other side of the color line brought its own set of costs, however. The persistent anxiety of hiding the past is shown in a newspaper account of the meeting of Eston's son John Wayles Jefferson, then a Lieutenant Colonel of the 8th Wisconsin, with a citizen of Chillicothe, Ohio, his former residence. "He begged me," recalled the writer, "not to tell the fact that he had colored blood in his veins, which he said was not suspected by any of his command."[11] Like Madison Hemings's sons, John W. Jefferson remained a bachelor, as did two of his nephews, one of whom was a suspected suicide; the other walked down the railroad tracks and "vanished off the face of the earth." The early deaths of an unusual number of Eston Hemings Jefferson's male descendants, if not attributable to genetic factors, may be symptomatic of the pressures of passing.

D S W : *It was December 1993, in Chillicothe, Ohio, the beginning of the Getting Word project, and we nervously awaited guests invited to a reception for descendants of Madison Hemings and his cousin Joseph Fossett. There were flakes of snow in the straight black hair of the first person to arrive. He rubbed long*

*white fingers over his face and perfectly angled nose. I hated to send him back out-
side into the snowstorm, but I could not avoid telling him that the reception was
only for descendants of the black people who lived at Monticello when Thomas
Jefferson was alive.*

"Yes, I know. That's why I am here. I am one of them."

*The next day, mindful that people are not as they appear, I approach every-
thing with caution—even the old photographs strewn across the table.*

*Madison Hemings's granddaughter and her family were there, early in this
century, standing and sitting in a farm's yard, facing the camera, their community, and me. There were no smiles; no one was touching. Two hunting dogs filled
the space between the father and the son.*

*There was something else. I knew this family to be black. They looked white.
The mother and daughters had clustered themselves at one side of the image. The
brother stood alone at the opposite edge of the picture. Time and folding had
creased the father. He appeared to be split into two parts.*

Since that reception in 1993 we have learned that Sally Hemings's children and their descendants had been changing, reconstructing, or reinforcing their racial identities through all the generations from the time of
slavery until the present. The light-skinned offspring of miscegenation in
slavery had maintained their distinctiveness by marrying others who
shared their physical appearance and its accompanying social status. In
this way, subsequent generations of Sally Hemings's descendants continued to resemble their famous ancestor, who was described as "mighty
near white."[12] Madison and Mary Hemings's descendants in Ohio were
part of an endogamous community of very light-skinned blacks that has
continued for more than a century. Only recently has this self-perpetuat-
ing group living suspended between two worlds begun to blend into the
rest of society, by expanding their marriage choices to include darker-
skinned spouses.

Our interviews with Madison Hemings's descendants, all of whom
identify themselves as people of color, reveal both the significance of light
skin and a deeply-felt allegiance to the black community. Similarities of appearance and social background were prerequisites for prospective mates,
and parents admonished their children of dating age to befriend only those
who looked like themselves. One descendant said: "I think it is who you
married. Those that were fair, perhaps, at the time married more white,

because it was the way." Another descendant, recalling his first dating experiences as recently as the 1980s, told how his parents expressed their displeasure when he brought darker-skinned girls home; they let him know that his one experiment in dating a white girl was also unacceptable.

This pattern over two centuries—miscegenation in slavery, endogamy accompanied by some passing for white, and assimilation into black culture—was broken in one branch of Madison Hemings's family. His youngest daughter, Ellen Wayles Hemings, married a man described in the family as having "no white blood"; he was "pure African," "Nubian black." Some of Ellen's descendants tell an interesting story about the origin of this union: Madison Hemings, old and infirm, arranged this marriage for his last unmarried daughter, joining her, possibly against her will, with a much older man he recognized as able to support her. Ellen and Andrew J. Roberts's marriage record,[13] however, is dated a year after Madison Hemings's death and reveals Roberts to be only five years older than his wife. The story appears to be a family effort to explain the unusual choice of a dark-skinned husband.

A. J. Roberts, a schoolteacher at the time of his marriage, did indeed provide well for his wife and family. He took them to southern California where he started a very successful family mortuary business, "the pioneer establishment in the State." He and his son Frederick Madison Roberts, the first black member of the California legislature, are featured in a 1919 work, *The Negro Trail Blazers of California*.[14] But the variations of skin color within this family seem to have been a factor in shaping personal worth. Ellen Hemings Roberts, described in her family as looking like a white woman, seemed to prefer her grandchildren with Caucasian features. One brown-skinned granddaughter recalled the special favors given her brother, with his pale skin and golden curls, while she herself was called "little black gal." In another branch of Madison Hemings's family, a woman who married a dark-skinned man was remembered as having "stuck the wrong color into their family" and her brown-skinned daughters considered themselves the "black sheep" of the family.

Color prejudice was present in the black community outside the family as well. One of Sarah Hemings Byrd's descendants said that "the blacks don't like it because you're light skinned and the whites know you're black so you're just stuck there." Her mother, in her seventies, remembered the hostility of her black schoolmates: "They used to call us white niggers."

No matter their complexion, Madison Hemings's descendants were emphatic in their identification with blackness. Many elected to remain a part of the black community even when their appearance made passing possible. For one Sarah Byrd descendant World War II provided two defining moments. When he enlisted in the navy, he was "really hurt" when he was recorded by the local recruiter as a negro of "dark" or "black" complexion. When he reached his assignment point, however, he adamantly refused to be placed in a white unit at the recommendation of the assigning officer, who was struck by his appearance. This forceful claim to African American identity was made in what seems to be a common scenario, in which a white person is eager to offer a passport to white identity and the privilege it provides to blacks who appear white. One of Ellen Hemings Roberts's descendants, when asked if she had ever considered passing for white, responded: "Absolutely not! It was how we were brought up to take pride in who we were." She also was often told by white people that she could be "anything" she wanted, as if no sane person would wish to be black. This tendency of whites to want to make the rules about race is shown in a particularly revealing case, where a neighborhood street became a battleground over control of racial categories. Every summer evening in the 1970s a white boy pounced on Madison Hemings's great-great-great-grandson, knocked him to the ground, and pummeled his chest, shouting, "You're white. I know you're white." "No, I'm not. I'm black," was the response. After protesting his blackness over and over, he finally confessed to being what he knew he was not in order to bring the daily ritual to an end.

D S W : *A shadowbox containing a fifty-odd-year-old twist of tobacco and an ear of yellow corn, only a year or two younger, sits on a fireplace mantel in my office. My paternal grandfather grew them both in one of the Piedmont, Virginia, fields he sharecropped. Before the shadowbox came to this Monticello office, its contents had hung against the wall of my parents' kitchen for decades. My grandfather gave them to my parents' home when they married and moved north. Tobacco and corn were symbols for my ancestors—of how hard they worked and who they were. They are now markers for me.*

L C S : *I cherish and display—at risk to its existence—one piece of family memorabilia that has come down to me: a framed document inset with a small photograph of a young man in uniform. He is my paternal great-grandfather, ap-*

pointed in the document as acting master in the Confederate navy, 1863. By fram-ing these fading manuscripts, someone in the family had chosen to mark his deci-sion to leave his inland home in the Union state of Kentucky for the seacoast and the Confederacy. And I had chosen to exhibit them, emblems of the slaveowning side of my family; my maternal ancestors were all Yankees. Other ancestors on my father's side had produced a Georgia plantation mistress who neglected to tell her slaves that the war was over and they were free, as well as a Pulitzer Prize–winning journalist who fought the Ku Klux Klan. Master Stanton stares out of the frame at the twentieth century, telling me that every American is impli-cated in the aftermath of slavery.

We attach our memories to markers—people, places, events—that de-fine and determine our identities.[15] Very much like icons on a computer screen, these familiar sites of memory can be opened to reveal a multi-tude of motifs and messages that influence our ideas and actions. These landmarks of the past usually undergo regular revision, changing their shapes and meanings as each new generation navigates its course toward identity. Thomas Jefferson remained a primary reference point for Eston Hemings's descendants, while in his brother Madison's family Sally Hem-ings survived as an additional marker of equal importance. For both fam-ilies, however, the unacceptability of a significant part of their family tree has led to the suppression of the links and associations that might nor-mally accompany sites of memory.

Whatever other parts of himself he left behind when he departed Chillicothe for Wisconsin, Eston Hemings took with him his connection to Thomas Jefferson. Although it was widely "rumored" in southern Ohio that he was Jefferson's son, he is not known to have made an un-equivocal statement of his parentage, as did his brother Madison. When asked by another Chillicothe resident to comment on his "perfect and striking" resemblance to Jefferson, his response was more ambiguous: "'Well,' answered Hemings quietly, 'my mother, whose name I bear, be-longed to Mr. Jefferson,' and after a slight pause, added, 'and she never was married.'"[16] He made his most direct statement on the issue by sup-pressing his mother's name to a middle initial *H* and taking the surname of the man he so closely resembled. Unlike most who passed for white, who closed the door on their past and created new family histories, Eston Hemings risked exposure by adopting this well-known surname and sustaining the memory of his tie to Jefferson. This seems to indicate a strong identification with the man he knew as his father. They shared physical appearance and unusual stature, mastery of the violin, and the tunes to go with it. Eston Hemings may also have had Jeffersonian tastes, as he purchased a set of silver spoons at an estate sale in 1827, when about to leave Virginia.[17]

Passing usually required discarding the past and the creation of a new family story untainted by connection to blackness. Eston H. Jefferson's children, however, preserved their connection to Thomas Jefferson and Monticello. His son Beverly, who died in 1908, was described by a friend as Thomas Jefferson's grandson in an addendum to a Chicago newspaper obituary.[18] Within a few decades, however, a new history had been created by weaving fiction into core truths that were important to family identity. The Jefferson connection was preserved, but the pedigree was revised to prevent discovery by those who knew that Jefferson and his wife had no surviving sons. Growing up in the 1940s, Eston Hemings's great-great-granddaughter heard that she was related to Thomas Jefferson, not through direct descent but collaterally, through his uncle. Other small alterations were made to the past: Eston's name became Estis; Virginia remained the home state, but Albemarle County became Fairfax; and all references to the fifteen-year residence in Ohio, where the family had lived as blacks, were eliminated. Sally Hemings is conspicuously absent from this story.

Madison Hemings never took the Jefferson surname and his recollections do not suggest that he identified with Jefferson in any way. He even pointed out their physical dissimilarity: "He [Jefferson] was a much smarter man physically, even at that age, than I am." But his several references to promises, and how they were broken by "white folks," indicate that, for him, Jefferson differed from other whites; he kept his promises. Referring to Jefferson's "solemn pledge" made in Paris to induce Sally Hemings to return with him to Virginia, he said: "We all became free agreeably to the treaty entered into by our parents before we were born." Because he remained a man of color, Madison Hemings did not have to twist Jefferson's relationship to him or to exclude his mother in his accounts of his history. Equal in importance, both parents appear in his 1873 recollections to a white journalist and in the stories told his children.

They and succeeding generations were left to pass it on or to deny it according to their own racial and personal identities.[19]

Memory and personal identity are inextricably linked. One Madison Hemings descendant, the daughter of a California legislator, understands her father in terms of her ancestor's calling: "My father was a public servant, so it seemed kind of natural. My great-great-grandfather was a public servant. It came on down to my father." Another descendant said that, had he known of his connection to Thomas Jefferson while he was in architecture school, he never would have dropped out. Eston Hemings's descendants see their family's multiple talents and interest in the arts and music as links with their Jefferson heritage. Descendants now living on both sides of the color line described Thomas Jefferson in glowing terms. Young and old alike called him "a great man" and many described him as "brilliant," the brightest of our presidents. Younger descendants called him "interesting" and "contradictory," while their elders found ways to understand Jefferson's complicity in slavery. Two sisters living on different continents for the last thirty-five years shared the same view that Jefferson was not a "mean" master, but he was "caught" in his time and "was just torn about what to do." His family relationship mediated his role as a slaveholder: "Blood is thicker than water," as one sister said.

Even though no visual images of Sally Hemings exist, she is clearly present in the minds, memories, and identities of Madison Hemings's descendants. She is described by these, mostly female, descendants as "bright" and "intelligent," "very special" and "extraordinary." "I'd like to know more about her" or "I wish I could have met her" are common responses. They see the people and situations in their own lives through the lens of Sally Hemings. A human resources worker considers Sally Hemings in the context of her own workplace, with its concerns of sexual harassment and equal opportunity. Another descendant reviewed the parallels in the lives of Sally Hemings and her mother and grandmother, all single parents, and concluded: "My mother felt the same thing Sally did." One woman, a deputy sheriff in a large city, perceived her ancestor as "strong" and "independent."

A third marker for Madison Hemings's descendants was the relationship itself, the nature of the link between Jefferson and Sally Hemings. One descendant, confessing her imperfect recollection of her great-aunt's

version of the family history, did remember that "it was more of a romantic story, it was about this captain of a ship." In two other branches there
is a particularly strong oral tradition of a deep and abiding love between
Jefferson and Hemings. As Ellen Hemings Roberts's granddaughter said,
Sally Hemings was "dearly loved" by Jefferson. "This was passed down,
down, down the oral history." In its most elaborated form, this version of
the story removed the stain of illegitimacy by pointing to the laws that
prevented Jefferson and Hemings from marrying, thereby allowing Sally
Hemings to become a positive role model, in spite of her marital and social status.

In the 1940s Ellen Roberts's niece Nellie Johnson Jones wrote a two-
page family history for a cousin, in which she said her grandfather was
"the son of Thomas Jefferson" (she was the daughter of Madison Hemings's daughter Mary Ann Hemings Johnson). While it is not known how
widely she spoke of her actual descent from Jefferson outside of her family, she was not averse to making her connection to Monticello known.
She had inherited from her mother several articles that had been Jefferson's—spectacles, a buckle, and an inkwell—and placed them for display
in shopfronts in Illinois and houses in Los Angeles. In 1938 she wrote for
advice to President Roosevelt and the postmaster general in her efforts to
find the most appropriate location for these objects. Stating that they had
descended to her from her great-grandmother Sally Hemings to Madison
Hemings and then to her mother, and without directly mentioning Jefferson's paternity, she offered to sell the mementos to the Thomas Jefferson
Memorial Foundation at Monticello: "Knowing the esteem in which
Thom. Jefferson is held; being a historical character who will live as long
as America endures, I decided that some one might want these articles."
She regretted her inability to donate them. The chairman of the board
did not ask to view the objects and declined Mrs. Jones's offer; their current whereabouts is unknown.[20]

Nellie Jones's efforts to establish an almost public dimension for her
connection to Jefferson were very much the exception. Her belief in a
love story thwarted by unjust laws freed her to break the silence guarded
so carefully by others of her generation. For the majority of Madison
Hemings's descendants the paternity story remained a private matter, and
its persistence in a hostile environment of disbelief is a striking demonstration of the strength of the oral tradition. One of the by-products of

the public denial of the family's history was a potent and pervasive silence, both inside and outside the family circle. Descendants of three of
Madison Hemings's daughters report that their elders talked little about
the Jefferson-Hemings history. One heard the story from her father at the
age of twelve: "But he said 'but we don't talk about it.' And I never mentioned it again to him and he never spoke about it. My grandmother did-
n't talk about it either." Personal encounters with skepticism reinforced
the suppression of the story. As one man related: "It was never really, really talked about. You tell people and they would kind of laugh at you or
didn't believe you or it would pass over their heads."

For members of an African American community where orality is
honored and respected, silence became a family trait. The silence of the
mysterious, staring son of Madison Hemings has been mentioned before.
His sister is remembered as a loving presence, but her voice is forgotten.
She was "very, very quiet." In describing their father and grandfather,
three sisters used the word "quiet" over a dozen times, and a descendant
in another branch stated: "You've been taught all your life to be quiet."
The repressive climate of disbelief engendered a number of stories of
documents or family Bibles that could have proved the Jefferson descent
that had either disappeared or been burned in fires or car wrecks.

Society's repudiation was matched by denial within the family. Slavery
itself was considered a shameful topic until recently and the specter of illegitimacy further stifled discussion of the past. Said one descendant of
her elders' injunctions to silence: "They seemed to feel because it was an
illegitimate relationship that they didn't want it known." Many stories
that might have flourished in a different climate vanished in the pervasive
silence. Madison Hemings's woodworking talents were forgotten, his
wife's freeborn status was lost, and no family accounts bearing on personality survive. Interestingly, the only information about Hemings's character comes from descendants of his white neighbors.[21]

Only the most important story, the one that was the hardest to believe,
was held onto with remarkable tenacity. Because people pass on stories as
part of the formation of identity, the account of descent from Thomas
Jefferson and Sally Hemings became something very different from tales
told around the dinner table or at bedtime to lull children to sleep. Madison Hemings's descendants chose the moments of transmittal carefully.
They waited until children were old enough to understand, or until they

reached an important transition point, or until their lives intersected with history. For Sarah Hemings Byrd's granddaughter, it was an occasion of both family pride and historical association that impelled her to pass on the story to her granddaughter. It was only when her granddaughter won a history prize in high school, sponsored by the Daughters of the American Revolution, that "she mentioned that we were related to the third president of the United States, Thomas Jefferson. She just took a lot of pride in the fact that we got that type of recognition. And she saw a connection there."

While Madison Hemings's descendants who remained black could openly identify with their slave ancestor, in order to erase their racial origins Eston H. Jefferson's descendants had to hide or deny her existence. It is apparently no accident that Dr. Eugene Foster, in pursuit of DNA samples, could find exclusively male-line descendants of Eston Hemings Jefferson but not of his brother Madison. In the Eston H. Jefferson branch, both the Y-chromosome and the memory of Thomas Jefferson were transmitted from generation to generation. The male markers of Madison Hemings's descendants seem to have disappeared as some men made the choice to pass for white and left no traces, while the women who remained behind never forgot Sally Hemings. The genetic markers in each line thus match the markers of memory.

DSW: *So much of what I've learned since the beginning of this project, I've learned around kitchen tables. It was around Beverly Gray's kitchen table in Chillicothe, Ohio, that I first heard the phrase "bringing children out of Egypt." It was used in describing the deliberate behavior of enslaved women to gain freedom for their children. Bev Gray told me that "children could be brought out of Egypt or slavery" by having a father who could and would free them, or by having skin light enough not to appear black.*

Bev's comment set my thinking of enslaved women on its head. In my mind, only Harriet Tubman and Sojourner Truth had such agency. Sally Hemings, Liberator. An interesting idea. If she and other enslaved women deliberately sought to "bring their children out," they were in some way doing what only God could do—freeing powerless people. A novel concept, to say the least. Those without power exercising it, and those with power letting it seep away through sexual acts they were privileged to have simply because they were in power.

LCS: *I am sitting over breakfast reading about the natural world, in which I find so many metaphors for human behavior. Dianne and I have been talking, writing, and reading together for weeks in connection with preparing this essay, but at this moment I am, I believe, far away from Monticello and its messages. The monarchs are on the move in Mexico. Clouds of butterflies waft north to California and their summer feeding grounds. But many never complete their appointed journey. They alight and give birth and die, leaving their children to carry on the voyage and the family. Unbidden, Betty Hemings, and her daughters Mary and Sally come to mind, making their long migration to freedom and fulfillment for their children.*

A number of Madison Hemings's female descendants are fascinated by the most evident moment of choice in Sally Hemings's life. Why did she leave freedom in Paris to return to slavery in Virginia? By her son's account, she refused to leave France until Jefferson promised her "extraordinary privileges" and "made a solemn pledge that her children should be freed at the age of twenty-one years. In consequence of his promise, on which she implicitly relied, she returned with him to Virginia."[22]

While we might find it hard to imagine making such a choice based on the fates of one's unborn children, Sally Hemings may have felt she was part of a continuum. Madison Hemings used the same term *concubine*, for both his mother and his grandmother Elizabeth (Betty) Hemings. If, through her connection to John Wayles, Betty Hemings had brought her children from the fields to the great house, could she, Sally, take her own one step further and bring them out of Egypt? Her sister Mary achieved this for some of her children when she formed a quasi-conjugal relationship with the white merchant who hired her in 1787. Thomas Bell, described by Thomas Jefferson as a "man remarkeable for his integrity," freed Mary Hemings, acknowledged his two children by her, and left them his substantial estate.[23]

Sally Hemings had partially accomplished her mission by 1822, when her oldest children Beverley and Harriet shed their slave identities and quietly left Monticello, evidently with Jefferson's blessing. Because they also discarded their African American identities, their emancipation required exile from their home. While proximity to family was sacrificed for the sake of freedom, it is apparent from their brother's recollections that Beverley and Harriet Hemings remained in touch with their mother and siblings. The close ties of this family are further indicated by the recurring names of siblings in the next generation, as well as actions after Jefferson's death in 1826. When Madison and Eston Hemings became free according to the terms of Jefferson's promise and his will, they and their mother took up residence together in Charlottesville, first in a rented house and then in one they purchased and, perhaps, built.[24]

Although no document granted Sally Hemings her freedom, she was evidently given "her time" by Jefferson's daughter Martha Randolph.[25] She lived to see a grandchild born in a house owned by her family. As property herself, she had little to give to her children, but she had negotiated to give them back what her enslaved condition had taken from them—their freedom. While the other men freed by Jefferson's will were in their forties and fifties, Madison and Eston Hemings began their adult lives as free men.

L C S : *From the time I read Dorothy Redford's* Somerset Homecoming *I could not help imagining a similar event at Monticello, bringing back descendants of all its former residents.[26] In the summer of 1997, Dianne and I took a first step in achieving such a goal, inviting the participants in the Getting Word project to come to Monticello for a weekend. We knew we wanted to have a naming ceremony, to acknowledge those who were unable to leave lasting records of their existence, whose talent and labor contributed to the creation and operation of Jefferson's house and plantation.*

As the date approached, I realized that projected attendance was nearing 130—the number of men, women, and children who lived in bondage at Monticello at Jefferson's death in 1826. I prepared 130 small cards, each imprinted with a name, and we placed them in a handmade white-oak basket.

D S W : *What we called the Getting Word Gathering provided an opportunity to end the silence before it was too late. When this project began I did not know that one of our tasks would be to encourage the transmission of information through oral stories. The telling of stories—the speaking of things and events— was so much a part of African American experience, there should have been no need to promote it. There was. Decades of disbelief and unwelcoming reception had produced a righteous silence that threatened the magic and charm of black orality. The Gathering would give descendants a chance to speak their ancestors back into existence in the same way the Bible says that God spoke the world into being.*

A poem by a West African philosopher-poet, Birago Diop, came to mind.

Those who are dead are never gone;
They are there in the thickening shadow.
The dead are not under the earth;
They are in the tree that rustles,
They are in the wood that groans,
. . . .
They are in the hut,
They are in the crowd,
The dead are not dead.

And so it was that a joint vision of a naming ceremony at the end of the Getting Word Gathering took form. On a warm clear evening in June, descendants and their families assembled on the mountaintop lawn, before the West Portico, with members of the Monticello staff. One of the fifty Betty Hemings descendants present spoke a prayer drawn from the Book of Timothy, encouraging each person to press on. Reminded of another verse in the same biblical chapter, a woman exclaimed that the Getting Word project had "come before winter," before all the memories were gone, before they were lost forever. Dianne read "The Dead Are Not Dead" and passed around the basket, from which everyone took a name card. One by one, descendants called out the names of those who had gone before, those 130 people who, on Independence Day 1826, were painfully aware that their fates hung in the balance. The economic realities of Jefferson's encumbered estate brought a train of events—appraisals, advertisements, and sales—that swiftly and harshly severed them from their homes and families. Sally Hemings and her sons were the only ones who were not separated from spouse, children, or parents. Her fifth great-granddaughter, a tow-headed ten-year-old, read out the name on the card in her hand—Sally Hemings—speaking her back into existence, breaking the silence.

NOTES

Getting Word, Monticello's African American Oral History Project, was begun in the fall of 1993, with Lucia Stanton as project director, Dianne Swann-Wright as project historian, and Beverly Gray as consultant. Continuously supported by the Thomas Jefferson Memorial Foundation, it was initially funded by the Virginia Foundation for Humanities and Public Policy and received additional funding from Coca-Cola. The last two years of the project have been supported by a grant from the Ford Foundation. Beverly Gray, an educator and historian in Chillicothe, Ohio, has generously shared her papers, her knowledge, and her insights, all of which have contributed so much to the project and to this chapter.

1. Our information is derived from interviews with twenty descendants of three daughters of Madison Hemings and four descendants of a son of Eston Hemings Jefferson, as well as documentary material relating to a branch of Madison Hemings's family through a fourth daughter. We would like to express our deep appreciation to the Hemings descendants who have so generously welcomed us into their homes and shared the thoughts, feelings, and memories that have made this chapter possible.

2. Albemarle County Deed Book 29: 276–77. A receipt in the University of Virginia Proctor's Papers notes payment to Eston Hemings for a violin case (receipt, June 1833, Box 10, Proctor's Papers). We are grateful to C. Allan Brown for pointing out this source.

3. Marriage licenses, 1831–1832, Albemarle County Clerk's Office; Lucia Stanton, "Monticello to Main Street: The Hemings Family and Charlottesville," *Magazine of Albemarle County History,* 55 (1997), 105–8.

4. *Daily Scioto Gazette,* 1 Aug. 1902; *Chillicothe Leader,* 26 Jan. 1887, typescript; Jefferson manuscript music, University of Virginia Library, Acc. No. 5118. Both newspaper sources were brought to light by Beverly Gray and the second one is in her collection.

5. Until 1910 Virginia law declared that a free person with more than three-quarters white heritage was white; in Ohio the legal situation was more ambiguous, with some cases decided for mulattoes with more than one-half white heritage until the 1859 visible admixture law. Eston Hemings's cousin Robert Scott, grandson of his aunt Mary Hemings Bell, lost a lawsuit in 1892 because his family, although legally white, was deemed "socially black" (Stanton, "Monticello to Main Street," 124–25); Stephen Middleton, *The Black Laws in the Old Northwest: A Documentary History* (Westport, 1993). Madison and Eston Hemings were listed as white in the 1830 Virginia census and as mulattoes in a special Virginia 1833 census and in the Ohio censuses of 1840 and 1850.

6. *Cleveland American,* undated, cited in the *Liberator,* 19 Dec. 1845, a reference brought to our attention by Micah Fink.

7. Madison Hemings recollections, Appendix; Ross County Deed Book, Ross County Courthouse, Chillicothe, Ohio, 68: 562–63; Madison Hemings estate, Ross County Probate Court records. His estate included, besides house, outbuildings, and land, a wagon and black mare, seven hogs, several plows, a large supply of lumber and wagon spokes, a workbench and tool chest, and assorted planes, augers, and chisels. Hemings's word as "his bond" was communicated by Beverly Gray, who interviewed a descendant of one of Hemings's white neighbors.

8. Fawn M. Brodie, "Thomas Jefferson's Unknown Grandchildren: A Study in Historical Silence," *American Heritage,* 27 (Oct. 1976), 95; Nellie Johnson Jones manuscript family history, private collection.

9. Unless otherwise noted, all quotations are from interviews and notes of conversation in the Getting Word project files.

10. Brodie, "Jefferson's Unknown Grandchildren," 95.

11. *Daily Scioto Gazette,* 1 August 1902.

12. Isaac Jefferson recollections, in James A. Bear, Jr., *Jefferson at Monticello* (Charlottesville, 1967), 4.

13. In private collection.

14. Delilah L. Beasley, *The Negro Trail Blazers of California* (Los Angeles, 1919), 40–41, 137, 215–16, 255–56.

15. Our thoughts about memory have been enriched by the authors who made imaginative use of Pierre Nora's concept of *lieux de mémoire* in *History and Memory in African American Culture,* ed. Geneviève Fabre and Robert O'Mealy (New York, 1994).

16. *Daily Scioto Gazette,* 1 Aug. 1902.

17. Stanton, "Monticello to Main Street," 113.

18. Judith Justus, *Down from the Mountain: The Oral History of the Hemings Family* (Perrysburg, Ohio, 1990), 93–94.

19. "Memoirs of Madison Hemings," Appendix A in this volume.

20. Nellie Jones to Stuart Gibboney, 29 July, 10 Aug. 1938; Gibboney to Jones, 1 Aug., 1 Nov. 1938, University of Virginia Library.

21. Personal communication of Beverly Gray, Chillicothe, Ohio.

22. "Memoirs of Madison Hemings" (Appendix A).

23. Stanton, "Monticello to Main Street," 97.

24. "Memoirs of Madison Hemings" (Appendix A).

25. Stanton, "Monticello to Main Street," 107–8.

26. Dorothy Spruill Redford, *Somerset Homecoming: Recovering a Lost Heritage* (New York, 1988).

PART III

Civic Culture

CHAPTER 8

"Denial Is Not a River in Egypt"

Clarence Walker

Most Americans, regardless of their color or sexual persuasion, do not handle interracial sex easily.[1] Despite all the progress made in race relations over the past fifty years, interracial sex is still a flashpoint of unease and disquiet. This is particularly true when the relationship involves blacks and whites. A Knight-Ridder poll taken in May 1997 revealed that although the people surveyed were for the most part favorably disposed toward intermarriage, "fully 3 in 10 respondents opposed marriage between blacks and whites."[2] The old query, "How would you like to have your daughter marry one?" may not be voiced as publicly as it once was, but it continues to play a powerful role in the way Americans, black and white, choose their mates.[3] This issue also colors the way we look at the American past.

I have been teaching American history for twenty-five years. When I take up the subject of miscegenation in my black American history class there is always some discomfort expressed by both black and white students. When I taught at Wesleyan University in Connecticut in the 1970s, a white student asked me what mulattoes looked like and when I explained that they were only one permutation in a range of racial intermixture the student became agitated. He wanted to know how a mulatto looked, and when one of his black peers in a moment of irritation yelled,

"Like your grandmother!" the class broke out in nervous laughter. At Wesleyan and at Davis, where I now teach, other students, both black and white, have become disturbed by the subject of racial intermixture and told me so after class: "Professor Walker, how could you talk about that?" My answer has always been that America was never a white nation, and that the idea that this was ever the case is a fantasy. I am quick to remind them that from the time of exploration, colonization, settlement, and creation of the American republic, the United States was a place where racial intermixture took place with greater frequency than many historians are willing to acknowledge. The disavowal of this legacy of colonialism has everything to do with the way historians of early American history have dealt with the Sally Hemings–Thomas Jefferson affair.

Thomas Jefferson occupies a central place in our nation's pantheon of heroes. Author of the Declaration of Independence, third president of the republic, and exemplar of the Enlightenment, Jefferson embodies all the gentlemanly virtues that we are supposed to associate with the Virginia aristocracy. These qualities in the popular mind are honor, refinement, and probity—in short, all things associated with whiteness. The recent revelation that this American icon was the father of a mulatto child has uncovered a deep fault line in how the nation thinks about Jefferson, interracial sex, slavery, and history—in brief, how we think about race.

Slavery played a central role in the history of the United States. Indeed, the country would not have been founded without some recognition of slavery as a protected institution. Black women were exploited both for their labor and reproductive capabilities. They were both workers and objects of sexual exploitation. This latter facet of slave women's lives has been captured in some of the most powerful slave narratives. Works such as *Incidents in the Life of a Slave Girl* and *Twelve Years a Slave,* by Solomon Northup, indicate that the plantations were sites of more than labor exploitation. Thirty-nine years ago, Severn Duvall, in a brilliant article, explored this side of slavery; the essay was called "Uncle Tom's Cabin: The Sinister Side of the Patriarchy," and explored an implicit theme of Harriet Beecher Stowe's powerful novel.[4]

As a proper Victorian lady, Stowe only obliquely hinted at what was sexually "going down" on Simon Legree's plantation. Legree, like Jefferson, was involved in a love relationship that "dare not speak its name." What I want to argue here is that the metaphor of the "closet" also obtains in the hetero-normative world and is not the exclusive invention of homosexuals. A number of heterosexual interactions are also conducted clandestinely and interracial sex in America has historically been one of these. This was particularly true in the seventeenth, eighteenth, and nineteenth centuries, when the mythology that upper-class white men were averse to black "trim" (sex) was part of the common-sense ideology to which white Americans hypocritically subscribed. I reference white American hypocrisy here because it speaks to the twin processes of denial and attraction that have informed white American attitudes about the subject of interracial sex.

In white discourse, the black body has historically been an object of simultaneous desire and repulsion. Jefferson gave voice publicly to the negative side of this sensibility when he wrote in *Notes on the State of Virginia* that Negroes "have less hair on the face and body. They secrete less by the kidneys, and more by the glands of the skin, which gives them a very strong and disagreeable odour."[5] Before he made these observations, Jefferson expressed an idea that speaks to white anxiety about black sexuality, that is, its supposed animality. Jefferson articulated the belief that black women coupled with orangutans. According to Jefferson, "the preference of the Oran-ootan for the black women over those of his own species" was well known. Black women were so unlike white females that they attracted both men and beasts. Even the sex act of blacks was described in terms that projected it beyond the bounds of normality. Black sex was "more ardent." The use of these words conjures up the image of animals in rut. In making these statements, Jefferson also repeated a long-held European belief that black women's bodies were both beautiful and monstrous.[6] In a sense, if we read this last observation as an intimation of things to come, Jefferson was comparing himself to an ape.

Like Oscar Wilde's Dorian Gray, Jefferson had a secret life which for both political and cultural reasons had to remain "closeted." According to a Virginia statute of 1662, stiff fines would be levied against "any Christian [who] shall commit fornication with a negro man or woman."[7] In Jefferson's Virginia, white men, in theory, could not sleep with black women openly. To do so publicly would have resulted in legal punishment and, more damaging, social ostracism. We know that some white men violated the anti-miscegenation law and were never prosecuted for doing so. But given his social and political position, Jefferson could flaunt neither the law nor public opinion. Whatever feelings Jefferson may have had for Sally Hemings were circumscribed by a set of cultural and political taboos that made the "personal political."

We have no record of the Sally Hemings–Thomas Jefferson affair. But what we do know about slavery and the sexual exploitation of black women under that system makes it easy to believe that the Hemings-Jefferson relationship was exploitative, with a powerful white man taking advantage of a powerless black female. Yet this may not have been the case. It is also possible that both parties had something to gain from the relationship. Hemings, for instance, may have used sex to get her children's freedom. Harriet Jacobs did this when she took a lover outside her master's household. "Of a man who was not my master I could ask to have my children well supported; and in this case, I felt confident I should obtain the boon. I also felt quite sure they would be made free."[8] It is also possible that white men and black women in slavery loved each other, a point often forgotten in our cynical and highly politicized readings of the past. My point here is that in the study of the subaltern, too much emphasis can be placed on overt forms of resistance.[9] How can we more fruitfully understand Jacobs's strategies of resistance to both slavery and sexual exploitation?

Jacobs, for example, simultaneously resisted and accommodated herself to the sexual blandishments of white men. She spurned the sleazy importunings of Dr. Flint and was seduced by the overtures of Mr. Sands. Jacobs thus exercised the full range of her sexual agency as a female slave. Sally Hemings may have done the same thing with Thomas Jefferson. Again, just what the internal dynamics of this relationship were, we do not know. Sex is a complex, often irrational impulse and just why some people find other people attractive remains a mystery. Writing about this issue recently, Paul Robinson has observed, "sex . . . is a rudely physical, indeed animal, need for the pleasure we get doing particular things with particular parts of our bodies. This is as true for intellectuals as it is anyone else. Sex is an often humbling experience for intellectuals precisely because it reminds them, so unconditionally, of the extent to which they are not pure *geist*."[10] In the case of Sally Hemings and her eminent paramour, all we know is that they produced a child. How the two lovers interacted with each other is a mystery. Jefferson and his mistress did not leave a written record of their relationship that would shed light on its in-

terior dynamics. I make this point because the Hemings-Jefferson relationship was not preserved for posterity as was, for example, the romance
and marriage of Hannah Cullwick and Arthur Munby.[11] Although their diaries deal with a romantic duo who lived after the death of Jefferson, the
story of Cullwick and Munby bears a close resemblance in several crucial
respects to the "Sage of Monticello's" secret affair. Cullwick was a maid
and Munby an upper-class British barrister and *literateur.* They were lovers
for fifty-four years, and no one knew. The romance was not a Jane Austen
love story filled with beautiful women and handsome swains. What we
know about this couple derives from the diaries left by the two lovers.
Munby liked "butch" working-class women. He was, Liz Stanley points
out, obsessed "with lower-class women who were truly working women,
whether in the coal pits of Wigan or digging the roads of London."[12]
Munby had no interest in the women of his own class, and his obsession
with working-class women parallels the *idée fixe* of male homosexuals of
his own time who were obsessed with the vitality of lower-class men.
This obsession is examined most sympathetically in E. M. Forster's novel
Maurice and is also the subtext of D. H. Lawrence's *Lady Chatterley's Lover,*
where the female protagonist's sexuality is brought to maturity by her
working-class gardener. Cullwick and Munby seem to have inhabited the
netherworld of "nonvanilla sex," drawn to sexual practices outside the
range of supposedly hetero-normative sexuality. "For years up until their
marriage Hannah wore a padlock and chain around her neck, to which
only Munby had the key."[13] She also called him "Massa," blackened her
face, and from time to time "licked his boots" and "washed his feet."[14]
These interactions, with their overtones of slavery, today would be labeled kinky by the prosaic and morally self-righteous. But in the Victorian
world they were all part of a vast sexual underground in which both the
bourgeoisie and the aristocracy participated.[15] I make this point because
what we know about this transgressive Victorian duo stands in sharp contrast to how little is known about Jefferson and Hemings. American historians can learn much about sexual relationships between upper-class men
and lower-class women by studying this affair. It illuminates some of the
problems attendant upon studying Jefferson and making claims that recent evidence has shown to be questionable. Horror of horrors, what if,
like Munby, Thomas Jefferson, one of the fathers of our country, was
bored by women of his own race and class and took a black woman slave

as his lover. I advance this speculation only as a "suspicion," and will have more to say about this problem in my conclusion.

All we know about Hemings and Jefferson is that they slept with each other, and that the world into which their offspring were born did not value black and white sexual interactions because couplings of blacks and whites eroded the boundary separating what were thought of as two essentially distinct and antithetical categories of people. In Jefferson's era, sex between whites carried no negative connotations because it was sanctified by marriage. This was not the case with black sex or the sex of other racialized subjects in the United States. What these people did in bed occupies a space marked by negative signifiers, even when they were married. Jefferson entered this world when he cohabited with Sally, and by coupling with a "beast," he dishonored himself, according to the codes of his class and race.

In colonial Virginia, white people married and blacks copulated, as Brenda Stevenson has recently reminded us.[16] Thus, Jefferson could never accord Sally Hemings the respect Virginia society expected a gentleman to display toward a white woman. Marriage for members of Jefferson's class was deeply invested with ideas of honor and claims to respectable standing in society. Fornication with a black woman was a statement about virility and not honor, an expression of white male domination of an inferior people. White men had access to both black and white women, a privilege not extended to black men in southern society. Indeed, sexual relations between the master race's women and black men were perceived as assaults on whiteness as embodied in both property and biology. All the preceding has to be taken into account when assessing the recent consternation expressed over the revelation that Jefferson was the lover of a black woman and the father of one of her children. Jefferson has been "outed," and this does not sit well with some conservative white Americans. Most black Americans have an entirely different point of view about Jefferson and his slave lover.

In black America, the story of Jefferson's dangerous liaison has been in circulation for some two hundred years. *Ebony*—the black version of *Look* and *Life* magazines—recently reported that the descendants of Thomas Woodson, Sally Hemings' putative first child, have kept alive the story of their great-great-great-grandmother's supposed affair with the third president of the United States. Within the Woodson clan, the magazine observed, the story was known "like religion." Unfortunately for the Wood-sons, their claim to be Jeffersons has been discredited by the recent DNA study.[17] Outside the Woodson family, the nineteenth-century black novel-ist and historian William Wells Brown in 1853 published his novel, *Clotel; or, The President's Daughter*.[18] In Brown's tale, Clotel is the daughter of Jeffer-son and his slave housekeeper. The idea that Jefferson's relationships with black people were more than platonic also constitutes the central theme of Barbara Chase-Riboud's fictional account of the life of Sally Hemings.[19]

The most outrageous appropriation of Jefferson for racial purposes is to be found in an obscure volume by Dr. Auset Bakhufu published in 1973. Although this text was published in the United States, I found the book in a small, progressive bookstore in Manchester, England. Titled *The Six Black Presidents*, with the subtitle *Black Blood: White Masks U.S.A.*, the vol-ume asserts without qualification many of the slanderous political ca-nards that circulated about Jefferson during his public life—for example, the accusation that Jefferson was black because his father, Peter Jefferson, "was half Black and half Indian."[20] Jefferson's father, the author notes, was fond of Indians and "found much pleasure in their company." One con-clusion that might be drawn from this quotation is that Jefferson had some genetic attraction to people of color because of his ancestry. This is not stated explicitly in the text, but if we read Peter Jefferson as an eigh-teenth-century precursor of contemporary "whiggerism"(white niggers), my reading of this passage is consonant with Bakhufu's interpretation of American history. What her book does is rehearse a number of the claims made by J. A. Rogers in *World's Great Men of Color*, an analysis of world history that has told black Americans for fifty-three years that many of the great personages of both ancient and modern history were black, an idea that has resurfaced in the contemporary Afrocentric movement.[21]

The point of all this is not an excursus in the arcanum of either black literature or history, because the works of William Wells Brown, Barbara Chase Riboud, J. A. Rogers, and even Dr. Bakhufu point to a fact of black life that undermines the commonly held idea of a pure black race, as ex-pressed in the lyric: "The blacker the berry the sweeter the juice I wants a real black woman for my special use."[22] What this song voices is a hope, not a reality, because there is no pure (real) black race just as there is no pure white race, and Jefferson contributed to this process.[23] Jefferson, in short, was a father of the United States in more than one way. He contributed to the process of remaking the nation racially, a process that would proceed throughout the nineteenth century. This is the source of what I referred to above as the "recent consternation."

Jefferson was a man of honor. At least this was his front, as the people I grew up with used to say when speaking about a prominent person, whether black or white. Within the world of the Tidewater aristocracy of Virginia, appearance was everything. Members of this elite comported themselves as though their model were Calpurnia, Caesar's wife, who was said to be "above suspicion." In societies governed by such a code, Kenneth Greenberg writes, members "project themselves through how they look and what they say. They are treated honorably when their projections are respected and accepted as true. The central concern to such men in such a culture is not the nature of some underlying reality but the acceptance of their projections."[24] One facet of Jefferson's public persona was that of devoted family man, long-suffering widower, and concerned father of two young daughters. Dumas Malone, Jefferson's greatest hagiographer, gave voice to this sentiment in his comments about the Jefferson-Hemings affair:

[The charges of a sexual relationship with Sally Hemings] are distinctly out of character, being virtually unthinkable in a man of Jefferson's moral standards and habitual conduct. . . . It is virtually inconceivable that this fastidious gentleman whose devotion to his dead wife's memory and to the happiness of his daughters and grandchildren bordered on the excessive could have carried on through a period of years a vulgar liaison which his own family could not fail to detect.[25]

Malone's comments reflect a profound naiveté about men, sex, race, and life in general. First, he cannot see beyond Jefferson's "front," or public persona. But DNA has "outed" or "unmasked" Jefferson and shown him to be a man whose passions were more than cerebral. Realization of this fact makes Malone's assertions risible. He fails to acknowledge that Jefferson lived in a world where upper-class men regularly exploited lower-class women, regardless of their color. And being husbands, fathers, politicians, and gentlemen did not deter them from seducing their servitors. These pillars of society were not troubled by bourgeois sensibilities of respectability. Black people have known this historically because their families include members who were products of "massa's" adventures in the quarters. Stated another way, Malone's denial of the Jefferson-Hemings affair represents a reading back into the eighteenth century of values more appropriate to the world of "Ozzie and Harriet," where sex was not the subject of either polite or public conversation.

Monticello was not "Falconhurst Plantation," the subject of Kyle Onstott's prurient 1958 novel *Mandingo*. Onstott bred thoroughbred dogs in Sacramento, California, and let this experience color his interpretation of antebellum slavery. Falconhurst was a stud farm where both black and white men worked at producing children for the slave market. No one in his right mind would suggest that Jefferson was running a slave-breeding plantation. But sexual encounters between blacks and whites did occur at Monticello and are as much a part of the Jeffersonian legacy as the Declaration of Independence. What, then, caused the Jefferson-Hemings romance to be a "vulgar liaison"—its illicit nature or the issue of race?

I think we have to go with race. If it had been revealed that Jefferson was the father of a white servant's child, this might have raised some eyebrows. Bastardy is something that can be forgiven white men, as the cases of Benjamin Franklin and Grover Cleveland indicate. While some might hold these indiscretions against them, the crossing of racial boundaries would have been more damaging still. Franklin and Cleveland were just "sowing wild oats," or, as the saying goes, "boys being boys." But had these two white men produced mixed-race children, the magnitude of their indiscretions would have increased markedly. Miscegenation, not bastardy, would be the issue foremost in the minds of their critics. And this is the issue that now haunts Jefferson's reputation. An icon of the nation has been revealed to have had a clandestine sexual affair with a woman who was not a member of his race or class. If Jefferson slipped, who else in the "Teflon White House" has strayed from the path of white middle-class rectitude?

Joseph J. Ellis should have had this query in mind when he wrote his recent, uninformed bromides about Jefferson and Hemings. Some of the language Ellis uses to discuss the Jefferson-Hemings affair is as unfortunate as that of Dumas Malone. I take exception, for example, to his pronouncement that "[in the] murkier world of popular opinion, especially within the black community, the story appears to have achieved the status of a self-evident truth."[26] Ellis ignores the possibility that what he dismisses as "a self-evident truth" was both true and evident to black people because of the palpable history of miscegenation in America. The fact that this case involved the third president of the United States did not make it improbable to black Americans. Black people, because of their historical and cultural experiences, have a different perception of American historical personages than white college professors and white people generally. Many of us honor these men but do not idealize them. We know them to be men with all the frailties of being human. This is particularly true of black Americans who have family connections in the South, where white men have been sleeping with black women since the seventeenth century. In claiming Jefferson as one of their ancestors, the Woodsons were proclaiming their "American-ness."

In his attempt to deny the Woodsons' Jeffersonian heritage, Ellis reveals a curious lack of understanding about male sexual performance. In an effort to deny Jefferson's sexual potency, Ellis also errs in affirming Henry Adams's statement that Jefferson's temperament was "almost feminine."[27] The word *temperament* occupies a different analytical space than does the term *sexuality,* and the two concepts should not be conflated. Temperament is not sexuality. Moreover, feminine does not mean passive or mild. Ellis obviously has never met a "Sugar Pimp," a man who is effeminate in manner but aggressive sexually with women. Nor does he take into account gay men, called "queens," who are "tops" or "punchers." Feminine men, in short, can be quite priapic. Ellis simply ignores the full range of human sexuality when he observes that:

When scholarly defenders like Dumas Malone and Merrill Peterson claimed that Jefferson was "not the kind of man" to engage in illicit sex with an attractive mulatto slave, they were right for reasons that went deeper than matters of male gallantry and aristocratic honor. Jefferson consummated his relations with women at a more rarefied level, where the palpable realities of physical intimacy were routinely sublimed to safer and sentimental regions. He made a point of insulating himself from direct exposure to the unmitigated meaning of both sex and slavery, a lifelong tendency that an enduring liaison with Sally Hemings would have violated in ways he found intolerable.[28]

Ellis has been compelled to abandon this position in light of the recent DNA discoveries.[29] But his earlier commitment to this line of argument illustrates the power of denial in the historical profession and an anxiety about interracial sex in the general public. Finally, what the Jefferson-Hemings affair shows is the difficulty some white Americans have in dealing with their own racial heritage, which may or may not include a dark-skinned ancestor.

NOTES

I would like to thank Professor Thelma W. Foote for an incisive and critical reading of this essay. I should also like to thank Professors Henry Abelove, James Rose, and John Sweet for some suggestions, and my graduate student, George Jarrette, for computer help.

1. *Interracial sex,* as I use the term here, refers to sex between blacks and whites.

2. Michael Lind, "The Beige and the Black," *New York Times Magazine* (16 Aug. 1998), 39.

3. Mary C. Waters, *Ethnic Options* (Berkeley, 1990), 104–05.

4. Severn Duvall, "Uncle Tom's Cabin: The Sinister Side of the Patriarchy" in *Images of the Negro in American Literature,* ed. Seymour L. Gross and John Edward Hardy (Chicago, 1966), 163–80.

5. For this and subsequent quotations from *The Notes on the State of Virginia,* see Appendix D in this volume.

6. Jennifer Morgan, "Some Could Suckle over Their Shoulder: Male Travelers, Female Bodies, and the Gendering of Racial Ideology, 1500–1700," *William and Mary Quarterly,* 54 (1997), 168.

7. Quoted in James Hugo Johnston, *Race Relations in Virginia and Miscegenation in the South 1776–1860* (Amherst, 1970), 167.

8. Harriet A. Jacobs, *Incidents in the Life of a Slave Girl,* ed. Jean Fagan (1881; Cambridge, 1987), 55.

9. On this point, see Michael Brown, "On Resisting Resistance," *American Anthropologist,* 98 (1996), 729–35.

10. Paul Robinson, *Gay Lives* (Chicago, 1999), xi.

11. Hannah Cullwick, *The Diaries of Hannah Cullwick,* ed. Liz Stanley (New Brunswick, N.J., 1984). For a more expansive reading of the diaries, see Anne McClintock, *Imperial Leather* (New York, 1995), 75–180.

12. Cullwick, *The Diaries of Hannah Cullwick,* Introduction, 14.

13. Ibid., 13.

14. Ibid.

15. For discussions of this underworld, see Steven Marcus, *The Other Victorians* (New York, 1964); Judith R. Walkowitz, *Prostitution and Victorian Society* (Cambridge, U.K., 1980) and *City of Dreadful Delight* (Chicago, 1992); and Jeffrey Weeks, *Sex, Politics, and Society* (London, 1981).

16. Brenda E. Stevenson, *Life in Black and White: Family and Community in the Slave South* (New York, 1996), 141.

17. Laura B. Randolph, "The Thomas Jefferson/Sally Hemings Controversy," *Ebony,* Feb. 1999, 189–94. See also Eugene Foster et al., "Jefferson Fathered Slave's Last Child," *Nature,* 196 (5 Nov. 1998), 27–28, for the DNA evidence.

18. William Wells Brown, *Clotel, or the President's Daughter* (1853, New York, 1970).

19. Barbara Chase-Riboud, *Sally Hemings* (New York, 1979).

20. Quoted in Dr. Auset Bakhufu, *The Six Black Presidents* (Washington, D.C., 1993), 3, see also 1–19.

21. J. A. Rogers, *World's Great Men of Color,* (1946; New York, 1972).

22. Quoted in Lawrence W. Levine, *Black Culture and Black Consciousness* (New York, 1977), 288.

23. For a valuable and wide-ranging collection of essays that deal with the problem of

sex and love across interracial boundaries, see Martha Hodes, ed., *Sex, Love, Race* (New York, 1977).

24. Kenneth S. Greenberg, *Honor and Slavery : Lies, Duels, Noses, Masks, Dressing as a Woman, Gifts, Strangers, Humanitarianism, Death, Slave Rebellions, the Proslavery Argument, Baseball, Hunting, and Gambling in the Old South* (Princeton, 1996), 7.

25. *New York Times*, "Word for Word/The History Books," 8 Nov. 1998.

26. Joseph J. Ellis, *American Sphinx* (New York, 1997), 305. For an insightful critique of earlier writings about this controversy, see Annette Gordon-Reed, *Thomas Jefferson and Sally Hemings: An American Controversy* (Charlottesville, 1997).

27. Ibid.

28. Ibid., 306.

29. See Joseph Ellis, "When a Saint Becomes a Sinner," *U.S. News and World Report*, 9 Nov. 1998, 67–69.

CHAPTER 9

Presidents, Race, and Sex

Werner Sollors

'Tis evening now; beneath the western star
Soft sighs the lover through his sweet cigar,
And fills the ears of some consenting she
With puffs and vows, with smoke and constancy
The patriot, fresh from Freedom's councils come,
Now pleas'd retires to lash his slaves at home;
Or woo, perhaps, some black Aspasia's charms,
And dreams of freedom in his bondmaid's arms.*

*The "black Aspasia" of the present ******** of the
United States, inter alia Avernales haud ignotissima
nymphas[i] has given rise to much pleasantry among the
anti-democrat wits in America.

—Thomas Moore, "To Thomas Hume, Esq. M.D.
  from the City of Washington" (1807)

In the first 223 years of the world's oldest ongoing republic, a relatively small pool of the population has been surprisingly successful in filling presidential slots: white, generally well-to-do, Christian, and (with one exception) Protestant men. While constitutional monarchies have made do with many queens, at times recruited from foreign stock, and while other democracies have been run by the likes of Margaret Thatcher, Indira Ghandi, or Golda Meir, the United States has continued its practice of cautious selectivity in choosing the highest officeholder.

Has this selectivity been enforced by a checks-and-balance system of gossip? For more than two centuries, American politics has been permeated by gossip that would seem calculated to connect presidents with the other—the *non*presidential—sex and, surprisingly often, the nonpresidential race. Such gossip may be presented as deeply shocking, upsetting, and unique, even when expressed repeatedly or appearing in the guise of "scientifically proven," but it has been part of the din of American democracy. Could it be a stabilizing element that, while it seems to challenge positions of political power (though never too much), actually makes more palatable the exclusion from the highest office of those social groups who are, by gossip, symbolically connected to the sites of power, if only in personal liaisons?

Thomas Jefferson may merely be the most famous case. The story of his relationship with his slave Sally Hemings was recently rekindled with the (not unquestionable) authority of DNA research, but the story of the slave-holding author of the declaration that "all men are created equal" has been told and retold for a very long time. In his *History of the United States of America during the Administrations of Thomas Jefferson* (1889–1891), Henry Adams reports how the Scotch adventurer James Thomson Callender, having been imprisoned for some months for the publication of the libelous volume *The Prospect before Us* and then pardoned by his political ally Jefferson, expected a reward and was referred for it to Madison in 1801. Callender "was in love," Henry Adams reports (not quite accurately),

and hinted that to win the object of his affection nothing less that the post-office at Richmond was necessary for his social standing. Meeting with a positive refusal, he returned to Richmond in extreme anger, and became editor of a newspaper called "The Recorder," in which he began to wage against Jefferson a war of slander. . . . He collected every story he could gather, among overseers and scandal-mongers, about Jefferson's past life,—charged him with having a family of negro children by a slave named Sally.

Adams saw this as mere slander, concluded that the rumor about "Black Sally" "seems to have rested on a confusion of persons," and claimed, earlier in his *History*, that Thomas Moore, "but an echo of fashionable England in his day," had "embalmed" Callender's slanders in the poetic lines (that appear here as epigraph), "as though to prove that the Old World knew what grossness was."[2] Omitting the opening lines about the presidential cigar, Adams comments on Moore's poem:

To leave no doubt of his meaning, he explained in a footnote that his allusion was to the President of the United States; and yet even Moore, trifler and butterfly as he was, must have seen, if he would, that between the morals of politics and society in America and those then prevailing in Europe, there was no room for comparison,—there was room only for contrast.[3]

For Henry Adams, the motive for advancing such slander lay in Callender's opportunism and in fashionable European hypocrisy toward American democracy.

Yet there was also an internal dynamic that kept the Jefferson-Hemings story alive, made it controversial and particularly gossip-worthy in American memory, a dynamic created by the coexistence of racial slavery and democracy. Antislavery authors in the United States and abroad were drawn to a story that dramatized this paradox at the foundation of American democracy. Captain Frederick Marryat's *Diary in America* (1839) drew attention to Jefferson in a general critique of white slaveholders' failure to recognize their slave children when he wrote:

I suspect that I have read more of Mr. Jefferson and other American authors than ever the Reviewer has; and I consider the writings of this Father of Democracy, opposed to his private life, to be a remarkable type of democracy in theory and in practice. To borrow a term from the Reviewer, those writings are "brave words" to proceed from an infidel, who proved his ardent love of liberty by allowing his own children to be put up to auction at his death, and wear away their existence in misery and bondage.[4]

An anonymous 1839 poem, entitled "Jefferson's Daughter," made the point emphatically:

> The daughter of Jefferson sold for a slave!
> The child of a freeman, for dollars and francs!
> The roar of applause when your orators rave
> Is lost in the sound of her chain as it clanks.

In six other stanzas the contrast is drawn between the icons of revolutionary patriotism (Lexington, Niagara, Liberty, stripes and stars) and the shameful legacy of racial slavery, as the slavery-supporting "blasphemers of Liberty's name" are exhorted to change their hearts and minds. The poem was authenticated by the following comment: "It is asserted, on the authority of an American newspaper, that the daughter of Thomas Jefferson, late President of the United States, was sold at New Orleans *for 1000 dollars.*"[5]

The first African American novel, William Wells Brown's *Clotel; or, The President's Daughter* (1853), developed fully the national implications of the story of Jefferson, the presidential slaveowner who left his beloved slave woman (here called Currer) in order "to fill a government appointment," and who failed to provide legal recognition for her or their children, exposing them to the extraordinary cruelties of slavery.[6] This story was, for abolitionists, the embodiment of a paradoxical country that was both an egalitarian republic and a slave-holding state.

Not only Jefferson's political opponents and antislavery writers were intrigued by the interracial dimension that was suggested by Callender's report, but also those twentieth-century historians who set out to refute the story. R. R. Burg has shown convincingly how the expressions of their hostility to Callender were only surpassed by such odd semantic choices as describing the reputed affair as a "vulgar liaison" or characterizing the Hemings descendants as "brood" and identifying their "pathetic wish for a little pride" as a motive for their claiming Jefferson as ancestor.[7]

Presidential relations across the color line have been viewed as particularly reprehensible and scandalous in more than one of Jefferson's successors.[8] Rumor had it that President John Tyler had an illegitimate mixed-race daughter who

ran away with the man of her choice in the United States. The lovers were captured, and she was brought to His Excellency, her father, who sold her to a slave-trader. From that Washington slave-pen she was taken to New Orleans by a man who expected to get twenty-five hundred dollars for her on account of her great beauty.[9]

Andrew Johnson was publicly accused of having a colored concubine. In his case no smoking DNA-gun has emerged, and David Warren Bowen summarized the state of affairs as follows:

[A]ny relationship of a sexual nature that Johnson might have had with his female slaves is hidden in the fog always surrounding that delicate subject. There is simply no conclusive evidence one way or the other. This is particularly regrettable because sex plays such an important part in racist mythology. If Dolly, for example, had been purchased for purposes other than domestic, it might clarify the nature of Johnson's personality as well as explain the kind treatment of her half-brother Sam or her children, Liz and Florence. If the converse is true, that Dolly and her counterparts, under the theoretically absolute power of the master, were not exploited in such a manner, it could possibly say a great deal about the strength of Johnson's personality and his feeling toward blacks.[10]

The list goes on. Even vice presidential candidates were measured by the yardstick of "miscegenation." As Richard Hildreth reported in 1856, the Kentuckian Richard M. Johnson had failed in his bid as a candidate in the 1835–1836 campaign, because he had *not* followed the common gentlemen's pattern and was, the narrator feels, "too much of a democrat to suit the tastes of the Virginians" when he acknowledged his liaison with Julia Chinn.

Mr. Johnson, being a bachelor, with no white wife or white children to control him, and, withal, one of the best-natured men in the world, must needs so far imitate the example of the patriarchs as actually to recognize a number of colored daughters as his own children. He has raised and educated them in his own house. He has even made efforts to introduce them into respectable society. The spirit of Kentucky women—the women, you know, are all natural aristocrats—defeated him in that; but he has procured white husbands for them, and their children, under the law of Kentucky, will be legally white, and entitled to all the rights and privileges of white persons. . . . If honest Dick Johnson had not acknowledged those children to be his, do you suppose that any body—unless by way of joke—would have ventured to charge them upon him? His offence consists not in having the children, but in owning them.[11]

Johnson was, in Hildreth's view, simply too honest for the presidency; such connections were to take place secretly and without acknowledgment—subject only to gossip, not to authoritative confirmation. Yet in the long run, this gossip did not hurt Johnson's vice presidential career—nor, in fact, did such stories hurt any of the presidential officeholders from Thomas Jefferson to William Jefferson Clinton.

Still, continuing through and long after the end of slavery, presidents either had to confront stories of "miscegenation" or profess to be firmly opposed to interracial love and marriage in general, most famously perhaps with Abraham Lincoln's recoiling from the possibility of interracial marriage in the context of the debates with Stephen Douglas. In the speech on "The Dred Scott Decision," delivered at Springfield, Illinois on June 26, 1857, Lincoln said: "But Judge Douglas is especially horrified at the thought of the mixing of blood by the white and black races: agreed for once—a thousand times agreed. There are white men enough to marry all the white women, and black men enough to marry all the black women; and so let them be married. On this point we fully agree with the Judge."[12] And Lincoln's well-known remarks in a similar vein of September 18, 1858, also include a sarcastic reference to Richard M. Johnson:

I do not perceive . . . that because the white man is to have the superior position, that it requires the negro should be denied everything. I do not understand that because I do not want a negro woman for a slave I must necessarily want her for a wife.[13] [Cheers and laughter.—*Tribune*] My understanding is that I can just leave her alone. I am now in my fiftieth year, and certainly never have had a black woman either for a slave or wife, so that it seems to me that it is quite possible for us to get along without making either slaves or wives of negroes. . . . I recollect of but one distinguished instance that I have heard of a great deal so as to be entirely confident of it, and that is the case of my friend Douglas's old friend, Co. Richard M. Johnson. . . .

I will add to the few remarks that I have made, for I am not going to enter at large upon this subject, that I have never had the least apprehension that I or my friends would marry negroes if there was no law to keep them from it [Laughter.—*Tribune*], but as my friend Douglas and his friends seem to be under great apprehension that may be they might if there was no law to keep them from it. I give him the most solemn pledge that I will to the very last stand by the law in this State that forbids the marriage of white folks with negroes. [Continued laughter and applause.—*Tribune*][14]

As the modern editor of the text of the debate put it, such comments "have since come to haunt [Lincoln's] reputation, with many historians citing them to dispute his legendary status as an enlightened emancipator."[15]

Somewhat more predictably, the shrillest Southern segregationist radicals made the fear of White House miscegenation central to their paranoid fantasies. In their minds, the fear of miscegenation extended to include even interracial dining. Public scandals surrounding miscegenation thus had their early twentieth-century equivalent in Theodore Roosevelt's famous lunch with Booker T. Washington in the White House on October 18, 1901. On the surface this appears harmless enough, but it caused a public stir against interracial meals and what they seemed to stand for. Many white voices professed "horror that a white gentleman can entertain a colored one at his table." The day after the meal, the *Baltimore Sun* editorialized on its front page, under the somewhat misleading headline, "The Black Man to Be Put on Top of the White Man," that this form of association on the basis of "social equality" was unacceptable in the South since the "inevitable result of this association is the intermarriage between black men and white women and white men and black women." The *Sun* continued:

This touches the point why the people of Maryland and the South feel concerned about the introduction of negroes into the White House upon the terms of social equality. The colored population in the Northern States is so insignificant in comparison with the white that the few marriages which take place between whites and blacks can have but little effect or significance. But once let social barriers overcome in the South, where a fourth to more than half of the population is negro, the result would be a calamity to the race. Intermarriage with negroes would destroy one of the finest races of people who ever inhabited any country—the Anglo-Saxon people of the South. The result would be a mongrel population inferior to both parent races.[16]

The paper asked provocatively, "if the President of the United States, with all his wealth and his aristocratic antecedents, is willing to have his family sit at dinner with a negro, how is the poor white man in the South to maintain his position of social superiority to the negro? If one negro man can be upon terms of social equality with the President why cannot another negro be on terms of social equality with the white farmer in the South and aspire to the hand of his daughter in marriage?"

Roosevelt was surprised by the public reaction to the affair and wrote to Albion W. Tourgée that he had not devoted much thought to the invitation, but, "As things have turned out, I am very glad that I asked him, for the clamor aroused by the act makes me feel as if the act was necessary. . . . I do not intend to offend the prejudices of anyone else, but neither do I intend to allow their prejudices to make me false to my principles."[17] However, a radical racialist novelist did connect a presidential meal in mixed company with an ill-fated miscegenation story involving the (fictitious) United States president's daughter. In Robert Lee Durham's novel *The Call of the South* (1908) the president invites to lunch at the White House a black bishop and a character called Dr. Woods—who looks like W. E. B. Du Bois—and the president's daughter Helen misunderstands this as a signal that it is all right for her to fall in love with and marry the Harvard-educated footman Hayward, who has "black blood."[18]

Even in the second half of the twentieth century, presidents and miscegenation have remained a theme. For example, such a strong supporter of racial integration as Harry S. Truman answered a journalist's question whether interracial marriage was becoming widespread in the United States with the blunt answer, "I hope not; I don't believe in it," adding the clichéd question to the journalist, "Would you want your daughter to marry a Negro?" When the reporter answered that his daughter should marry the man she loved, Truman continued, "Well, she won't love someone who isn't her color," and went on to express his belief that interracial marriage ran against the Bible.[19] As recently as 1992, when Bill Clinton ran for office, he had to declare, "Listen, I don't have a black baby."[20] It was a rumor that was recirculated several times in 1998 and 1999 and that was brought to cinematic life in Mike Nichols's R-rated *Primary Colors* (1998). I hardly have to remind readers that such gossip, or any work of art based on it, still has little effect on presidential popularity, even though the accusations took on a rather serious form in this case.

Meanwhile, American writers also have kept the Jefferson story alive. It was probably no coincidence that William Faulkner called the capital of his fictional Yoknapatawpha County "Jefferson," and in *Absalom, Absalom!* (1936) gave his sinister white patriarch Sutpen the first name "Thomas." One of the crazy people in the Golden Day in Ralph Ellison's *Invisible Man* (1952) says this about the white philanthropist whom the narrator has brought to the bar: "He's Thomas Jefferson and I'm his grandson—on the 'field-nigger' side."[21] And, though little cited in the recent revival of the Jefferson debates, Barbara Chase-Riboud has undertaken a full fictional exploration of Jefferson in her book *Sally Hemings* (1979). James Ivory's costume drama *Jefferson in Paris* (1995) is only the most recent PG-13 installment ("adult situations, nudity, violence") of a long-standing fascination with the Jefferson-Hemings tale.

The recent revelations have not led to a new examination of the 1786 Virginia bill, drafted by Thomas Jefferson, which stipulated that "a marriage between a person of free condition and a slave, or between a white person and a negro, or between a white person and a mulatto, shall be null."[22] Nor have they inspired scholars to go back to Jefferson's strange calculus of color chart that he sent to Francis Gray on March 4, 1815, and that examines the consequences of interracial sexuality over three generations, or "crossings."[23] In this document Jefferson alternates between natural (actually, incest) metaphors from the animal realm and the language of slavery and freedom, when he explains:

Thus a Merino ram being crossed, first with a country ewe, second with his daughter, third with his granddaughter, and fourth with his great-granddaughter, the last issue is deemed pure Merino, having in fact but ⅛ of the country blood. But observe, that this does not re-establish freedom, which depends on the condition of the mother, the principle of the civil law, *partus sequitur ventrem,* being adopted here. But if *e* [the one-eighth descendant of a Negro *a*] be emancipated, he becomes a free *white* man, and a citizen of the United States to all intents and purposes.

His blending of a faith in scientific principles with certain culturally shaped, and internally inconsistent, racial assumptions makes Jefferson a figure who has not lost his relevance today; and one yearns for more imaginative and contemplative writing that would try to re-create a fuller sense of the universe of the Jeffersons and the Hemingses.[24]

The historical and literary stories surrounding Jefferson's relationship with Sally Hemings may have done little more than raise the question whether or not the rumors could now be verified; it is to this question that the DNA debate has made a new contribution. The late historian Nathan Huggins seems to have anticipated this development when he argued ten years ago: "The evidence is circumstantial; we will never get at a truth everyone will accept. Custodians of the Jefferson legacy seek to protect his historical reputation and demand substantial and irrefutable evidence." Yet Huggins continued boldly: "I venture to say that most black people *know* the rumors are essentially true despite gaps and problems with the evidence." Whether or not Callender's assertion was *"actually true,"* the story was *"symbolically true,"* and for a good reason: "Like other legitimizing myths, the Sally Hemings story ties a people to the founding of the nation, reinforcing birthright claims."[25] These claims—and their continued denial—have permeated the discussions about Jefferson and about presidents, sex, and race. Huggins saw in the "desire to merge national and racial identity into a single myth" the reason for the "compelling persistence of the story of Sally Hemings." One wonders what stories will emerge once legitimizing national myths derive not only from Thomas Jefferson but also from Sally Hemings, not only from Richard M. Johnson but also from Julia Chinn, and not only from Andrew Johnson but also from Dolly, Liz, and Florence? Will a dramatic enlargement of the pool of contenders for highest office, beyond the current confines set by race and sex, also change the nature of political gossip in this country?

NOTES

I am grateful to Jan Lewis, Jessica Hook, and Aviva Taubenfeld, as well as to the participants in the conference, for suggestions, sources, and comments.

1. "Not the least well known among other infernal nymphs."

2. Henry Adams, *History of the United States of America during the Administrations of Thomas Jefferson*, ed. Earl N. Harbert (1889-1891; New York, 1986), 219–20.

3. Ibid., 113–14. Adams quotes a somewhat different version of the last four lines of the poem that serves as epigraph here.

> The weary statesman for repose hath fled
> From halls of council to his negro's shed;
> Where, blest, he woos some black Aspasia's grace,
> And dreams of freedom in his slave's embrace.

4. Capt. Marryat, *A Diary in America: With Remarks on Its Institutions* (London, 1839), vol. III, 300–301. See also his general remarks, vol. III, 56–58.

5. *Tait's Edinburgh Magazine* (July 1839), 452; the author is identified only by the initial "E." "Jefferson's Daughter" is discussed in William Edward Farrison, *William Wells Brown: Author and Reformer* (Chicago, 1969), 125–26.

6. William Wells Brown, *Clotel, or the President's Daughter* (1853; New York, 1969), 60.

7. R. R. Burg, "The Rhetoric of Miscegenation: Thomas Jefferson, Sally Hemings, and Their Historians," *Phylon* 47 (1986), 128–38.

8. Many of the following examples have been taken from contributions to Werner Sollors, ed., *Interracialism: Black-White Intermarriage in American History, Literature, and Law* (New York, forthcoming in 2000).

9. Jane Grey Swisshelm, *Half a Century* (Chicago, 1880), 129; cited in Carter G. Woodson, "The Beginnings of Miscegenation of the Whites and the Blacks," reprinted in Sollors, ed., *Interracialism*.

10. David Warren Bowen, *Andrew Johnson and the Negro* (Knoxville, 1989), 55.

11. Richard Hildreth, *Archy Moore, The White Slave; or, Memoirs of a Fugitive* (New York and Auburn, 1856), 316, 318, 319. See Thomas Brown, "The Miscegenation of Richard Mentor Johnson as an Issue in the National Election Campaign of 1835–1836," *Civil War History*, 39 (1993), 5–30.

12. Roy P. Basler, ed. *Abraham Lincoln: His Speeches and Writings* (Cleveland and New York, 1946), 363. Lincoln goes on to say that slavery results in mulattoes born of black mothers and white fathers and concludes that "these statistics show that slavery is the greatest source of amalgamation; and next to it, not the elevation, but the degeneration of the free blacks."

13. Harold Holzer, ed., *The Lincoln-Douglas Debates: The First Complete, Unexpurgated Text* (New York, 1993), 189. This sentence follows the version in the *Tribune*. The transcript actually reads: "I do not perceive because I do not court a negro woman for a wife, that I must necessarily want her for a wife" (p. 189). The sentence as such does not make sense, though Lincoln's slip at this moment in his speech is in and of itself not uninteresting, especially since Lincoln had used more or less the same phrasing before: on 26 June 1857, for example, he said: "I protest against that counterfeit logic which concludes that, because I do not want a black woman for a *slave* I must necessarily want her for a *wife*." See Mario Cuomo and Harold Holzer, eds., *Lincoln on Democracy* (New York, 1990), 90.

14. Cuomo and Holzer, eds., *Lincoln on Democracy*, 189–90.

15. Ibid., 188.

16. *Baltimore Sun,* 19 Oct. 1901.

17. Theodore Roosevelt Papers, Library of Congress. Tourgée had written a letter dated 21 Oct. 1901, and Roosevelt's response is dated 8 Nov. 1901.

18. Robert Lee Durham, *The Call of the South* (Boston, 1908), 383–85.

19. William D. Zabel, "Interracial Marriage and the Law," reprinted in Sollors, ed., *Interracialism.*

20. Curtis Wilkie, "33 Days That Defined a Candidate," *Boston Globe Magazine* (22 July 1992), 12. Presidential candidate Clinton at a closed-door meeting with Chicago Democrats, in an "attempt to put down one persistent rumor," as he answered "uncomfortable questions by quietly acknowledging he had been involved in extramarital affairs."

21. Ralph Ellison, *Invisible Man* (1952; New York, 1972), 77.

22. Bill no. 86, Revisal of the Laws, 1776–1786, in Julian P. Boyd et al., eds., *The Papers of Thomas Jefferson,* 27 vols. to date (Princeton, 1950–), 2:557.

23. See Appendix C in this volume. This letter is also reproduced in Werner Sollors, *Neither Black nor White yet Both: Thematic Explorations of Interracial Literature* (1997; paperback ed., Cambridge, 1999), 113–14.

24. Jan Lewis's essay in the present collection is a good example of what I have in mind. It also deserves mention that Barbara Chase-Riboud includes Jefferson's letter to Francis Gray in her novel *Sally Hemings: A Novel* (New York, 1979).

25. Nathan Irvin Huggins, *Revelations: American History, American Myth,* ed. Brenda Huggins (New York, 1995), 277. Huggins interestingly generalizes: "Legitimizing myths and myths of national origins are commonly set in illicit sexual unions."

CHAPTER 10

Our Jefferson

Jack N. Rakove

❧

John Adams was only half wrong when he uttered his last words: "Thomas Jefferson still lives." In fact, the "Sage of Monticello" had predeceased his predecessor as vice president and president by a matter of hours. Jefferson's own supposed last words were a query: "Is it the Fourth?" His good sense in going out on that note helps explain why Adams was also half right. Jefferson remains alive for us—"us" being both scholars and the public—to an extent and with an attractive power that none of his contemporaries can rival: not Madison, with his more deeply probing intellect; not Washington, struggling with the importance of being George; not even Franklin, the other self-fashioned sage whose inner life rivals Jefferson's in its elusiveness. Long before the formation of historical memories became a hotly fashionable subject, Merrill Peterson had already traced the twistings and turnings of the great man's reputation.[1] Jefferson's survival is due to many sources, including our fascination with the tangled issue this volume addresses. But the foremost reason why Jefferson still lives surely reflects his association with the principle of equality whose creed he embedded in the preamble to the Declaration of Independence, the first of the three achievements memorialized on his tombstone.

It was also a stroke of genius that Jefferson and Adams contrived to expire on the fiftieth anniversary of that document. Even if the "Era of Good Feelings" was already waning by 1826, a casualty of the political competition between John Adams's direct heir (his son John Quincy) and Jefferson's unlikely political one (Andrew Jackson), their good timing in choosing so portentous a date of death left Americans feeling good. Who could possibly deny the providential implications of so stunning a coincidence? Was this not proof that the deity—or what the authorities of Jefferson's university alternately call the "ultimate reality"[2]—had looked down on this republican handiwork and found it good?

A very different kind of providence—more of the star- (or Starr-) crossed kind—recently conspired to allow results of scientific tests increasing the likelihood that Jefferson fathered children by Sally Hemings to appear just as evidence of the sexual frolics of his partial namesake, William Jefferson Clinton, was being disseminated on the air- and e-waves. That Clinton, too, stood condemned by the wonders of DNA was only one of the ironies that attended the concurrence of these two events. Could Clinton's folly be excused or mitigated by the new evidence that Jefferson, too, had transgressed, not only by evading the oath he had reputedly sworn to his dying wife, but also by crossing the racial boundaries he had seemingly surveyed in that most troubling passage in all his writings, the racialist explanation of the necessity for deporting the African Americans whom he wished (or so he said) to see freed? What kind of ultimate reality would permit such a conjunction of events? Earlier generations of Americans, imbued with a belief that all such coincidences must have meaning, might have concluded that the time for national repentance was at hand. President Clinton certainly thought so: his first public appearance following the sensational release of the referral of the independent counsel was to seek contrition at the National Prayer Breakfast, the closest (if inverted) approximation Americans now have to the fast days of old.[3] And indeed, just as the November 1998 elections demonstrated how strongly the impulse to forgive the president beat within the African American community, so some African American commentators interpreted the Jefferson-Hemings developments as a call for racial reconciliation—another recognition that they and their ancestors had always been part of the national story. Yet amid the ongoing unpleasantness in Washington, the city that Jefferson had done so much to plan, it was hard to escape the suspicion that this Providence might prefer the

monologues of Lenny Bruce to the harmonies of the Mormon Taberna-
cle Choir.

The ironic coincidence of these two stories also reflected a deeper stra-
tum of our contemporary political culture: the much-discussed merger of
the personal and political, the private and public, in ways that make us increasingly uncomfortable (insofar as we are all liberated libertarians) but
that we also find difficult to resist or at least ignore (insofar as we are all
prurient puritans). That merger does not accord with the principle that
James Madison enunciated when he instructed an eager journalist that
the life of a public man must revolve largely around his public deeds.[4] Yet
Madison, in this respect, did not speak entirely for his generation. He certainly did not speak for Jefferson or John Adams, both of whom make far
more engaging subjects for biography than Madison because they carefully preserved a hefty archive of personal correspondence (and, in Adams's
case, a diary and autobiography) that affords ample opportunity for psychological inspection. Had Jefferson and Adams not wanted us to examine their hearts and minds as well as their public deeds and writings, they
would have purged their literary estates of much of the material that will
sustain the publication of the letterpress editions of their papers long after the computer on which I am writing will be a relic of the neolithic age
of information technology.

Yet the deeper issue is not whether we would be better off adhering to
Madison's archaic and prim standard, for obviously all facets of our subjects' lives are grist for the intellectual mill. Nor would it make sense to
retreat to the decorous treatment of Jefferson's private life for which first
Fawn Brodie and more recently Annette Gordon-Reed have faulted an
earlier generation of scholars.[5] With Jefferson, private and public are
hopelessly entwined—as Herbert Sloan's book on Jefferson and debt so
brilliantly explains.[6] None of us could imagine discussing Jefferson's public writings on slavery and race without simultaneously considering how
his extravagant ambitions for Monticello, his deepest love, coupled with
his disastrous treatment of the estate of which Sally Hemings was a part
and the debt problems compounded by the Treaty of Paris, all ensnared
him ever more relentlessly—yet ever so voluntarily—in the tragic juxtaposition of American slavery and American freedom.[7]

The issue, rather, is how we *weigh* the different elements of the Jeffersonian legacy—how we balance personal and political, public and pri-

vate—so that our current preoccupations do not prevent our seeing the problem whole. The Jeffersonian legacy is complex and multistranded, and its resonance in the contemporary world extends well beyond the preoccupations that lie at the heart of the Jefferson-Hemings fascination. There is, in my view, something profoundly troubling about the extent to which our condemnations of Jefferson's failings, often resting on uncritical assumptions of our own moral superiority, blind us to critical truths that Jefferson grasped better than any of his contemporaries—perhaps even better than his friend James Madison. And I would like to use the generous invitation that Peter Onuf and Jan Lewis have extended to me to reflect broadly on my vision of Jefferson to explain why, my known leanings toward Madison notwithstanding, I find myself growing more partial to Jefferson with each year.

❦

Let me begin with my reflections on the Jefferson-Hemings relationship, once deemed so improbable, now seemingly so much more likely if not completely proven.

There was always an obvious circularity in the earnest and labored denials that a man like Jefferson could ever have engaged in a longstanding sexual relationship—whether affectionate, convenient, or even coerced—with a paramour like Sally Hemings. At bottom, all these denials rested on the same assumption: it would simply have been out of character for Jefferson to indulge himself in this way. Whether from a permanent grief over his wife Martha's early death, or devotion to the life of the mind over the impulses of the heart, or distaste for the fruits of miscegenation—oh-so-evident in his father-in-law's life—character, temperament, intellect, and self-respect all prohibited it. Yet if, in fact, Jefferson and Sally carried on a relationship—call it a liaison, romance, affair, or concubinage—all those assumptions about his character would have been wrong, or at least radically incomplete. True, in the nature of things, the evidence for this relationship would be exponentially more elusive than that for any of the other numerous facets of Jefferson's life that so intrigue us—but so what? Living as we do in an age when public sexual confession and the explicit presentation of sexuality in everyday life are central aspects of our culture, even we cannot ignore the essentially private nature of sexual longing that remains hidden away from outside view but so active an element of interior mental life, conscious and self-conscious alike.

We need to take this dimension of sexuality seriously, not only because it will help us to rethink the question of Jefferson's character and personality, but also because there is a curious yet striking connection between the interior nature of sexual desire and one of those great principles to which Jefferson was so strongly and publicly committed: freedom of conscience. The juxtaposition seems, at first glance, ironic, not to say downright perverse—the more so when we think how ardently religion labors to constrain sexuality itself. Yet, in fact, the psychology of sexuality and religious belief are closely related in one critical way: both are essentially concerned with inner states of mind that resist external examination. Jefferson's commitment to disestablishment and to freedom of conscience rested upon the powerful philosophical insight that John Locke formulated so well in his *Letter Concerning Toleration.* Religious belief can never be coerced because it is a completely inner conviction; one's nagging doubts that all ideas about the supernatural are matters of opinion at best and outright fantasies or opiates at worst can always be disguised through outward conformity to prescribed rituals. One can beam contentedly during a sermon, looking visibly attentive for all the world to see, while privately wondering where all this malarkey came from, or why YHWH would ever have chosen such out-of-the-way precincts as the desert of Sinai or the hill country of Judea, three thousand and two thousand years ago, to arrange the performance of the miracles whose authenticity Jefferson so much doubted. And what is to stop one from raptly joining in the service, in all its solemnity, while inwardly contemplating any of a number of raptures involving the cute young thing two pews over?

For however much we think we know about other people, we rarely glimpse, much less comprehend, their interior sexuality—that state of mind we sometimes equate with fantasy, but that embraces much more. Of course, when men and women write or speak at great length about their sexual feats and defeats, we have something to go on—although probably less than meets the eye or ear, for we cannot neatly separate leaps of the imagination and braggadocio from the details of performance. But when the record is sparse or silent for years—nay, decades—at a time, we remain clueless. We can speculate that sexual longing has been completely suppressed or sublimated, or search for displaced Freudian clues in other places, but the reality is that we simply do not know. If nothing else, Jefferson's flirtation with Maria Cosway in 1786–1787 demonstrates that Martha's death five years earlier did not mark the passing of his sexual desire. Jefferson carefully presents his dialogue between the head and the heart as a lament over the departure of the Cosway *couple,* but who could possibly think that when Jefferson turned from Maria's carriage "more dead than alive," it was the prospect of going without Richard Cosway's company that distressed him?[8] Anyone who can recall in his or her own life the frustrated pangs of an unfulfilled love will immediately know why Jefferson gives his heart the best lines.

As President Clinton, speaking under some duress, has mused, when we talk about sexuality, we enter one of the most mysterious realms of our existence (all the attention it receives notwithstanding). Whatever we think we now know or can plausibly imagine about a Jefferson-Hemings relationship remains little less speculative than it was before. We cannot know whether the patriarch of Monticello crudely commandeered the pleasures of Sally's body—seizing the part of many a plantation lord—or whether Sally set out to seduce her owner and brother-in-law, demonstrating in the cool of a Parisian evening, with a fire roaring in the hearth, or in the heat of a sultry Virginia night, that his flesh might be willing even when the spirit was weak, or that the reason of the head need not always prevail over the tug of the heart and associated organs. We cannot know whether Jefferson saw in Hemings a living embodiment of the departed wife whom he had loved so passionately, or whether Hemings saw in Jefferson the legal husband she could have had were it not for the fact that a single one of her four grandparents was black. We cannot know whether common memories of Paris formed a foundation for their romance, as Annette Gordon-Reed suggests,[9] or whether the slings and arrows of public life encouraged Jefferson to seek other forms of private release at Monticello than his endless projects for home improvement. We can speculate as much as we want about the possible forms this relationship might have taken, drawing probabilistic inferences on the basis of what other contributors to this volume have reconstructed of patterns of interracial sex on the plantation, yet never conclusively know whether this liaison was typical or unique. What we can surmise, I think, is that any simple reconstruction of this relationship based on the stereotype of the lustful white planter forcing the submission of a fearful slave mistress probably misses the mark. The familial, racial, and psychological dynamics of this relationship will always elude us.

For my part, I have to confess to rather hoping that Thomas and Sally enjoyed something like the romance that Gordon-Reed offers as an antidote to the denials of earlier scholars. Why should the rights and opportunities of the living generation—or simply the living—not take precedence over obligations to the dead, in matters of sex as well as debt? Why should Jefferson have consigned himself, at age forty, to a life of chastity, forever grieving for his departed wife? Many a widow or widower, surviving a marriage blessed with such happiness that remarriage to another initially seems inconceivable, soon learns otherwise. And for her part, what better alternative did life present to Sally Hemings? Even conceding that the relationship was obviously not one of equals, or that an undertone of coercion could still have clouded the possibility of consent, how would Sally have fared better in life? The short answer, of course, is that freedom is to be prized above all else—its price is beyond rubies, its value is absolute, and its denial can never be justified.[10] Yet we cannot know whether Sally Hemings would have answered that question in the same way. Why would a relatively sheltered life with Jefferson and her children at Monticello not be less precarious (and more precious) than the fruits of freedom, especially if, as Gordon-Reed argues, a promise of freedom for those children was a condition of Sally Hemings's consent?

Posing the problem in this way leads me to my final observation on Jefferson and Hemings. Our fascination with their relationship has led us to slight what is arguably its most striking element. The issue is effectively encapsulated in a single passage of Lucia Stanton's brilliant essay on Jefferson and his slaves. In an age when the "one-drop" rule was not the law, the children of Sally Hemings, Stanton observes, "had seven-eighths white ancestry and were thus white by Virginia law, which declared that a person 'who shall have one fourth part or more of negro blood, shall . . . be deemed a mulatto.'" As Jefferson well knew, and explicitly calculated, that did not make them free, because their status still followed that of their mother; they would become free only if emancipated (as the Hemings children, alone of Jefferson's slaves, were). If Hemings's children were also Jefferson's, the master of Monticello was holding his own children as slaves, but once freed, such a former slave would enter society (as Jefferson explicitly observed) as "a free *white* man, and a citizen of the US. to all intents and purposes."[11] Yet even if Jefferson was tacitly rearing his children for a life of freedom, hoping they could pass quietly into the ranks of free society—and possibly even free white society—it was a free-dom very different than the one that his children by Martha enjoyed.

❦

As absorbed as we are in our speculations about Jefferson and Hemings, a skeptic might well wonder whether an absolute verification of the rela-tionship would alter our understanding of the one member of the found-ing generation who still lives most vividly in our historical imagination. Obviously we would have to adjust our views of the "character" of the "inner Jefferson," hitherto deployed to support a conclusion opposite to the one that will now be sustained. Obviously, too, we would have to won-der how Jefferson could allow his children by Sally to disappear into a sort of netherworld of free society without providing his posterity with the full measure of liberty they deserved. No doubt the recent findings will help keep the Jefferson industry thriving well into the new millennium.

Yet what else does the Jefferson-Hemings relationship really add to the basic problem that has confronted us all along, which is simply to reconcile Jefferson's egalitarian commitments with the reality of his life as a slave-holder and his inability to discipline his reckless expenditures in the princi-pled cause of emancipating his own slaves? As much as the relationship complicates and enlarges the problem of understanding Jefferson's *private* life, including the psychology of slaveholding, it does not fundamentally al-ter the essential *public* dilemma. Jefferson professed to hate slavery, first and foremost for its effects on the republican citizen, but also, in more modest degree, for its effects on the slave; he drafted a bill for emancipation that corresponded with the best enlightened opinion of his age; he publicly affirmed that the freed slaves deserved settlement in a country of their own. Yet he never emancipated any slaves but those of the Hemings fami-ly; he never agitated for enactment of the bill he had drafted; he reacted with the deepest alarm to the slave revolt in Santo Domingo and to the growth of a (somewhat) more militant antislavery sentiment in the United States; and his notion of exactly where the freed slaves might be resettled continually receded as his "empire for liberty" progressively expanded.[12] For the nineteenth-century South, his legacy included the flirtation with nullification in the Kentucky Resolutions of 1798 and the avowal of a pro-to-scientific theory of racial inferiority in his *Notes on the State of Virginia*—both foreshadowing critical elements of the new militance the South would project as slavery came under renewed and more fervent assault.

For the historian, it will not do to lump Jefferson's failings together under a valedictory judgment of hypocrisy. After all, hypocrisy is only a
characterization of how we act, not an explanation of the sources of our
actions. Nor is there much advantage to be gained by pursuing Jefferson
with the sort of prosecutorial zeal exemplified in the work of Paul Finkelman. True, Finkelman and other likeminded critics have performed yeoman service by demonstrating just how easily Jefferson subordinated his
ostensible abhorrence of slavery to more pressing considerations, both
public and private. Yet does that disturbing evidence truly warrant the
conclusion that "no one bore a greater responsibility for that failure [to
place the nation on the road to liberty for all] than the author of the Declaration of Independence—the Master of Monticello"?[13] Given the depth
of the southern commitment to the peculiar institution as the bedrock of
its economic, legal, social, and moral order, and the fact that its abolition
ultimately required the outside intervention made possible only by the
Civil War, it beggars the imagination to see how the engaged opposition
to slavery that Jefferson admittedly never mounted would have made any
difference in the fate of slavery. Judgments of moral responsibility and political agency are not always interchangeable.

Yet they are always troubling, and never more so to historians than
when they feel impelled to encourage their students to suspend the impulse to judge in the interest of cultivating the need to understand. The
one occasion on which I regularly confront our Jefferson problem comes
when I make "Thomas Jefferson and the American Dilemma" the subject
of the lecture that closes my course on colonial and revolutionary America. In that capacity, I act more as a teacher than a scholar; or rather, I try
to bring my perspectives as a scholar of the eighteenth century to bear on
my vocation of a teacher. As a scholar, it is not especially important to me
to judge the morality of the actors of the past. Those judgments, if one
wishes to make them, come easily and are not very challenging; explaining the sources of the acts committed is more difficult. As a teacher, however, I feel an obligation not only to answer my students' natural concern—even anxiety—to know how to think about Jefferson but, more
important, to challenge their natural presumption that the moral values
of our own enlightened age are superior to those of the Age of Enlightenment that Jefferson helped to illuminate.

In casting my Jefferson lecture in these terms, I confess to being much influenced by a passage that Gordon Wood wrote about the efforts of our mutual teacher, Bernard Bailyn, to write a "tragic" history of the American Revolution that would deal fairly with the most interesting of its real "losers": Thomas Hutchinson, penultimate royal governor of Massachusetts. Here Wood argues that Americans do not really

want to hear about the unusability and pastness of the past or about the latent limitations within which people in the past were obliged to act. They do not want to hear about the blindness of people in the past or about the inescapable boundaries of their action. Such a history has no immediate utility and is apt to remind us of our own powerlessness, of our own inability to control events and predict the future.

The discipline of history, Wood continues, does not fully share the common project of other social sciences. Where these disciplines

try to breed confidence in managing the future, the discipline of history tends to inculcate skepticism about people's ability to order their destinies at will. History that reveals the utter differentness and discontinuity of the past tends to undermine that crude instrumental and presentist use of the past that Americans have especially been prone to. And history that shows that the best-laid plans of people in the past often went awry and that most people struggled against forces which they never clearly understood or over which they had little control tends to dampen that naive conquer-the-future spirit that Americans above all other peoples possess.

And yet, Wood concludes, it is only by understanding those limitations—and not by imposing arbitrary degrees of freedom that the past never really enjoyed—that we can understand what "makes true freedom and moral choice—and wisdom—possible."[14]

What draws us to Jefferson—and what most troubles us about him—is that our Jefferson problem embodies the incompatible poles of historical consciousness that Wood identifies. That Jefferson was embedded in a vicious institution that he inherited but had not created goes without saying; that his doubts about it fell far short of what was demanded or morally correct is just as apparent. Yet who better represents the American conviction that the past is something from which we can be liberated—indeed should be liberated—than Jefferson?[15] There is more wit and irony in Franklin; a more prudent accounting of the possibilities and perils of popular government in Madison; a more realistic grasp of public policy and foreign relations in Hamilton; and a more insightful under-

standing of human nature in John Adams. But Jefferson speaks to us as
the great optimist, the apostle of equality and democracy, the believer in
the power of reason and the opponent of superstition and hidebound tradition. It is Jefferson who tells us we should have confidence in our own
judgment, when his friend Madison warns us—as he warned Jefferson—
that the play of public opinion on politics has to be carefully checked, that
people more often act out of impulsive passion or selfish interest than a
prudent regard for their own or the public good. As Wood has elsewhere
noted, none of his contemporaries was more optimistic, or more inclined
to prefer the promise of the future to the errors of the past. "He was a
virtual Pollyanna about everything," Wood observes; he "had little understanding of man's capacity for evil and had no tragic sense whatsoever."[16]
Hence Jefferson embodied, even helped to create, that very impoverish-
ment of a historical sense that Wood decries—but which we arguably
need to apply if we are ever to come to grips with our Jefferson problem.
It is precisely the difficulty we experience in looking at Jefferson in this
way that makes his failure to come to grips with the problem of slavery so
troubling. If Jefferson, with his belief in reason and equality and progress,
could do no better, then what could be expected of the rest of American
society?

I have come to suspect—although I cannot prove—that Jefferson understood this quandary better than we have realized. Far from dismissing
the contradiction between Jefferson's public condemnation of slavery and
the possessive individualism of his own slaveholding as rank hypocrisy, I
now regard his inability to imagine how whites and blacks could ever coexist as an act of moral honesty. Having looked into his own heart (again)
and seen the depth of the prejudice that resided there, how could he have
imagined that his countrymen would prove more enlightened?

Treating Jefferson not as a hypocrite or slacker but as someone grappling with questions he could solve neither intellectually nor morally may
help us to think anew about that passage in his writings which disturbs us
most: the discourse on racial difference in Query XIV of the *Notes on the
State of Virginia.*[17] Jefferson opened his discussion of the logic of linking
his proposed scheme of gradual emancipation with a plan to colonize the
freed population elsewhere by noting that "It will probably be asked,
Why not retain and incorporate the blacks into the state, and thus save
the expence of supplying, by importation of white settlers, the vacancies

they will leave?" Jefferson initially answered this rhetorical question in a single, remarkably direct if grimly pessimistic sentence: "Deep rooted prejudices entertained by the whites; ten thousand recollections, by the blacks, of the injuries they have sustained; new provocations; the real distinctions which nature has made; and many other circumstances, will divide us into parties, and produce convulsions which will probably never end but in the extermination of the one or the other race." What Jefferson was arguing, in effect, was that this relationship was already so tainted, indeed poisoned, that it could never be made right; that the currents of mutual fear and justifiable resentment were likely to run so deep and strong that no stable society could ever be reconstructed with this disturbed history as its foundation—much less a republican society requiring strong bonds of fraternity to provide the cohesion that an absent aristocracy would not be available to offer.

Had Jefferson stopped there, or merely elaborated this point, we could still fault him for a lack of remorse and a failure of moral nerve, but we would also have to credit his willingness to confront the problem of creating a biracial society with a painful if disturbing honesty. But Jefferson did not stop there. He immediately plunged on to offer a further point: "To these objections, which are political, may be added others, which are physical and moral." From here Jefferson quickly descended into his discussion of the physical and intellectual differences that must long discourage the free white and black citizens of one polity from ever coexisting on conditions of equality. The account Jefferson offers, however, is frankly a mess. From a brief speculation about the possible physical sources of differences in complexion, he quickly passes on to a merely aesthetic opinion about the relative beauty and expressiveness of the two races, the one capable of changing color to reveal emotion, the other "veil[ed]" in an "eternal monotony" of "the countenances." Then Jefferson recovers and returns to "other physical distinctions," which turn out to offer a rather loosely defined category of analysis, including some extraordinarily subjective impressions about the emotional state of Africans. Some of the observations are downright foolish. First Jefferson notes that blacks "seem to require less sleep," being inclined to stay awake "for the slightest amusements"; then, a few sentences later, he illustrates the observation that "their existence appears to participate more of sensation than reflection" by associating it with "their disposition to sleep when abstracted from their diversions, and unemployed in labour." What else were they supposed to do in the intervals between the labor demanded by their master and the casual leisure they expropriated for themselves: crack open copies of *The Iliad* or *Tristram Shandy*, or manuals of personal improvement—and to what end? A further comparison of the poetry of Phillis Wheatley and Ignatius Sancho with the artistic accomplishments of the slaves of antiquity also seems like an extended digression.

From our vantage point, we have good reason to wish that Jefferson might have allowed a sense of discretion to get the better part of his intellectual valor. Yet the confusions of this passage instruct us to read it with some care. For starters, it is essential to understand that Jefferson's foray into a proto-scientific racism was made in defense not of slavery but of emancipation. That by itself distinguishes it significantly from the more virulent expressions of racism that would be offered in later generations, for then observations of racial difference were more commonly made to explain why enslavement was in fact a logical and natural condition for an entire people. Jefferson's concern is rather with explaining the problem that emancipation of a racially distinct population would pose for the future of republican citizenship. Moreover, by shuffling awkwardly between different modes of comparison and analysis, Jefferson conveys his self-conscious embarrassment about the implications of the position he is tentatively espousing, and this becomes even more manifest when Jefferson closes his discussion on a note of uncertainty. The conclusion he is suggesting, Jefferson warns us, "must be hazarded with great diffidence," not least because its acceptance might work to "degrade a whole race of men from the rank in the scale of beings which their Creator may perhaps have given them." Jefferson then undermines his conclusion even further by questioning the basis of his own reasoning. "To our reproach it must be said, that though for a century and a half we have had under our eyes the races of black and of red men, they have never yet been viewed by us as subjects of natural history." In other words, as plausible as everything Jefferson has just alleged about racial difference may be, it is little more than speculation resting on an incomplete and inadequate empirical foundation.

This impression of Jefferson's intellectual embarrassment draws further corroboration from the other section of the *Notes on the State of Virginia* addressed to the "particular customs and manners that may happen to be received in that state."[18] It is not self-evident that Jefferson needed to answer that query by discussing the effect of slavery on the character of the free citizenry. Surely that broad heading could have sustained other possible answers that would have skirted the slavery question entirely—as if blacks were merely the objects of white control, not active participants in society. Instead, Jefferson invokes slavery as a fundamental threat to republican citizenship, and in terms that simultaneously elevate the subject race to the condition of a people capable of freedom. "And with what execration should the statesman be loaded," Jefferson asks, "who permitting one half the citizens to trample on the rights of the other, transforms those into despots, and these into enemies, destroys the morals of the one part [the masters], and the amor patriae of the other [the slaves]." To speak of the enslaved as the other half of the citizenry, possessing rights at least *in potentia,* is a revealing usage, and so is the concession that "love of country" is something that slaves can be desired to possess but not expected to acquire. This language echoes one of the opening sentences of the earlier discussion of emancipation, where Jefferson imagines how the preparations for freedom will end. When the younger members of the enslaved race reach the appointed age (eighteen for women, twenty-one for men), "they should be colonized to such place as the circumstances of the time should render most proper, sending them out with arms, implements of household and of the handicraft arts, feeds, pairs of the useful domestic animals, &c."—and further, those making this colonization possible should also take care "to declare them a free and independant people."[19] The echo of 1776 is unmistakable, for what the Declaration of Independence finally declared was that the colonies were now "Free and Independent States." A truly free and independent people following the example of 1776 should not, of course, have independence declared for it, but declare it for itself, making its own Lockean appeal to heaven because slavery, by Locke's own terms, cannot be established as a hereditary condition.[20] That was a prospect that Jefferson, fearful of slave rebellion, could conceive but not countenance. Yet Jefferson's doubts about the capacities of a freed population to be integrated as equal citizens in a republican polity cannot completely outweigh his recognition that they were equally entitled, as a people, to reclaim the rights of self-government their enslavement had denied them.

In both queries, Jefferson's brief for emancipation takes an avowedly political cast, resting on the dual assumption that just as blacks cannot be expected to take the part of equal citizens, so whites reared in the habits of domination cannot be expected to acquire the attributes desired of republican citizens. Yet in the later query, Jefferson strikes an entirely different and surprising note. Now when he "tremble[s] for my country," it is divine, not civil justice that he invokes, conjuring the order of a morally governed universe where neither a mechanistic deity nor a politically correct ultimate reality reigns, but a justice-dispensing God. If not quite a God of revelation or miracles—for what miracle could rescue Americans from this sin?—it is still an almighty clothed in the mantle of the Old and New Testament, and ominously capable of intervening in human history to permit "a revolution in the wheel of fortune" through an act of "supernatural influence!" Lay this passage aside Lincoln's second inaugural, which pronounces the sentence that God has just (and justly) executed on *both* parties to the Civil War as "true and righteous altogether," and their symmetry is perfectly complementary. So is the deeper irony linking their authors: two men who had escaped the blinders and shackles of doctrinal creed or denominational loyalty, yet who had absorbed the language of a Protestant moralism and who understood its hold on the consciences of their countrymen.

The way in which Jefferson's troubled and troubling treatment of slavery and race in these passages implicates his commitments to equality, self-government, and the rights of conscience provides the larger context within which, I believe, Americans need to reflect on the complexity of the Jeffersonian legacy. It is to restoring this complexity that I now turn.

❧

Disclosure of the new scientific evidence relating to Jefferson and Hemings coincided with the thirtieth anniversary of the publication of one of the truly epochal works of American historical scholarship: Winthrop D. Jordan's *White over Black: American Attitudes toward the Negro, 1550–1812*.[21] The single chapter that Jordan devoted to Jefferson still shapes the basic definition of our Jefferson problem. Jordan not only placed the intellectual and psychological dimensions of Jefferson's grappling with race at the heart of the concluding arguments of his book, which emphasized the centrality of questions of race to the very definition of postrevolutionary American nationhood; he also used the ambiguities and ambivalence of Jefferson's position to link his attitudes to our own—"our"

equating with the white population who hold the "American attitudes" of
the subtitle, projected upon a black population that appears in the book as
the object of white perception and action. Jefferson embodies, for Jordan,
the very mentality that an even more momentous work, Gunnar Myrdal's
An American Dilemma, had examined a generation earlier. Jordan closed his
work by echoing the supposition upon which Myrdal had founded his:
"Within every white American who stood confronted by the Negro," Jordan observed, "there had arisen a perpetual duel between his higher and
lower natures." Myrdal had framed his dilemma in nearly identical terms:
"The Negro problem in America would be of a different nature," Myrdal
wrote, "if the moral conflict raged only between valuations held by different persons and groups of persons. *The essence of the moral situation is,
however, that the conflicting valuations are also held by the same person.*"[22]

In one critical respect, Myrdal and Jordan differed in their assessment
of Jefferson. In a passing comment, Myrdal described Jefferson's "guarded
treatment" of racial difference in Query XIV as "a high point in the early
history of the literature on Negro racial characteristics. In critical sense
and in the reservation for the results of future research, it was not surpassed by white writers until recent decades." By contrast, Jordan, after
much closer consideration, concluded that "it constituted, for all its qualifications, the most intense, extensive, and extreme formulation of anti-
Negro 'thought' offered by any American in the thirty years after the Revolution." Yet that harsh view was not quite Jordan's final judgment, for he
went on to add that Jefferson's longer-lasting legacy may have inhered in
"his prejudice for freedom and his larger equalitarian faith." Jordan thus
raised, but did not pursue, a puzzle that lies at the heart of any effort to
appraise the moral dimensions of human action: How do we balance
judgment of the intentions of the actors with knowledge of the consequences—good or ill, unforeseen and inadvertent—to which their actions
led?

Completing his work in the mid-1960s, just as the promise of integration and the second reconstruction was souring in the face of racial riots
and new antagonisms, Jordan thus helped to make Jefferson a touchstone
for the persisting confusion of our own attitudes. Ever since, it has been
impossible to deny the commanding place that Jefferson holds, as both
historical actor and symbol, in the great American dilemma. In the intervening period, it is true, our perspective on Jefferson has shifted. Where

Jordan was fascinated by the psychology of racial attitudes, with a special emphasis on sexuality, we are more inclined to frame the problem in moral terms, as a test of character, the better to measure the gap between professed principles and practiced behavior. In an age of rampant confession, the sources of sexuality no longer beguile us, but the character issue still does, especially when we are dealing with our leaders. Character and leadership are qualities that we judge, not merely explain; they necessarily engage us in moral and political discourse, in ways that the mere task of accounting for historical change does not. It is one matter to explain why slavery took hold in the colonies in the late seventeenth century, or why it remained essential to the plantation economy of the South a century later. It is another matter to assess an individual's moral and political responsibility in confronting, or failing to confront, the evils of his age.

I do not know whether historians have any special credentials in this respect; I tend to doubt that we do. Yet one cannot avoid thinking in moral terms even when one is diffident about reaching moral judgments; and it may well be that we cannot avoid applying moral norms despite our inclinations to don a veil of analytical objectivity. If I explain the origins of the three-fifths clause of the Constitution as a sensible, expedient compromise, have I not also adopted a moral stance that says that the political urgency of reconstituting the Union trumped any ethical imperative to deny slavery formal recognition in the national compact?[23] Moreover, an unwillingness to consider frankly the moral dimensions of past action, or an inclination to invoke the logic of *tout comprendre est tout pardonner,* may only demonstrate one's own "moral obtuseness."[24]

But judgments of moral responsibility can be no more selective than any other form of historical explanation. Indeed, insofar as the impulse to judge requires us to think even more broadly about the sources, nature, and consequences of human action, it imposes additional burdens. In a case like this, that obligation becomes all the more incumbent because we run the risk of assigning to the past a responsibility we would not, and in fact do not, demand of ourselves in the present. Its acts ironically become easier to judge than our own; ours become easier to explain because we can readily identify all the constraints under which we labor, including those that lead us to act in less moral ways than the better angels of our nature might demand. Arguably the impulse to judge the past reverses the moral order of things. The moral judgments that matter most are those we need to make of ourselves, because we still face the option of choice—a luxury the past has lost. Judging the past, again, is actually quite easy; explaining it is far more difficult.

But judge Jefferson we must—or so it seems—so the question remains, on what basis can we do so?

We should begin by recognizing that our current absorption with Jefferson stems almost entirely from our preoccupations with matters of race.[25] The flood of Jefferson scholarship that pours ceaselessly from the presses reminds us that our general interest in Jefferson has other, less vexed sources. But the urgency of our concern is tied to race—and indeed to the persistence of exactly the same dualist conflict that both Myrdal and Jordan located in the American head and heart. That conflict demands resolution, and resolution means a rendering of historical justice. We can bring Jefferson and his generation to a dock of historical judgment, holding them responsible for a failure of moral and political imagination that entrenched slavery ever more deeply in the fabric of national life. In that case, we enjoy the advantage of a moral superiority, sometimes bordering on smugness, that eases the conscience because it enables us to distance our struggles for redemption from the original sin we only inherited from our fallen forebears. Or else, probing more deeply, we face the disquieting recognition that earlier problems remain our own, and more intractably than we can comfortably admit.

Something like this insight is what animated, I think, Jordan's grim concluding judgment of 1968 that "there was little in [the] historical experience" of the white man "to indicate that he would succeed" in the long overdue effort to overcome the burden of racial prejudice;[26] it is certainly implicit in Gordon Wood's speculation about the disquiet Americans feel in contemplating human incapacity to transcend the flawed structures of belief and behavior in which our lives are embedded. In this putative tale of two Thomases we can afford to treat Hutchinson's inability to comprehend the American Revolution as a personal tragedy meriting an empathetic reading, but Jefferson's failure may remind us too much of our own. Hence our tendency to project onto his generation shortcomings we have not escaped. In either case, there is something avowedly presentist in the formulation—a reminder of what J. R. Pole once described as Americans' unhappy knack for trying to maintain a dialogue with the past while forgetting that the past can neither listen, much less respond to any-

thing we say.[27] It cannot remind us of the limits of our historical knowledge, nor parry our devastating thrusts, nor enjoy the benefits of our
hindsight. It simply sits in the dock, inertly and insensibly awaiting our
judgment.

So if we are to judge the past by rules of due process, we have to ap-
point ourselves its patient defenders as well as its zealous prosecutors and
then appeal to the audience—our readers and students—to pass judgment. In the case of slavery, the likely defense is fairly evident. We would
recall that Jefferson was born into a world that was only beginning to understand that slavery was an evil of a kind radically different from the other wrongs of life; that most slaveholders remained convinced that their
"people" were their chattels; that it was reasonable to ask whether a stable republican polity could rest upon the foundation of a biracial or multiracial society. Or we might mount a more aggressive defense still, challenging the capacity and right of later generations even to sit in
judgment. Which century, the eighteenth or twentieth, tolerated the
greater injustices or inflicted the greater injuries to life and limb? Which
generation had the greater capacity to alleviate human misery but failed
to do so?

There is, however, another mitigating line of defense that the historian
turned attorney might mount for Jefferson, and it does not involve the in-
vidious and morally pointless exercise of comparing genocides (were the
cattle cars to Auschwitz worse than the Middle Passage?) or other sins and
sufferings.

Whatever his shortcomings on matters of slavery and race, there were
other urgent political matters that Jefferson saw with absolute clarity, and
which he happened to solve, I think, correctly. One was that he understood, better than any member of his generation, that all legitimate government must ultimately rest on the principle of popular consent, freely
expressed by subjects who should properly acquire the mantle of citizens.
The other was that coercion of religious belief and punishment of religious dissent were absolutely unjustifiable. At the close of our own miserable century of tyranny, devastation, and persecution, the strength of Jefferson's commitment to these principles remains not only impressive in
itself, but deeply puzzling. For why should a planter coming from a back-
water marchland like Virginia, a beneficiary of the same system of enslavement we find so offensive, nevertheless acquire and act upon libertar-

ian convictions whose fate in recent decades has proved far more precarious than our fin-de-siècle gloating about the triumph of democracy can
admit? Wrongly assuming, as we so naturally and uncritically do, that
freedom is the normal condition of mankind from which slavery must be
the deviation requiring explanation, our judgmental approach to Jefferson
risks getting the real problem exactly backward. Why he should have
come to question slavery at all, or why he should have developed so deep
a commitment to principles of equality, are more difficult questions than
explaining why his practice fell so disappointingly short of his convictions. It may well be true, as Edmund Burke once noted and Edmund
Morgan has more recently argued, that possession of slaves may have the
perverse effect of making their owners more sensitive to the preservation
of their own freedom;[28] but a commitment to equality may be another,
more surprising matter.

In pondering this element of the Jefferson legacy, we should begin
with the document that his attorney would submit first in his defense: the
Declaration of Independence. We may concede, with Pauline Maier, that
the editorial revisions that Congress imposed on his draft greatly improved it, or that the multiple declarations that Americans made during
the spring and summer of independence are as important and revealing as
the ultimate declaration.[29] Even so, we should hesitate to deny Jefferson
his due. For if there is, any longer, a master narrative of American history,
Jefferson's fortuitous authorship of the declaration might even itself be a
sufficient source of his importance in the national memory. That such a
narrative can any longer be written is something we are increasingly
asked to question and doubt; yet to deny its common-sense existence
would be a characteristic act of academic myopia. That narrative hinges
on the concept of equality, on both its promise and its denial, on the
hopes it engenders and the disappointments it inevitably produces. Something of its power rests in turn, one might suggest, on Jefferson's good
sense in converting the elusive and prudent statement of equality and
rights expressed in the Virginia Declaration of Rights into more direct,
concise, and always memorable language.

Of course, the impeachers of Jefferson's hypocrisy can quickly respond
that deeds speak louder than words—that in the scale of justice Jefferson's
professions of equality weigh only lightly against his practice of inequality. No doubt they are morally right to do so. Yet as historians, we are tied

to a belief in the inadvertent and unintended consequences of human action, and here there is room aplenty to contemplate the consequences of Jefferson's authorship. Whatever Jefferson thought he meant by his self-evident statement of equality and rights, whatever the limits of his vision, his words acquired a completely independent force of their own. Initially the Declaration of Independence was not the Urtext that modern commentary has made it. But even before Jefferson's death, it was coming to acquire the moral authority it has long since exercised, as its language was appropriated by new claimants—freed blacks, abolitionists, the early advocates of women's rights—until it received decisive transformation in the hands of Lincoln at Gettysburg. One does not know how well Jefferson would have anticipated this, much less intended it; yet I think he certainly would have appreciated its thrust. For equality, by its nature, is an explosive and corrosive force; once unleashed in one realm, it cannot easily be contained from spilling over into others. Once one deploys the concept of equality to attack one form of privilege—say the idea of aristocracy, or established religion, or the innate right of the state to grant monopolistic privileges—it is nearly impossible to prevent it from being directed against others—say the dominions of gender, or genealogy, or even race—and even against those forms of dominion that you might be inclined to accept as part of the natural order of things.

In one important sense, the concept of equality that Jefferson evoked in the declaration was far less liberal than ours, for it was tied less to notions of liberal individualism than to the collective right of the American people to govern themselves. While the Declaration of Independence builds its case for self-government on the natural rights foundation that all men are presumed individually to possess, its true concern is with the right of a people, denied the right to be governed by laws made with their own consent, to assert their authority to reconstitute themselves as a free and independent people. We have moved beyond that; our concerns lie more with notions of individual entitlement and fulfillment, or even with the capacity of minority communities to resist political or cultural amalgamation. In a world where a romantic nationalism is again extracting horrible vengeance on deviant groups, the nationalist impulses lurking in Jefferson's summoning an American people into existence cannot be ignored. Nor can we deny the manifest conclusion of Query XIV: that ineradicable memories and intractable differences would long, even forever, prevent one American people from being forged from two different races, however intimate their association.[30]

All this may be cause to distance Jefferson's evocation of the collective equality of a homogenized American people from our own notions. Yet such a distancing comes at great potential cost. It requires a distinctly American form of solipsism to ignore the universal truth incarnated in Jefferson's commitment to the principle of government by consent. Of all his contemporaries, none saw this principle more clearly than Jefferson. Perhaps his conviction drew something from those long walks in the French countryside, where he observed the *ancien regime* on its last legs and an immiserated peasantry who often depended on the largesse of the state to scrape their way through the winter. Perhaps it owed much to the disappointments of his last years, which drove him to think ever more nostalgically about the meaning of 1776 as the decline of Virginia society, so "dependent" on slavery, became apparent. Even so, where contemporaries doubted the capacities of other, less favored peoples to rule themselves by consent, Jefferson continued to regard the United States not as an asylum for the dispossessed but as a beacon to be emulated.

In that he was fundamentally correct—and we should not be embarrassed to affirm his vision. No government can ever be truly legitimate whose rule does not finally rest on the consent of its subjects, freely given, who must therefore also become its citizens. No government that relies on the rigid control of information and a monopoly of coercive force can ever secure the true allegiance or sustained loyalty of its subjects. Regimes that think they can do so will, at one time or another, discover the essential hollowness of their authority. Extracting obedience, which can be coerced, is not the same as commanding consent, which must be freely given. In this sense, the wellsprings of loyalty that form the basis of citizenship may not differ so much from the psychology of freedom of conscience; both presuppose that the inner beliefs of the sovereign, rights-bearing individual cannot be driven by the devices of coercion. Government is truly legitimate only when consent is freely given. That is the essential truth that has been vindicated in recent years in places like Berlin, Moscow, Vilna, Johannesburg, and Buenos Aires; it is the truth we still wait to see vindicated in Beijing, Rangoon, Hanoi, Havana, and Monrovia. All peoples are equally entitled to be ruled only by mechanisms of consent; all governments founded on any other principle, however urgent their pleas for order and stability, ultimately lack legitimacy, even if the conventions of diplomacy and the fictions of sovereignty induce us to render them a respect they do not deserve. All peoples, too, are equally entitled to throw off the shackles of arbitrary rule. When future generations write their narrative of twentieth-century American history, the rise and collapse of segregation will doubtless command a major place in the story; but for all its importance, this chapter will not outweigh the even more profound ideological struggles and acts of tyranny that have framed the narrative of world history over the same period.

The other truth Jefferson grasped was no less profound, and the world would be a better place if his position finally prevailed. Building upon Locke, but going beyond him, Jefferson and Madison understood that the solution to the religion problem depended on the simple recognition that no authority has the capacity to establish the truth of any statement of religious belief, and that the only basis upon which the state can legitimately act to regulate religious expressions requires the commission of overt harmful acts, and not mere statements of opinion. From this basic position, far-reaching implications followed. One was that acceptance of the doctrines of disestablishment and freedom of conscience marked the point at which the meaning of limited government first became clear. For the acceptance of those principles meant that an entire area of governance that no state had hitherto been able to renounce—because religion was too dangerous to be left to the marketplace of belief—could now be safely deregulated, and thus relegated to the sphere of private activity. A second implication, no less important, was that acceptance of freedom of conscience as an absolute right identified a true sphere of privacy and individuality wherein the authority of the state could not intrude. Recognition of other civil rights did not presuppose that the state could not act at all, only that when it acted it had to conform to known rules of law. Our homes may be our castles, but any deputy with a duly signed search warrant can search them. But the commitment to freedom of conscience went further. It identified a realm of behavior that was quintessentially liberal in nature, that allowed individuals to acquire a new form of sovereignty, or we might say property, in their own rights. It is the original source of the concept of privacy whose existence and extent so perplex us today, for its acceptance identified an inviolable sphere of autonomy that each of us absolutely retains. When Jefferson and Madison committed themselves to this principle, they were not simply building upon Locke's arguments for toleration; they were extending them in a radical way. Living as we do in the aftermath of the Holocaust, witnessing ominous revivals of religious persecution around the world, it seems strange to me that we shrink from appreciating the importance of this principle, which Jefferson grasped so clearly.

Jefferson affirmed his commitment to freedom of conscience and disestablishment in the hope that many forms of religious orthodoxy and sectarian loyalty would wither away, to be replaced by forms of belief owing less to revelation and priestcraft and more to a rational acceptance of the natural order of the universe and essential principles of (Christian) morality. That he was naive in that hope was one of the disappointments that soured his final years. Not only were Americans reviving some of their old faiths, making them more vigorous than they had been before the revolution, they were even inventing new religious traditions and the revelations to justify them. Imbued with a democratizing force that Jefferson had helped to inspire, unconstrained by a state that had lost all effective power to limit religious expression, hustling to compete in a marketplace of deregulated religion, American Protestants were heaven-bent on extending an empire for religious liberty, experimenting with new modes of conversion, paving new paths to salvation, and holy-rolling and snake-handling their way across a continent.

Jefferson would not have been pleased by this development, but I think he should have been, for in the vitality of American Protestantism lay a crucial element of the eventual answer to the contradiction between slavery and freedom that he never resolved. It was essential to the ultimate extinction of slavery that the political wrong it inflicted upon the principle of equality was compounded by the conviction of its utter sinfulness. To say that slavery was wrong because it violated basic principles or depraved the master was one step in its eradication, but not the decisive one, for then as now, there were many wrongs in the world to which most sensible people were easily inured. But when Americans in growing numbers could say that slavery was not merely wrong, but intolerably sinful, the balance of sentiment began to shift, and shift decisively. The recognition that slavery contradicted both republicanism and Christianity, with its primitive message of the new birth and the equality of believers, made it possible to mobilize a consensus against slavery strong enough to see the

Civil War through to completion and its logical conclusion, emancipation. Whether that perception of the intolerable sinfulness of slavery
would have taken hold had the Jeffersonian religious program not inad-
vertently created the antebellum spiritual hothouse is a fair question. This
was certainly not what Jefferson imagined, much less intended; yet it is
completely consistent with the appeal to religious conscience that Jefferson had enshrined in his strongest statement against slavery; and he may
deserve some credit for creating the conditions that made religion the
strongest agent of republicanism. The ultimate reality has been known to
work in more mysterious ways still.

NOTES

1. Merrill Peterson, *The Jefferson Image in the American Mind* (1960; Charlottesville, 1997).

2. As described by Associate Justice Anthony Kennedy in summarizing the university's
guidelines for the support of student organizations in *Ronald W. Rosenberger v. Rector and
Visitors of the University of Virginia*, 515 U.S. 819, 823 (1995).

3. James Bennet, "Testing of a President: Tearful Clinton Tells Group of Clerics: 'I
Have Sinned,'" *New York Times*, 12 Sept. 1998.

4. Madison to J. K. Paulding, April 1831, in Gaillard Hunt, ed., *The Writings of James
Madison*, 9 vols. (New York, 1900–1910), 9:451–52.

5. Fawn Brodie, *Thomas Jefferson: An Intimate History* (New York, 1974); Annette Gordon-
Reed, *Thomas Jefferson and Sally Hemings: An American Controversy* (Charlottesville, 1997).

6. Herbert Sloan, *Principle and Interest: Thomas Jefferson and the Problem of Debt* (New
York, 1995).

7. Ibid., 13–49; and see the provocative essay by Garry Wills, "The Aesthete," *New York
Review of Books*, 40, no. 14 (12 Aug. 1993), 6–10.

8. Thomas Jefferson (hereafter TJ) to Maria Cosway, 12 Oct. 1786, in Merrill D. Peterson, ed., *Thomas Jefferson: Writings* (New York, 1984), 866–77.

9. Gordon-Reed, *Jefferson and Hemings*, 172.

10. This point is made quite effectively—if a shade too succinctly—in Philip D. Morgan,
Slave Counterpoint: Black Culture in the Eighteenth-Century Chesapeake and Lowcountry (Chapel
Hill, 1998), 262. "Such claims of humane treatment of individual slaves by individual masters, however accurate and however widespread, go no way to lessening the inhumanity of
slavery as an institution, for the indictment rests, not on the issue of treatment, but on the
denial of freedom."

11. Lucia Stanton, "'Those Who Labor for My Happiness': Thomas Jefferson and His
Slaves," in Peter S. Onuf, ed., *Jeffersonian Legacies* (Charlottesville, 1993), 152.

12. Peter S. Onuf, "'To Declare Them a Free and Independant People': Race, Slavery,
and National Identity in Jefferson's Thought," *Journal of the Early Republic*, 18 (1998), 1–46.

13. Paul Finkelman, "Jefferson and Slavery: 'Treason against the Hopes of the World,'"
in Onuf, ed., *Jeffersonian Legacies*, 212. Reading Finkelman, one wonders whether he thinks
that slavery could actually have been put on the road to extinction by 1800 had the nation's
political elite, TJ foremost among them, simply committed themselves to the task then.

This strikes me as a counterfactual that might better be labeled a counterfantasy, but perhaps I am naive in overestimating the extent of the southern commitment to slavery.

14. Gordon S. Wood, "The Creative Imagination of Bernard Bailyn," in James A. Henretta, Michael Kammen, and Stanley N. Katz, eds., *The Transformation of Early American History: Society, Authority, and Ideology* (New York, 1991), 45–47.

15. Judith Shklar, "Democracy and the Past: Jefferson and His Heirs," in *Redeeming American Political Thought* (Chicago and London, 1998), 171–86; originally presented as the Robert Wesson Lecture in Democracy, Stanford University, April 1988.

16. Gordon S. Wood, "The Trials and Tribulations of Thomas Jefferson," in Onuf, ed., *Jeffersonian Legacies*, 413.

17. For quotations in this and the following paragraphs, see Appendix D in this volume.

18. See Appendix E in this volume.

19. See Appendix D.

20. That at least seems to be the inescapable conclusion to be drawn from Chapter XVI ("Of Conquest") of the *Second Treatise*, where Locke is at some pains to explain why the rights that even a lawful conqueror obtains over the initial objects of his conquest cannot be sustained over the family and descendants of the defeated. Locke, *Two Treatises of Government*, ed. Peter Laslett (1960; rev. ed., Cambridge, U.K., 1963).

21. (Chapel Hill, 1968).

22. Winthrop D. Jordan, *White over Black*, 581–82; Gunnar Myrdal, *An American Dilemma: The Negro Problem and American Democracy* (New York, 1944, 1964), lxix–lxx.

23. Jack N. Rakove, *Original Meanings: Politics and Ideas in the Making of the Constitution* (New York, 1996), 70–75, 92–93.

24. Bernard Bailyn, *Context in History* (Melbourne, Australia, 1995), 16.

25. Unless, that is, one drinks deeply from the dark draught of Conor Cruise O'Brien's delirious diatribe on TJ's enthusiasm for the French Revolution; O'Brien, *The Long Affair: Thomas Jefferson and the French Revolution, 1785–1800* (Chicago and London, 1996).

26. Jordan, *White over Black*, 582.

27. J. R. Pole, *Paths to the American Past* (New York, 1979), 250.

28. Edmund Burke, "Speech on Conciliation with America," 22 March 1775, in Philip Kurland and Ralph Lerner, eds., *The Founders' Constitution* (Chicago and London, 1987), 1:4; Edmund S. Morgan, *American Slavery, American Freedom: The Ordeal of Colonial Virginia* (New York, 1974).

29. Pauline Maier, *American Scripture: Making the Declaration of Independence* (New York, 1997), 47–153.

30. Onuf, "'To Declare Them a Free and Independant People.'"

CHAPTER II

"The Memories of a Few Negroes"

Rescuing America's Future at Monticello

Annette Gordon-Reed

❧

For the better part of the entire month of November 1998, citizens of the United States of America were treated to, and participated in, an intense conversation about race and the history of slavery in America. The publication of the results of DNA tests that bolstered the thesis that the third president of the United States, Thomas Jefferson, had fathered a family of children with Sally Hemings, an enslaved woman on his plantation, presented the perfect occasion to talk about what has happened—was happening—between blacks and whites in America.

My interest in the results of these tests, and the public reaction to them, was quite high because I had recently published a book about Jefferson and Hemings that was extremely critical of the way American historians had presented this story to the world. I stated flatly that they had mishandled the issue for the more than 150 years they had been writing about it, casting the story as a mere slander against Jefferson's character, supported only by one fuzzy-minded female historian, a black female novelist with an axe to grind, and a black public too irrational to separate fantasy from reality.[1] Winthrop D. Jordan's balanced appraisal of the matter in his 1968 seminal work, *White over Black: American Attitudes toward the*

Negro, 1550–1812, was far too lightly passed over by those who took it upon themselves to fashion Jefferson's image.[2]

My look at the historiography revealed two things: first, there never had been a systematic and fair consideration of the matter by those who could be called Jefferson scholars. Had they set out on that path, and been willing to go forthrightly where the evidence took them, they would most probably have come to the second conclusion that I reached: the weight of the evidence clearly suggested that the Jefferson-Hemings liaison was more likely historical fact than fiction. The DNA tests had the potential for showing, with a great deal more finality than is typical in historical debates, whether I was right or wrong about a truth that I thought could easily have been discerned.

Why didn't historians discern it? There is no one answer equally applicable to all who wrote on this subject. In some cases the problem seemed to have stemmed from a potent combination of adherence to white supremacy, class bias, and hero worship. Traditional Jefferson scholars were simply ill-equipped to see the humanity of blacks as equal to that of Jefferson and his white family. Madison Hemings and Israel Jefferson—Sally Hemings's son and a former slave at Monticello, respectively—gave accounts that supported the existence of the relationship. Neither document was treated as of serious historical import. These men, when written of at all, were often presented as mental or moral cripples telling childish tall tales. Why was it necessary to ascertain if such people were telling the truth?

In sorting this matter out, one must also look to the near total identification with and inclination to protect the reputations of Jefferson and those members of his family who provided an alternative explanation for the paternity of Sally Hemings's children. The honor of Jefferson and the Randolphs was so important that they were to be given the benefit of every doubt—no matter how unreasonable. At the same time, the honor and dignity of Madison Hemings and his family were of little consequence. There was a lack of true empathy with black Americans' efforts during slavery to preserve their families in the face of the depredations of the slave system. Moreover, some historians failed to understand how deeply that loss and threatened loss of identity is felt by black Americans even until this day. In the unspoken cost-benefit analysis the question was simple: whose interests do we most mind hurting, the Jeffersons' and Randolphs' or the Hemingses'?

Given Jefferson's great importance to America the choice might seem obvious. But it is less clearly so when we consider the relationship that the Jeffersons and Randolphs bore to the Hemingses. They owned them, and even they recognized that ownership as an aggression against the innocent. It is the normal impulse, when confronted with aggressors and victims, to reserve one's greatest concern for the victim. By this standard, evidence of one slave family's success in escaping the obliteration of their identity should have been treated with respect and care. Certainly, the interests of those who wrongly held them in slavery should not have been protected with such zeal and unquestioned vigilance. In this case, however, the identity of the slave family was pushed aside and portrayed as a grab for power and privilege by those presumed unworthy of the blood of an American icon.

No doubt a degree of professional inertia and deference to the cult of the Jefferson scholar—individuals who have supposedly "figured Jefferson out"—prevented a more clearheaded assessment of the Hemings matter. For scholars writing near the end of the twentieth century, the basic outline of Jefferson's personal life had been set for well over one hundred years. Even if there was reason to suspect that the overall outline was probably dated, most historians were of the view that only a few, inconsequential items were likely candidates for revision. A Jefferson with Sally Hemings as his longtime mistress could not be considered an inconsequential alteration to his life story. It would require, for those who doubted the truth of the liaison, a major reassessment of Jefferson and his life at Monticello.

Finally, account must be taken of the role that centuries of white supremacy played in the handling of this story. A central tenet of that doctrine is that whites must control the shaping of reality. Any reality offered by blacks that conflicts with the desires of whites is to be put down. As far as we have come, we have not yet rid ourselves of this feature of American life. There is little wonder why some historians may have reacted too strongly against (or blithely ignored) Madison Hemings's attempt to state the truth of his life. That truth would have drastically altered the agreed upon truths of Jefferson's life.

James Callender may have written the first words specifically about Jef-

ferson and Hemings, but as one who was at Monticello and who was intimately involved with Jefferson and Hemings, Madison Hemings's recollections about his life on the mountain are the Rosetta Stone of this story.
As I wrote, I knew that if Madison Hemings was truthful (and every bit of
information I found and every avenue I pursued indicated that he was), almost all that had been written about Jefferson's private life and character
would have to be reexamined. Jefferson the father, Jefferson the grandfather, Jefferson the racist, Jefferson the asexual man of letters—all aspects
of him would look different.

If Jefferson's biographers had not seen the role that Sally Hemings
played in his life, what else hadn't they seen? It is not as if no one at the
time noticed that Jefferson had a mistress and numerous children with
her on his home ground. As Joshua Rothman has shown, Jefferson's
neighbors knew and gossiped about Sally Hemings and her children.[3] The
existence of this hole in the historical record is quite a commentary on
the way history and biography have been practiced.

A black man and former slave's version of life at Monticello was
squarely pitted against not only the cult of Jefferson, but also the separate
and distinct cult of the Jefferson scholar. It is easy to understand what
happened when Madison Hemings's memoir was rediscovered in the
1950s and when Fawn Brodie published it in its entirety in 1974. The document, standing by itself, was more than just a challenge to a particular
conception of Jefferson; it had to have been perceived as a challenge to
traditional authority, particularly when Brodie took it up and treated it as
a valid historical document. It could not have gone unnoticed that a white
woman was using the words of a black man to say that a group of white
males did not know what they were talking about. Two members of relatively powerless groups were contending for power in an arena from
which their kind had been largely excluded. There is little wonder Brodie
received the response that she did—and, it must be said, why it took others so long to say out loud that she was probably right and the others
were probably wrong.

It simply is not the case that Brodie's excursions into psychobiography
alone discredited *Thomas Jefferson: An Intimate History* in the eyes of historians. To an extent generally unacknowledged, psychoanalysis, or at least
psychological insights that derive from the principles of psychoanalysis,
form the basis of a great many Jefferson biographies—of all biographies,

really. This would almost have to be so. Jefferson was silent about many things that are of natural interest to people—like what he did for female company during the forty-five years or so after his wife's death. As desiring, seeking, and attaining companionship is typically considered a normal part of life, there had to be some way of dealing with Jefferson's silence on this matter. One could deal with it by ruling the question an irrelevancy that bordered on the prurient, to shame people out of attempting to discuss the question openly. In the alternative Jefferson could be psychoanalyzed from across the years and found to have had no real interest in those pursuits after his wife's death. In either formulation Jefferson would be seen as beyond or above a relationship with Hemings.

Both postures were comfortable and easy. With Hemings, Jefferson's life is a much more complicated business. Monticello, the place of Jefferson's serene refuge—the one thing that seemed sure, safe, and understandable—looks vastly different, no doubt an almost unimaginable place to some. It was a place where a man's two families (of different races and vastly different social status) lived together in what must have been some version of harmony that he virtually willed into existence. Who was this man?

To a great extent that question was being asked and answered with increasing urgency since the 1960s, which saw the beginning of a reassessment of Jefferson. In *Jefferson and Civil Liberties: The Darker Side,* Leonard Levy assailed Jefferson for not being as much the champion of freedom of speech as had been thought. Certainly his racial views had come under sustained attack since the publication in 1968 of Jordan's *White over Black,* which contained a detailed discussion of Jefferson's infamous passages about black people in *Notes on the State of Virginia.* By 1993, with the publication of Peter S. Onuf's *Jeffersonian Legacies* on the occasion of Jefferson's 250th birthday, it was clear that the era of worshipping Jefferson as an unblemished icon was largely over.[4]

Nevertheless, the Hemings matter resisted the full revisionist spirit. Fawn Brodie's, *Thomas Jefferson: An Intimate History,* which accepted the Hemings story as true, was well received by the public. Ultimately, however, the book worked no basic change in the scholarly presentation of Jefferson's life. On the question of the domestic life of Thomas Jefferson, scholars of another era were given almost complete deference. While the reasons for skepticism about the story largely shifted—with the tendency of more recent and less reverential scholars to focus on Jefferson's racism as the likely bar to the truth of the relationship—the basic hesitancy to treat the subject as a matter for serious inquiry remained. The two major studies of Jefferson's character published in the 1990s, one by Andrew Burstein, who was generally favorably disposed toward Jefferson and another by Joseph Ellis, who was less so, discounted the story in quite strong terms.[5]

After studying the matter closely for some years, it was apparent to me that the Jefferson and Hemings controversy had never really been about what could reasonably be deduced from historical inquiry. If it had been, it would not have taken until Fawn Brodie's biography of Jefferson in 1974 for a historian to say that the story was true. Certainly, the story that Jefferson's nephews, the Carrs, were the fathers of Hemings's children would never have taken hold to the extent that it did. In the absence of any systematic effort to gather evidence from the contemporary time, or to analyze closely the statements of contemporary witnesses, the conversation about Jefferson and Hemings seemed to turn largely on who had read the largest number of Jefferson letters.

For all these reasons, I knew that it would take something akin to divine intervention before Madison Hemings's statement, even supported as it was by an extensive amount of circumstantial and direct evidence, could be taken as historical fact. That should not be surprising, for assertions of blacks' equal humanity have often been treated as threats to the maintenance of white supremacy. One can always expect recalcitrance from some quarters, and that the recalcitrance will eventually be seen as a moral error when the passage of time allows for calm reflection. The apologies and attempts at reconciliation that sometimes follow often deepen the cynicism of blacks and their supporters, who cannot understand how so much damage could be inflicted for causes that were so comparatively trivial.

In a real sense, the Jefferson-Hemings saga amounts to an American version of the Dreyfus case, in which people have hitched their own individual hopes, fears, and anxieties to a story that was (is) at its most fundamental level really about a man, a woman, and the children they had together in the midst of a devastating social system that the man could have done more to help dismantle.

With all this in mind, I had been waiting for the results of the DNA test for well over a year and a half before they were announced. During the question-and-answer period after a talk I had given about Jefferson and Hemings in Jefferson's own home territory, Charlottesville, Virginia, a woman raised her hand and announced that she and a colleague were putting together a DNA test that would settle the matter once and for all. We could, she said, have the answer in as short a time as six months. Their idea was to draw blood from the descendants of the relevant families—Hemingses, Woodsons, Jeffersons, and Carrs—and then check their DNA to see what relationships, if any, existed between and among them. The introduction of science would complement the historical record in a way that could yield as definitive a result as would be needed to tell historians whether Jefferson was the most likely father of Hemings's children. We would have what we never have in history: scientific evidence of genetic links between individuals whom we believe from the historical record alone to have been related to one another.

The woman, it turned out, was Winifred Bennett, a resident of Charlottesville—and she was not kidding. The colleague she referred to was Dr. Eugene Foster, also of Charlottesville. It was Dr. Foster's test, and his article in the British journal *Nature* explaining the results of the test, that brought on the media frenzy in November. In a way, it seemed fitting that people from Charlottesville should weigh in on this matter, because that town had been the locus of another famous historical debate about identity: the mystery of Tsar Nicholas's supposedly long-lost daughter, Anastasia. DNA testing firmly established that Tsar Nicholas did not have a long-lost daughter. Or if he did, she was not Anna Anderson, the woman who lived in Charlottesville until the end of her life and who claimed along with devoted supporters that she was the child of Nicholas and Alexandra who had escaped the massacre of the Romanov family.

The prospect of bringing DNA evidence to bear on this matter was dizzying. It was, in truth, something I had fantasized about from the first time I learned of the remarkable strides that were being made toward understanding the intricacies of human genetics. Based on what I knew, I felt confident that science would one day provide an answer. Importantly, I understood that it would not require the exhumation of Jefferson's remains to do so. From time to time historians had suggested that we could never know whether Jefferson was the father of Sally Hemings's children until we dug him up, but that solution was never realistic. It always seemed (and seems) more designed to be obstructionist than anything else. What is accomplished by making the answer to a test—that one knows can never been taken—the sole determinant for resolving a historical controversy? It accomplishes the real objective whenever anyone engages in this type of tactic: it effectively takes resolution of the matter off the table, putting it beyond the realm of the possibility of an answer. *Did Thomas Jefferson and Sally Hemings have children together? That's just something we can never know.*

This approach was quite convenient for supporters of the status quo. Turning the story of Jefferson and Hemings into an unfathomable mystery that could never be resolved by the tools typically used by historians allows the historical consensus about the basic facts of Jefferson's private life to remain intact, no matter how much nonscientific—that is to say, historical—evidence could be amassed in support of an alternative vision of his private life. Scientists controlled the inquiry, and historians' work could never be good enough. This posture not only enshrines the conventional narrative of Jefferson's life, but has the added value of making the proponent of the scientific solution seem reasonable and broadminded, when in fact he or she is quite the opposite. *I'd be willing to accept this if only we had the right tools, which, by the way, I know we'll never have.* It also carries with it a built-in intimation of irresponsibility or mendacity on the part of those who believe that the conventional historical record as it stood could yield an answer.

But I knew that advances in technology would quickly overtake the "dig him up" ruse. If scientists could use genetic tests to track the existence of the genes of the early Africans throughout populations across the globe over thousands of years, surely there would come a time when it could be known whether the Hemings family and Jefferson family were genetically connected. Certainly that answer could come by the time the human genome is mapped during the first half of the next decade.

Despite my faith in the divine intervention of the god of science, and my firm belief, based on my own study of the matter, about what the results of the DNA tests would be—that there would be a genetic connection between the Jefferson and Hemings descendants, that there would be no connection among the Hemings and Carr descendants, and that there would be no connection between the Jefferson, Woodson, and Carr descendants—the idea of a scientific test of my convictions was, quite honestly, unsettling. First, there was the prospect that my mistake would bring a torrent of recrimination inundating me and any other black who might in the future argue strenuously that black testimony was a trustworthy source of important historical fact. The Rosetta Stone would become the Hitler diaries, and people would never tire of telling (and hearing) the tale.

The other source of my discomfort was the knowledge that once the test results came in, and if they were as I thought they would be, the matter would be settled. There could be no more retreats into the safety of "on one hand, but on the other hand," or "we may never know." This would affect not only my own statements, but my reaction to what others said as well. If others continued to treat the matter as still an open question, how could I continue to moderate my voice when faced with what could only be interpreted as even greater contempt and lack of concern for the history and interests of black people? Decisions would have to be made.

I also knew that DNA evidence would be persuasive to many of those in the historical community who had been doubters. Having stated so adamantly that the historiography on Jefferson and Hemings was flawed, and having come to the conclusion in my own mind that the relationship probably existed, I found myself somewhat unprepared to face the reality of a world without serious opposition to my beliefs. A genetic test, well in advance of the time I thought it possible, forced the issue before I had time to sort through all the possible ramifications of an historically accepted Jefferson-Hemings relationship. I would also be forced to think more clearly about what I thought of the two people at the heart of this controversy.

When the results of the DNA tests were announced and they were completely in line with the information presented in my book, the question was posed quite starkly for me and many others: What do we think of Jefferson now? All American citizens, indeed any citizen of the world, who sees himself or herself as having a stake in Jefferson in any way will have to ask that question. One could begin to see the contours of this process taking shape in the media reporting on the DNA results. Reporters, pundits, and newspaper editorialists weighed in on the question as if it were a matter of the gravest concern. If Jefferson's stock had declined in the historical community because of his involvement in slavery and some of his racist writings, the overwhelming evidence that he engaged in miscegenation seemed an occasion to argue even more strongly that he was damaged goods.

This sentiment seems to have been helped along because of the unfortunate fact that the DNA results were released near the approaching zenith of the President Clinton–Monica Lewinsky scandal. Some felt this was no mere coincidence. It was charged that the results were specifically timed to "help" Clinton, by pointing out at a critical moment that another American president—a beloved and respected one—had had problems of his own with a forbidden woman. Armed with the confirmation of Jefferson's indiscretion, Americans would go to the polls during the midterm election and vote for men and women who would turn back the effort to impeach the president who, after all, had only done what Jefferson had done.

In fact, the comparison was helped along because the historical commentary to Dr. Foster's article on the DNA results openly speculated that the findings might help President Clinton avoid impeachment. Jefferson and Hemings were swept up in the centrifugal force of the media's obsession with the Clinton scandal. The settling of a centuries-old controversy about one of the most important men in history—a controversy that raised profound questions about race, status, and the construction of historical reality—was treated by some as just another excuse for pundits to issue banalities about heroes with feet of clay.

Indeed, Jefferson had been set up for this type of treatment. Scholars had used assessments of his character as the primary shield to protect him from the truth of the liaison with Hemings. A person with a "good" character could not have been in such a relationship. To the extent that the DNA results combined with historical evidence proved that Jefferson *had* been in the relationship, the natural tendency would be to think that Jefferson had a "bad" character.

In practically every article, news report, or interview that dealt with the DNA test results in any depth the word *hypocrisy* appeared as a matter of course.[6] Jefferson was denounced as a "hypocrite." This sentiment was voiced and written with a great amount of passion, passion that probably said more about those who made the charge than about Jefferson himself. The central item of hypocrisy in Jefferson's life, of course, was his ownership of slaves even as he voiced sentiments against slavery and wrote with passion about the rights of man. But now there was something perhaps even more terrible to tell: while holding forth on the evils of miscegenation, Jefferson had been carrying on a long-term relationship with a black woman, Sally Hemings! It was difficult to say which part of the hypocrisy was so upsetting. Was it that Jefferson did not practice what he preached or that he preached what he did not practice? If the DNA test had turned out differently, would Jefferson have been more admirable because it would have shown that he made negative comments about race-mixing *and stuck to his guns?* Would people have breathed a sigh of relief because Jefferson's stated aversion to blacks was thorough, complete . . . and consistent?

As is often the case with discussions of this issue, one wonders what message was being imparted by these responses. How could descendants of slaves be expected to receive the news that a Founding Father's long-term sexual relationship with a slave would cause more expressed disappointment than his buying, selling, and making gifts of slaves? We know that Jefferson made women clean his house, cook his meals, and look after his children. Women harvested his crops while he sat writing letters and thinking great thoughts. When he died penniless, the majority of his female slaves were scattered to the four winds, losing family, home, and friends. All these actions—all these things done to black women—have been taken in and washed clean of their import for those who style themselves as the keepers of the Jefferson flame.

Yet, the knowledge that Jefferson became infatuated with a slave woman, entreated her to return to Virginia with him with promises of a life of privilege for her and freedom for their children, had children with her, and kept his promises about providing her with a life of relative privilege and giving their children freedom—that would put him beyond the pale—literally. There would be no way to wash him clean of the defilement. Conor Cruise O'Brien, in *The Long Affair,* his over-the-top condemnation of Jefferson, compared the Virginian's situation to that of colonial Englishmen who took up with African women or the women of all the other parts of the empire upon which the sun never set. They were said to have "gone native." They were no longer Englishmen, and, of course they were no longer white.[7] Has Jefferson met a similar fate? Can he be the symbol of the spirit of America if he has been, in some sense, blackened by Sally Hemings?

However one answers that question, it is likely that for the foreseeable future Jefferson will remain a primary focus of attention for scholars and the public. His ideas and his life interest us, and the Hemings matter further fuels that interest. It is a point of commonality between blacks and whites. Despite all the talk about hypocrisy and living a lie, what one heard over and over in the discussions about Jefferson and Hemings was that the liaison made Jefferson seem more human. This was not just because it indicated that he could make a "mistake," but because it confirmed that he had human feelings and desires. Jefferson's sexuality, so long denied and truncated, became remarkably present. Not only did he have sex. He had it for a long time, fathering his last child at age sixty-five. Moreover, he did all this with the very symbol of carnality: a black woman.

Many people, no doubt, will think less of Jefferson specifically because of his sexuality. At the same time, there is evidence that the revelation of Jefferson's liaison with Sally Hemings has actually improved his image in the eyes of some Americans. Sociologist Orlando Patterson said as much when he announced that knowing that Jefferson had been involved with Hemings made him feel closer to him. Jefferson was, through his part-black children, a member of "the family."[8]

This is a difficult business because, at some level, when thinking about the matter, one has to decide just what Jefferson did with or to Hemings. While the Hemings affair may make Jefferson more accessible in some respects, it necessarily stirs complicated feelings. Was he a rapist? Could there have been love between the two of them? Should that matter to us?

It matters now, it always has, and probably always will.

The traditional historical responses to the Hemings-Jefferson story suggest extreme discomfort with miscegenation. Exaggerated notions about the sexuality of black people (views that Jefferson himself clearly shared) particularly confounded those who viewed Jefferson as the model of probity in his private character. For them miscegenation is the opposite of probity. It is degeneracy by definition. If Jefferson was with Hemings, he may as well have been crawling around on all fours, baying at the moon. There could be no imaginative construction of the relationship (or of Hemings) that could save him from the fall. One can see the still powerful response that miscegenation invokes in the 1995 Merchant Ivory film *Jefferson in Paris*. The film treats the relationship as true, but its makers could barely bring themselves to allow the two characters to touch one another on screen, although Nick Nolte's Jefferson touched and kissed the *married,* but white, Maria Cosway throughout the movie.

Ambivalence about miscegenation is not the only reason for finding the Jefferson-Hemings affair offensive. There is the quite legitimate concern about the power differential that existed between a master in his mid-forties and a slave girl in her mid-teens. How could Hemings, no matter what she may have *thought* she was doing, really have consented to the terms of the "treaty" her son said she entered into with Jefferson? In this view, at the very least Jefferson had used his superior power and knowledge to take advantage of a young slave girl. That the terms of the treaty were fulfilled does not negate the way the whole thing started. For some, the issue is clear. This was rape, pure and simple.

How do we view the fact that Jefferson did not give Hemings her formal freedom? Was it an indication of blatant lack of regard for the woman with whom he had been involved for at least twenty years? Or were there other reasons rooted in the time and other aspects of Jefferson's personality that accounted for his failure in this regard? I believe the most probable answer is likely to trouble present-day sensibilities because it underscores Jefferson's patriarchal attitude, and his less than bold personal style. Jefferson believed that women should be under the protection (read *control*) of men. It was probably never in his contemplation to free Hemings if it meant (and given the circumstances it would have meant) that she would have to leave Monticello and be under the control of another man. When one adds the extreme social opprobrium that would likely have attended his formal filing of a document to free her and a petition to the legislature of Virginia to allow her to remain in the state, one can see how Jefferson, never given to martyrdom, would have chosen the more expedient route. It may be overly romantic to think that things could have been otherwise. And yet, one wishes, as is often the case with Jefferson, for something better.

If Jefferson the lover of Hemings presents problems, Jefferson the father of slave children takes us onto different, even more troubling terrain. What can one make of his attitude toward his offspring with Hemings? The only direct evidence we have is Madison Hemings's memoir in which he notes that Jefferson was not "in the habit" of showing him and his siblings "partiality" or "fatherly affection." Jefferson was kind to them, but he was "uniformly" kind to everyone.[9]

As were all the other slaves on his plantation, Jefferson's mistress and children were listed in his Farm Book as if they had no special meaning to him.[10] However, the Farm Book is not a good guide to Jefferson's relationships with individual slaves. One could read it from cover to cover and never know that at the end of Jefferson's life, Burwell Colbert would receive his freedom, three hundred dollars, and a house, or that John Hemings and Joe Fossett would receive similar bequests. We certainly would not know that Madison and Eston Hemings would be singled out for their freedom.

Consider Jefferson's treatment in his Farm Book of the departures of Beverley and Harriet Hemings. The notations beside their entries simply state that they ran away and lists the year. Beverley did not run away. He left according to the agreement that Jefferson made with Hemings to induce her to return to Virginia. We have an even greater sense of the gap between the words Jefferson put on paper and the actions he took when we consider what happened to Harriet. Jefferson had his overseer give Harriet money and purchase a ticket on a stagecoach to take her north to freedom. She did not run away, as Jefferson wrote in his Farm Book. He helped send her away. There was, evidently, much more going on at Monticello than can be discerned from notations in this cryptic text.

When I read the microfilm of Madison Hemings's memoir in the *Pike County (Ohio) Republican* to compare it with the transcription in Fawn Brodie's book I noticed several mistakes, but one in particular caught my eye. In at least one place where Brodie has Hemings saying "our father" when referring to Jefferson, in the original document Hemings actually referred to Jefferson simply as "father." I saw this as an important difference from an evidentiary point of view because it showed Hemings's deep connection with the story he was recounting. Either he was telling the truth or I was reading the words of a deeply disturbed individual. There was nothing else in the memoir that suggested that the latter was true.[11]

This difference is important for another reason. No matter how it may offend our present-day notions about family, it is clear that Madison Hemings viewed himself as has having been a member of a family. Sally Hemings was "mother." Jefferson was "father." Why would Madison Hemings think of Jefferson as father, even as he spoke of Jefferson's disinclination to show open affection for the Hemings children?

There are some possible answers. First, consider what Madison Hemings knew about white men and the way they treated their children with slave women. He knew that his grandfather, John Wayles, had died and left his children and mistress in slavery. He knew that his mother's life essentially consisted of looking after him and his siblings and attending to Jefferson's chamber and wardrobe. He knew, as others remarked upon, that his mother was treated as "much above" other slaves at Monticello. The promise of freedom was spoken of as something so certain that Hemings remembered that he and his siblings were "measurably happy" as children because they knew the promise would be fulfilled. How could he have been so sure? Most crucially, he knew that his father, unlike his grandfather, had given his children freedom as promised. Why wouldn't this be an important part of establishing his sense of a family connection to Jefferson? To Hemings, Jefferson was "father"—an imperfect one—but father, nevertheless.

Moreover, as I discovered while researching my book, the name of each of the Hemings children was significant. They had been named in the same manner that Jefferson's children with his wife had been named, the same way Jefferson named his grandchildren: for members of the Randolph family or for close friends. Certainly everyone in his community and family would have recognized the Randolph family names. Of course, everyone would know James Madison. Naming children in the eighteenth century, in black families and white, was a serious matter, a way to announce and preserve family origins and connections. The Hemings family was no different.

Was it mere chance that the Hemings boys were trained to a profession and an avocation, carpentry and the violin, for which Jefferson had a strong affinity? What of Beverley Hemings and his hot-air ballooning? Is it significant that Eston Hemings, the son who became a musician, made one of Jefferson's favorite songs a central part of his repertoire?

Madison Hemings would have known the answer to all these questions, but we cannot. It cannot be emphasized enough what a tragedy it is that the answers most likely will never be known, and that they will not be known for any reason that can be called a good one. What if instead of writing to Henry Randall to find out who Madison Hemings's father was, James Parton had put that question to Madison Hemings himself? There was a moment when a historian had the chance to rise above the prejudices of the day and let curiosity and open-mindedness, the lifeblood of history, give him the courage to take a chance. Hemings might have responded, and history would have been immeasurably richer for it. Similar moments of opportunity have existed from the very beginning, and the one who rose to the occasion—Fawn Brodie—was made the object of ridicule and scorn. What a lesson to be learned in all this!

It is true that we do not and will never have the details of what went on between Jefferson and Hemings and their children. This does not mean that we have nothing to go on. Perhaps the most persistent, and ultimately damaging, feature of the original debate over whether the relationship existed at all was the tight rein placed upon the historical imagination. One was simply not to let one's mind wander too freely over the matter. Brainstorming, drawing reasonable inferences from actions, attempting to piece together a plausible view of the matter were shunted into the category of illegitimate speculation, as grave an offense as outright lying. Yet, a good amount of history is necessarily based upon just this sort of methodology. Why the hesitancy about applying it to the Jefferson and Hemings relationship?

I suppose the answer stems from the knowledge that the public must eventually settle on some way to view Jefferson and Hemings. Jefferson's reputation depends upon how we think he conducted himself in this relationship. Given the enormous head start that Jefferson has in the public's affection, it is a safe bet that the terms of the settlement will be in his favor. When that happens, Jefferson will be even more powerful as a cultural touchstone than ever. Thomas and Sally, long the forbidden American myth, will become simply "the American myth."

There is no question that there is some anxiety about this prospect. The image of Jefferson and Hemings as multicultural heroes is fake. In the end, it will probably be left to novelists, playwrights, and poets, unencumbered by the need for footnotes, to get at the ultimate meaning of this story. That effort, done in the right way, will yield universal truths as important and real as any to be found in history books.

But historians must tell the story, too. While it is easy to think of the "larger issues" that Jefferson's relationship with Hemings raises, I suspect that the most difficult issues are the seemingly "small" ones. At the most fundamental level we now must face the question of how to accommodate the new knowledge into Jefferson's biography. There is no way to be a little bit pregnant on this score. The declaration of the new truths that must be stated are simple, and yet breathtaking, when one considers how long and hard they have been resisted over these many years. There is no doubt that seeing these words in print will rattle some to their cores. Thomas Jefferson had thirteen children, six of whom lived to adulthood. Some of his children were white and some of them were black. He had four sons born to him, three of whom lived to adulthood. He had three daughters who lived to adulthood, not two. Jefferson did not live in celibacy for the forty-five years after the death of his wife of ten years, Martha Jefferson. He had a thirty-eight-year, apparently monogamous, relationship with Sally Hemings, an enslaved black woman on his plantation, and fathered a child with her when he was sixty-five years old. There is no question that the lay of the land will change when historians write openly about this as part of our history, and not a simple legend. It is difficult to say what changes will occur, but at least we can embark on the project in a spirit of good faith that will allow us to improve on what was done before.

NOTES

The quotation in the title is from Merrill D. Peterson, *The Jefferson Image in the American Mind* (New York, 1960), 187.

1. I am referring to biographer Fawn M. Brodie, author of *Thomas Jefferson: An Intimate History* (New York, 1974); and Barbara Chase-Riboud, author *Sally Hemings: A Novel* (New York, 1979).

2. Winthrop D. Jordan, *White over Black: American Attitudes toward the Negro, 1550–1812* (Chapel Hill, N.C., 1968).

3. See Rothman, "James Callender and Social Knowledge of Interracial Sex in Antebellum Virginia," chapter 4 in this volume.

4. Peter S. Onuf, ed., *Jeffersonian Legacies* (Charlottesville, 1993); Leonard Levy, *Jefferson and Civil Liberties: The Darker Side* (Cambridge, Mass., 1963).

5. Andrew Burstein, *The Inner Jefferson: Portrait of a Grieving Optimist* (Charlottesville, 1995); Joseph J. Ellis, *American Sphinx: The Character of Thomas Jefferson* (New York, 1997).

6. See, for example, "The Destruction of Thomas Jefferson," *Port St. Lucie News*, 21 Nov. 1998; "The Big News Is of History—Not Sex," *The Richmond Times Dispatch*, 16 Nov. 1998; "Legacy of Slavery Breeds Hypocrisy and Corruption," *Houston Chronicle*, 15 Nov. 1998; "Self Evident Truths," *Chicago Sun Times*, 4 Nov. 1998; "DNA Test Finds Evidence of Jefferson Child by a Slave," *New York Times*, 1 Nov. 1998.

7. Conor Cruise O'Brien, *The Long Affair: Thomas Jefferson and the French Revolution* (Chicago, 1997)

8. "Jefferson the Contradiction," *New York Times*, 2 Nov. 1998.

9. "Memoirs of Madison Hemings," Appendix A in this volume.

10. Edwin Morris Betts, ed., *Thomas Jefferson's Farm Book, with Commentary and Relevant Extracts from Other Writings* (Charlottesville, 1987).

11. "Memoirs of Madison Hemings," Appendix A in this volume.

Appendices

Madison Hemings's Memoir

❧

"LIFE AMONG THE LOWLY, NO. 1,"

Pike County (Ohio) Republican, 13 MARCH 1873

I never knew of but one white man who bore the name of Hemings; he was an Englishman and my great grandfather. He was captain of an English trading vessel which sailed between England and Williamsburg, Va., then quite a port. My great-grandmother was a fullblooded African, and possibly a native of that country. She was the property of John Wales, a Welchman. Capt. Hemings happened to be in the port of Williamsburg at the time my grandmother was born, and acknowledging her fatherhood he tried to purchase her of Mr. Wales, who would not part with the child, though he was offered an extraordinarily large price for her. She was named Elizabeth Hemings. Being thwarted in the purchase, and determined to own his own flesh and blood he resolved to take the child by force or stealth, but the knowledge of his intention coming to John Wales' ears, through leaky fellow servants of the mother, she and the child were taken into the "great house" under their master's immediate care. I have been informed that it was not the extra value of that child over other slave children that induced Mr. Wales to refuse to sell it, for slave masters then, as in later days, had no compunctions of conscience which restrained them from parting mother and child of however tender age, but he was restrained by the fact that just about that time amalgamation began, and the child was so great a curiosity that its owner desired to raise it himself that he might see its outcome. Capt. Hemings soon afterwards sailed from Williamsburg, never to return. Such is the story that comes down to me.

Elizabeth Hemings grew to womanhood in the family of John Wales, whose wife dying she (Elizabeth) was taken by the widower Wales as his concubine, by whom she had six children—three sons and three daughters, viz: Robert, James, Peter, Critty, Sally and Thena. These children went by the name of Hemings.

Williamsburg was the capital of Virginia, and of course it was an aristocratic place, where the "bloods" of the Colony and the new State most did congregate. Thomas Jefferson, the author of the Declaration of Independence, was educated at

William and Mary College, which had its seat at Williamsburg. He afterwards stud-
ied law with Geo. Wythe, and practiced law at the bar of the general court of the
Colony. He was afterwards elected a member of the provincial legislature from
Albemarle county. Thos. Jefferson was a visitor at the "great house" of John Wales,
who had children about his own age. He formed the acquaintance of his daughter
Martha (I believe that was her name, though I am not positively sure,) and intimacy
sprang up between them which ripened into love, and they were married. They afterwards went to live at his country seat Monticello, and in course of time had born
to them a daughter whom they named Martha. About the time she was born my
mother, the second daughter of John Wales and Elizabeth Hemings was born. On
the death of John Wales, my grandmother, his concubine, and her children by him
fell to Martha, Thomas Jefferson's wife, and consequently became the property of
Thomas Jefferson, who in the course of time became famous, and was appointed
minister to France during our revolutionary troubles, or soon after independence
was gained. About the time of the appointment and before he was ready to leave
the country his wife died, and as soon after her interment as he could attend to and
arrange his domestic affairs in accordance with the changed circumstances of his
family in consequence of this misfortune (I think not more than three weeks thereafter) he left for France, taking his eldest daughter with him. He had sons born to
him, but they died in early infancy, so he then had but two children—Martha and
Maria. The latter was left home, but afterwards was ordered to follow him to
France. She was three years or so younger than Martha. My mother accompanied
her as a body servant. When Mr. Jefferson went to France Martha was just budding
into womanhood. Their stay (my mother's and Maria's) was about eighteen
months. But during that time my mother became Mr. Jefferson's concubine, and
when he was called back home she was *enciente* by him. He desired to bring my
mother back to Virginia with him but she demurred. She was just beginning to understand the French language well, and in France she was free, while if she returned to Virginia she would be re-enslaved. So she refused to return with him. To
induce her to do so he promised her extraordinary privileges, and made a solemn
pledge that her children should be freed at the age of twenty-one years. In consequence of his promise, on which she implicitly relied, she returned with him to Virginia. Soon after their arrival, she gave birth to a child, of whom Thomas Jefferson
was the father. It lived but a short time. She gave birth to four others, and Jefferson
was the father of all of them. Their names were Beverly, Harriet, Madison (myself),
and Eston—three sons and one daughter. We all became free agreeably to the
treaty entered into by our parents before we were born. We all married and have
raised families.

Beverly left Monticello and went to Washington as a white man. He married a
white woman in Maryland, and their only child, a daughter, was not known by the
white folks to have any colored blood coursing in her veins. Beverly's wife's family
were people in good circumstances.

Harriet married a white man in good standing in Washington City, whose name
I could give, but will not, for prudential reasons. She raised a family of children,
and so far as I know they were never suspected of being tainted with African blood
in the community where she lived or lives. I have not heard from her for ten years,
and do not know whether she is dead or alive. She thought it to her interest, on go-

ing to Washington, to assume the role of a white woman, and by her dress and conduct as such I am not aware that her identity as Harriet Hemings of Monticello has ever been discovered.

Eston married a colored woman in Virginia, and moved from there to Ohio, and lived in Chillicothe several years. In the fall of 1852 he removed to Wisconsin, where he died a year or two afterwards. He left three children.

As to myself, I was named Madison by the wife of James Madison, who was afterwards President of the United States. Mrs. Madison happened to be at Monticello at the time of my birth, and begged the privilege of naming me, promising my mother a fine present for the honor. She consented, and Mrs. Madison dubbed me by the name I now acknowledge, but like many promises of white folks to the slaves she never gave my mother anything. I was born at my father's seat of Monticello, in Albemarle county, Va., near Charlottesville, on the 19th day of January, 1805. My very earliest recollections are of my grandmother Elizabeth Hemings. That was when I was about three years old. She was sick and upon her death bed. I was eating a piece of bread and asked if she would have some. She replied: "No, granny don't want bread any more." She shortly afterwards breathed her last. I have only a faint recollection of her.

Of my father, Thomas Jefferson, I knew more of his domestic than his public life during his life time. It is only since his death that I have learned much of the latter, except that he was considered as a foremost man in the land, and held many important trusts, including that of President. I learned to read by inducing the white children to teach me the letters and something more; what else I know of books I have picked up here and there till now I can read and write. I was almost 21½ years of age when my father died on the 4th of July, 1826.

About his own home he was the quietest of men. He was hardly ever known to get angry, though sometimes he was irritated when matters went wrong, but even then he hardly ever allowed himself to be made unhappy any great length of time. Unlike Washington he had but little taste or care for agricultural pursuits. He left matters pertaining to his plantations mostly with his stewards and overseers. He always had mechanics at work for him, such as carpenters, blacksmiths, shoemakers, coopers, &c. It was his mechanics he seemed mostly to direct, and in their operations he took great interest. Almost every day of his later years he might have been seen among them. He occupied much of the time in his office engaged in correspondence and reading and writing. His general temperament was smooth and even; he was very undemonstrative. He was uniformly kind to all about him. He was not in the habit of showing partiality or fatherly affection to us children. We were the only children of his by a slave woman. He was affectionate toward his white grandchildren, of whom he had fourteen, twelve of whom lived to manhood and womanhood. His daughter Martha married Thomas Mann Randolph by whom she had thirteen children. Two died in infancy. The names of the living were Ann, Thomas Jefferson, Ellen, Cornelia, Virginia, Mary, James, Benj. Franklin, Lewis Madison, Septemia and Geo. Wythe. Thos. Jefferson Randolph was Chairman of the Democratic National Convention in Baltimore last spring which nominated Horace Greeley for the Presidency, and Geo. Wythe Randolph was Jeff. Davis' first Secretary of War in the late "unpleasantness."

Maria married John Epps, and raised one son—Francis.

My father generally enjoyed excellent health. I never knew him to have but one spell of sickness, and that was caused by a visit to the Warm Springs in 1818. Till within three weeks of his death he was hale and hearty, and at the age of 83 years walked erect and with a stately tread. I am now 68, and I well remember that he was a much smarter man physically, even at that age, than I am.

When I was fourteen years old I was put to the carpenter trade under the charge of John Hemings, the youngest son of my grandmother. His father's name was Nelson, who was an Englishman. She had seven children by white men and seven by colored men—fourteen in all. My brothers, sister Harriet and myself, were used alike. We were permitted to stay about the "great house," and only required to do such light work as going on errands. Harriet learned to spin and to weave in a little factory on the home plantation. We were free from the dread of having to be slaves all our lives long, and were measurably happy. We were always permitted to be with our mother, who was well used. It was her duty, all her life which I can remember, up to the time of father's death, to take care of his chamber and wardrobe, look after us children and do such light work as sewing, &c. Provision was made in the will of our father that we should be free when we arrived at the age of 21 years. We had all passed that period when he died but Eston, and he was given the remainder of his time shortly after. He and I rented a house and took mother to live with us, till her death, which event occurred in 1835.

In 1834 I married Mary McCoy. Her grandmother was a slave, and lived with her master, Stephen Hughes, near Charlottesville, as his wife. She was manumitted by him, which made their children free born. Mary McCoy's mother was his daughter. I was about 28 and she 22 years of age when we married. We lived and labored together in Virginia till 1836, when we voluntarily left and came to Ohio. We settled in Pebble township, Pike County. We lived there four or five years and during my stay in the county I worked at my trade on and off for about four years. Joseph Sewell was my first employer. I built for him what is now known as Rizzleport No. 2 in Waverly. I afterwards worked for George Wolf Senior. and I did the carpenter work for the brick building now owned by John J. Kellison in which the Pike County Republican is printed. I worked for and with Micajab Hinson. I found him to be a very clever man. I also reconstructed the building on the corner of Market and Water Streets from a store to a hotel for the late Judge Jacob Row.

When we came from Virginia we brought one daughter (Sarah) with us, leaving the dust of a son in the soil near Monticello. We have born to us in this State nine children. Two are dead. The names of the living, besides Sarah, are Harriet, Mary Ann, Catharine, Jane, William Beverly, James Madison, Ellen Wales. Thomas Eston died in the Andersonville prison pen, and Julia died at home. William, James and Ellen are unmarried and live at home in Huntington township, Ross County. All the others are married and raising families. My post office address is Pee Pee, Pike County Ohio.

SOURCE NOTE

Reprinted from Annette Gordon-Reed, *Thomas Jefferson and Sally Hemings: An American Controversy* (Charlottesville, 1997), 245–58.

James Callender's Reports

❧

It is well known that the man, *whom it delighteth the people to honor,* keeps, and for many years past has kept, as his concubine, one of his own slaves. Her name is SALLY. The name of her eldest son is TOM. His features are said to bear a striking although sable resemblance to those of the president himself. The boy is ten or twelve years of age. His mother went to France in the same vessel with Mr. Jefferson and his two daughters. The delicacy of this arrangement must strike every person of common sensibility. What a sublime pattern for an American ambassador to place before the eyes of two young ladies!

If the reader does not feel himself *disposed to pause* we beg leave to proceed. Some years ago, this story had once or twice been hinted at in *Rind's Federalist.* At that time, we believed the surmise to be an absolute calumny. One reason for thinking so was this. A vast body of people wished to debar Mr. Jefferson from the presidency. *The establishment of this* SINGLE FACT would have rendered his election impossible. We reasoned thus; that if the allegation had been true, it was sure to have been ascertained and advertised by his enemies; in every corner of the continent. The suppression of so decisive an enquiry serves to shew that the common sense of the federal party was overruled by divine providence. It was the predestination of the supreme being that they should be turned out; that they should be expelled from office by the *popularity* of a character, which, at that Instant, was lying fettered and gagged, consumed and extinguished at their feet!

. . . By this wench Sally, our president has had several children. There is not an individual in the neighbourhood of Charlottesville who does not believe the story; and not a few who know it. . . . Behold the favorite, the first born of republicanism! the pinnacle of all that is good and great! in the open consummation of an act which tends to subvert the policy, the happiness, and even the existence of this country!

'Tis supposed that, at the time when Mr. Jefferson wrote so smartly concerning negroes, when he endeavoured much to belittle the African race, he had no expectation that the chief magistrate of the United States was to be the ringleader in shewing that his opinion was erroneous; or, that he should chuse an African stock whereupon he was to engraft his own descendants. . . .

If the friends of Mr. Jefferson are convinced of *his* innocence, *they* will make an appeal of the same sort [that Callender had successfully made for public testimonials when he rebutted charges against him in connection with his putative role in the Alexander Hamilton–Maria Reynolds scandal]. If they rest in silence, or if they content themselves with resting upon a *general denial,* they cannot hope for credit. The allegation is of a nature too *black* to be suffered to remain in suspence. We should be glad to hear of its refutation. We give it to the world under the firmest belief that such a refutation *never can be made.* The AFRICAN VENUS is said to officiate, as housekeeper at Monticello. When Mr. Jefferson has read this article, he will find leisure to estimate how much has been lost or gained by so many unprovoked attacks upon

J. T. CALLENDER.

2. *Richmond Recorder,* 20 OCTOBER 1802

We are surprised at the petulance of some eastern editors in still affecting to doubt the truth of Sally's story. In this state, at least as far as we can learn, every body believes it. On the second day after the first publication, when the demos were denying the whole, a gentleman came into the district court, and offered to bet a suit of cloaths, or any sum of money, with any man present, that the charge was correct. He specified a small exception, which we have since noticed. Sally did not go to France in the same ship with our French ambassador. She went afterwards; and the gentleman said something about the black wench and the captain, which we do not think it necessary to repeat. Nobody would venture to take up this gentleman. He was known to be capable of paying a debt; and to have the best access to family information. If we had been mad enough to publish a tale of such enormous, of such inexpressible ignominy, without a solid foundation, the Recorder, and its editors must have been ruined. All decent men would have struck out their names. We have lost but five or six in Richmond. One of these is a young man, whose own father-in-law hath since actually subscribed. Some of those who gave up their papers have been since harassing their acquaintances to lend them the Recorder. "Why did you not keep the paper, when you had it?" said a gentleman to one of those borrowers. Twelve days after the publication of Sally's affair, Mr. Ralph Wormely, a gentleman whose wealth is as great as his probity, sits down, writes and subscribes a defence of the Recorder. He thanks us, in particular, for telling so much truth of political characters. Do you conceive, that a person of Mr. Wormely's standing would hazard the strong encomiums which he has bestowed, unless after the most serious premeditation? Since the publication of Sally, we have had at least an hundred and fifty new subscribers. Many of them are among the most respectable citizens of Virginia. Strange! If all these people subscribe with the previous certainty that the editors of this paper could have propagated a base calumny. Mr. Coleman of New York, and our corps of subscribers in that city, our friends in Philadelphia, about fifty subscribers in Baltimore, and sixty in New Jersy; may all rest assured that, upon Sally's business, as upon every other quarter, the reputation of our veracity is invulnerable.

SOURCE NOTE

Transcription by Joshua D. Rothman

Thomas Jefferson to Francis Gray, 4 March 1815

You asked me in conversation, what constituted a mulatto by our law? And I believe I told you four crossings with the whites. I looked afterwards into our law, and found it to be in these words: "Every person, other than a negro, of whose grandfathers or grandmothers any one shall have been a negro, shall be deemed a mulatto, and so every such person who shall have one-fourth part or more of negro blood, shall in like manner be deemed a mulatto["]; L. Vir'a 1792, December 17: the case put in the first member of the paragraph of the law is *exempli gratiâ*. The latter contains the true canon, which is that one-fourth of negro blood, mixed with any portion of white, constitutes the mulatto. As the issue has one-half of the blood of each parent, and the blood of each of these may be made up of a variety of fractional mixtures, the estimate of their compound may be intricate; it becomes a mathematical problem of the same class with those on the mixtures of different liquors or different metals; as in these, therefore, the algebraical notation is the most convenient and intelligible. Let us express the pure blood of the white in the capital letters of the printed alphabet, the pure blood of the negro in the small letters of the printed alphabet, and any given mixture of either, by way of abridgment in MS. letters.

Let the first crossing be of a, a pure negro, with A, pure white. The unit of blood of the issue being composed of the half of that of each parent, will be $a/2 + A/2$. Call it, for abbreviation, h (half blood).

Let the second crossing be that of h and B, the blood of the issue will be $h/2 + B/2$, or substituting for $h/2$ its equivalent, it will be $a/4 + A/4 + B/2$, call it q (quarteroon) being $1/4$ negro blood.

Let the third crossing be of q and C, their offspring will be $q/2 + C/2 = a/8 + A/8 + B/4 + C/2$, call this e (eighth), who having less than $1/4$ of a, or of pure negro blood, to wit $1/8$ only, is no longer a mulatto, so that a third cross clears the blood.

From these elements let us examine their compounds. For example, let h and q cohabit, their issue will be $h/2 + q/2 = a/4 + A/4 + a/8 + A/8 + B/4 = {}^3a/8 + {}^3A/8 + B/4$, wherein we find $3/8$ of a, or negro blood.

Let h and e cohabit, their issue will be $h/2 + e/2 = a/4 + \text{A}/4 + a/16 + \text{A}/16 + \text{B}/8 + c/4 = {}^5a/16 + {}^5\text{A}/16 + \text{B}/8 + c/4$, wherein $5/16\, a$ makes still a mulatto.

Let q and e cohabit, the half of the blood of each will be $q/2 + e/2 = a/8\ \text{A}/8 + \text{B}/4 + a/16 + \text{A}/16 + \text{B}/8 + c/4 = {}^3a/16 + {}^3\text{A}/16 + {}^3\text{B}/8 + c/4$, wherein of a is no longer a mulatto, and thus may every compound be noted and summed, the sum of the fractions composing the blood of the issue being always equal to unit. It is understood in natural history that a fourth cross of one race of animals with another gives an issue equivalent for all sensible purposes to the original blood. Thus a Merino ram being crossed, first with a country ewe, second with his daughter, third with his granddaughter, and fourth with his great-granddaughter, the last issue is deemed pure Merino, having in fact but $1/16$ of the country blood. But observe, that this does not re-establish freedom, which depends on the condition of the mother, the principle of the civil law, *partus sequitir ventrem,* being adopted here. But if e be emancipated, he becomes a free *white* man, and a citizen of the United States to all intents and purposes.

SOURCE NOTE

Andrew A. Lipscomb and Albert Ellery Bergh, eds., *The Writings of Thomas Jefferson,* 20 vols. (Washington, Thomas Jefferson Memorial Association, 1903–4), 14:267–71, excerpt (268–70).

Thomas Jefferson, Notes on the State of Virginia (London, 1787)

❧

QUERY XIV, LAWS (EXCERPT)

Many of the laws which were in force during the monarchy being relative merely to that form of government, or inculcating principles inconsistent with republicanism, the first assembly which met after the establishment of the commonwealth
appointed a committee to revise the whole code, to reduce it into proper form and
volume, and report it to the assembly. This work has been executed by three gentlemen, and reported; but probably will not be taken up till a restoration of peace
shall leave to the legislature leisure to go through such a work. . . .

[Among the measures considered by the Committee of Revisors was one "to
emancipate all slaves born after passing the act."] The bill reported by the revisors
does not itself contain this proposition; but an amendment containing it was prepared, to be offered to the legislature whenever the bill should be taken up, and further directing, that they should continue with their parents to a certain age, then be
brought up, at the public expence, to tillage, arts or sciences, according to their ge-
niusses, till the females should be eighteen, and the males twenty-one years of age,
when they should be colonized to such place as the circumstances of the time
should render most proper, sending them out with arms, implements of houshold
and of the handicraft arts, seeds, pairs of the useful domestic animals, &c. to declare them a free and independant people, and extend to them our alliance and protection, till they shall have acquired strength; and to send vessels at the same time to
other parts of the world for an equal number of white inhabitants; to induce whom
to migrate hither, proper encouragements were to be proposed. It will probably be
asked, Why not retain and incorporate the blacks into the state, and thus save the
expence of supplying, by importation of white settlers, the vacancies they will
leave? Deep rooted prejudices entertained by the whites; ten thousand recollections, by the blacks, of the injuries they have sustained; new provocations; the real
distinctions which nature has made; and many other circumstances, will divide us

into parties, and produce convulsions which will probably never end but in the extermination of the one or the other race.—To these objections, which are political, may be added others, which are physical and moral. The first difference which strikes us is that of colour. Whether the black of the negro resides in the reticular membrane between the skin and scarf-skin, or in the scarf-skin itself; whether it proceeds from the colour of the blood, the colour of the bile, or from that of some other secretion, the difference is fixed in nature, and is as real as if its seat and cause were better known to us. And is this difference of no importance? Is it not the foundation of a greater or less share of beauty in the two races? Are not the fine mixtures of red and white, the expressions of every passion by greater or less suffusions of colour in the one, preferable to that eternal monotony, which reigns in the countenances, that immoveable veil of black which covers all the emotions of the other race? Add to these, flowing hair, a more elegant symmetry of form, their own judgment in favour of the whites, declared by their preference of them, as uniformly as is the preference of the Oranootan for the black women over those of his own species. The circumstance of superior beauty, is thought worthy attention in the propagation of our horses, dogs, and other domestic animals; why not in that of man? Besides those of colour, figure, and hair, there are other physical distinctions proving a difference of race. They have less hair on the face and body. They secrete less by the kidnies, and more by the glands of the skin, which gives them a very strong and disagreeable odour. This greater degree of transpiration renders them more tolerant of heat, and less so of cold, than the whites. Perhaps too a difference of structure in the pulmonary apparatus, which a late ingenious experimentalist has discovered to be the principal regulator of animal heat, may have disabled them from extricating, in the act of inspiration, so much of that fluid from the outer air, or obliged them in expiration, to part with more of it. They seem to require less sleep. A black, after hard labour through the day, will be induced by the slightest amusements to sit up till midnight, or later, though knowing he must be out with the first dawn of the morning. They are at least as brave, and more adventuresome. But this may perhaps proceed from a want of forethought, which prevents their seeing a danger till it be present. When present, they do not go through it with more coolness or steadiness than the whites. They are more ardent after their female: but love seems with them to be more an eager desire, than a tender delicate mixture of sentiment and sensation. Their griefs are transient. Those numberless afflictions, which render it doubtful whether heaven has given life to us in mercy or in wrath, are less felt, and sooner forgotten with them. In general, their existence appears to participate more of sensation than reflection. To this must be ascribed their disposition to sleep when abstracted from their diversions, and unemployed in labour. An animal whose body is at rest, and who does not reflect, must be disposed to sleep of course. Comparing them by their faculties of memory, reason, and imagination, it appears to me, that in memory they are equal to the whites; in reason much inferior, as I think one could scarcely be found capable of tracing and comprehending the investigations of Euclid; and that in imagination they are dull, tasteless, and anomalous. It would be unfair to follow them to Africa for this investigation. We will consider them here, on the same stage with the whites, and where the facts are not apocryphal on which a judgment is to be formed. It will be right to make great allowances for the difference of condition, of education, of conversation, of the sphere in which they move. Many millions of them have been brought to, and born in America. Most of them indeed have been confined to tillage, to their own homes, and their own society: yet many have been so situated, that they might have availed themselves of the conversation of their masters; many have been brought up to the handicraft arts, and from that circumstance have always been associated with the whites. Some have been liberally educated, and all have lived in countries where the arts and sciences are cultivated to a considerable degree, and have had before their eyes samples of the best works from abroad. The Indians, with no advantages of this kind, will often carve figures on their pipes not destitute of design and merit. They will crayon out an animal, a plant, or a country, so as to prove the existence of a germ in their minds which only wants cultivation. They astonish you with strokes of the most sublime oratory; such as prove their reason and sentiment strong, their imagination glowing and elevated. But never yet could I find that a black had uttered a thought above the level of plain narration; never see even an elementary trait of painting or sculpture. In music they are more generally gifted than the whites with accurate ears for tune and time, and they have been found capable of imagining a small catch. Misery is often the parent of the most affecting touches in poetry.—Among the blacks is misery enough, God knows, but no poetry. Love is the peculiar oestrum of the poet. Their love is ardent, but it kindles the senses only, not the imagination. Religion indeed has produced a Phyllis Whately; but it could not produce a poet. The compositions published under her name are below the dignity of criticism. The heroes of the Dunciad are to her, as Hercules to the author of that poem. Ignatius Sancho has approached nearer to merit in composition; yet his letters do more honour to the heart than the head. They breathe the purest effusions of friendship and general philanthropy, and shew how great a degree of the latter may be compounded with strong religious zeal. He is often happy in the turn of his compliments, and his stile is easy and familiar, except when he affects a Shandean fabrication of words. But his imagination is wild and extravagant, escapes incessantly from every restraint of reason and taste, and, in the course of its vagaries, leaves a tract of thought as incoherent and eccentric, as is the course of a meteor through the sky. His subjects should often have led him to a process of sober reasoning: yet we find him always substituting sentiment for demonstration. Upon the whole, though we admit him to the first place among those of his own colour who have presented themselves to the public judgment, yet when we compare him with the writers of the race among whom he lived, and particularly with the epistolary class, in which he has taken his own stand, we are compelled to enroll him at the bottom of the column. This criticism supposes the letters published under his name to be genuine, and to have received amendment from no other hand; points which would not be of easy investigation. The improvement of the blacks in body and mind, in the first instance of their mixture with the whites, has been observed by every one, and proves that their inferiority is not the effect merely of their condition of life. We know that among the Romans, about the Augustan age especially, the condition of their slaves was much more deplorable than that of the blacks on the continent of America. The two sexes were confined in separate apartments, because to raise a child cost the master more than to buy one. Cato, for a very restricted indulgence to his slaves in this particular, took from them a certain price. But in this country the slaves multiply as fast as the free inhabitants. Their situation and manners place the commerce between the two sexes almost without restraint.—The same Cato, on a principle of oeconomy, always sold his sick and superannuated slaves. He gives it as a standing precept to a master visiting his farm, to sell his old oxen, old waggons, old tools, old and diseased servants, and every thing else become useless. . . . The American slaves cannot enumerate this among the injuries and insults they receive. It was the common practice to expose in the island of Aesculapius, in the Tyber, diseased slaves, whose cure was like to become tedious. The Emperor Claudius, by an edict, gave freedom to such of them as should recover, and first declared, that if any person chose to kill rather than to expose them, it should be deemed homicide. The exposing them is a crime of which no instance has existed with us; and were it to be followed by death, it would be punished capitally. We are told of a certain Vedius Pollio, who, in the presence of Augustus, would have given a slave as food to his fish, for having broken a glass. With the Romans, the regular method of taking the evidence of their slaves was under torture. Here it has been thought better never to resort to their evidence. When a master was murdered, all his slaves, in the same house, or within hearing, were condemned to death. Here punishment falls on the guilty only, and as precise proof is required against him as against a freeman. Yet notwithstanding these and other discouraging circumstances among the Romans, their slaves were often their rarest artists. They excelled too in science, insomuch as to be usually employed as tutors to their master's children. Epictetus, Terence, and Phaedrus, were slaves. But they were of the race of whites. It is not their condition then, but nature, which has produced the distinction.—Whether further observation will or will not verify the conjecture, that nature has been less bountiful to them in the endowments of the head, I believe that in those of the heart she will be found to have done them justice. That disposition to theft with which they have been branded, must be ascribed to their situation, and not to any depravity of the moral sense. The man, in whose favour no laws of property exist, probably feels himself less bound to respect those made in favour of others. When arguing for ourselves, we lay it down as a fundamental, that laws, to be just, must give a reciprocation of right: that, without this, they are mere arbitrary rules of conduct, founded in force, and not in conscience: and it is a problem which I give to the master to solve, whether the religious precepts against the violation of property were not framed for him as well as his slave? And whether the slave may not as justifiably take a little from one, who has taken all from him, as he may slay one who would slay him? That a change in the relations in which a man is placed should change his ideas of moral right and wrong, is neither new, nor peculiar to the colour of the blacks. Homer tells us it was so 2600 years ago. . . .

> Jove fix'd it certain, that whatever day
> Makes man a slave, takes half his worth away.

But the slaves of which Homer speaks were whites. Notwithstanding these considerations which must weaken their respect for the laws of property, we find among them numerous instances of the most rigid integrity, and as many as among their better instructed masters, of benevolence, gratitude, and unshaken fidelity

—The opinion, that they are inferior in the faculties of reason and imagination, must be hazarded with great diffidence. To justify a general conclusion, requires many observations, even where the subject may be submitted to the Anatomical knife, to Optical glasses, to analysis by fire, or by solvents. How much more then where it is a faculty, not a substance, we are examining; where it eludes the research of all the senses; where the conditions of its existence are various and variously combined; where the effects of those which are present or absent bid defiance to calculation; let me add too, as a circumstance of great tenderness, where our conclusion would degrade a whole race of men from the rank in the scale of beings which their Creator may perhaps have given them. To our reproach it must be said, that though for a century and a half we have had under our eyes the races of black and of red men, they have never yet been viewed by us as subjects of natural history. I advance it therefore as a suspicion only, that the blacks, whether originally a distinct race, or made distinct by time and circumstances, are inferior to the whites in the endowments both of body and mind. It is not against experience to suppose, that different species of the same genus, or varieties of the same species, may possess different qualifications. Will not a lover of natural history then, one who views the gradations in all the races of animals with the eye of philosophy, excuse an effort to keep those in the department of man as distinct as nature has formed them? This unfortunate difference of colour, and perhaps of faculty, is a powerful obstacle to the emancipation of these people. Many of their advocates, while they wish to vindicate the liberty of human nature, are anxious also to preserve its dignity and beauty. Some of these, embarrassed by the question "What further is to be done with them?" join themselves in opposition with those who are actuated by sordid avarice only. Among the Romans emancipation required but one effort. The slave, when made free, might mix with, without staining the blood of his master. But with us a second is necessary, unknown to history. When freed, he is to be removed beyond the reach of mixture.

Thomas Jefferson, Notes on the State of Virginia *(London, 1787)*

❧

QUERY XVIII, MANNERS

It is difficult to determine on the standard by which the manners of a nation may be tried, whether *catholic,* or *particular.* It is more difficult for a native to bring to that standard the manners of his own nation, familiarized to him by habit. There must doubtless be an unhappy influence on the manners of our people produced by the existence of slavery among us. The whole commerce between master and slave is a perpetual exercise of the most boisterous passions, the most unremitting despotism on the one part, and degrading submissions on the other. Our children see this, and learn to imitate it; for man is an imitative animal. This quality is the germ of all education in him. From his cradle to his grave he is learning to do what he sees others do. If a parent could find no motive either in his philanthropy or his self-love, for restraining the intemperance of passion towards his slave, it should always be a sufficient one that his child is present. But generally it is not sufficient. The parent storms, the child looks on, catches the lineaments of wrath, puts on the same airs in the circle of smaller slaves, gives a loose to his worst of passions, and thus nursed, educated, and daily exercised in tyranny, cannot but be stamped by it with odious peculiarities. The man must be a prodigy who can retain his manners and morals undepraved by such circumstances. And with what execration should the statesman be loaded, who permitting one half the citizens thus to trample on the rights of the other, transforms those into despots, and these into enemies, destroys the morals of the one part, and the amor patriae of the other. For if a slave can have a country in this world, it must be any other in preference to that in which he is born to live and labour for another: in which he must lock up the faculties of his nature, contribute as far as depends on his individual endeavours to the evanishment of the human race, or entail his own miserable condition on the endless generations proceeding from him. With the morals of the people, their industry also is destroyed. For in a warm climate, no man will labour for himself who can make another labour for him. This is so true, that of the proprietors of slaves a very small proportion indeed are ever seen to labour. And can the liberties of a nation be thought secure when we have removed their only firm basis, a conviction in the minds of the people that these liberties are of the gift of God? That they are not to be violated but with his wrath? Indeed I tremble for my country when I reflect that God is just: that his justice cannot sleep for ever: that considering numbers, nature

and natural means only, a revolution of the wheel of fortune, an exchange of situation, is among possible events: that it may become probable by supernatural interference! The Almighty has no attribute which can take side with us in such a con-
test.—But it is impossible to be temperate and to pursue this subject through the
various considerations of policy, of morals, of history natural and civil. We must be
contented to hope they will force their way into every one's mind. I think a change
already perceptible, since the origin of the present revolution. The spirit of the
master is abating, that of the slave rising from the dust, his condition mollifying, the
way I hope preparing, under the auspices of heaven, for a total emancipation, and
that this is disposed, in the order of events, to be with the consent of the masters,
rather than by their extirpation.

CONTRIBUTORS

ANNETTE GORDON-REED, of New York Law School, is the author of *Thomas Jefferson and Sally Hemings: An American Controversy* (1997).

RHYS ISAAC, of LaTrobe University, Melbourne, Australia, is the author of many works, including *The Transformation of Virginia, 1740–1790* (1982), which was awarded the Pulitzer Prize in history.

WINTHROP D. JORDAN, of the University of Mississippi, is the author of *White over Black: American Attitudes toward the Negro, 1580–1812* (1968), which won the National Book Award, and other works.

JAN ELLEN LEWIS, of Rutgers University, Newark, is the author of *The Pursuit of Happiness: Family and Values in Jefferson's Virginia* (1983) and other works.

PHILIP D. MORGAN, of the College of William and Mary, is the editor of the *William and Mary Quarterly* and the author of *Slave Counterpoint: Black Culture in the Eighteenth-Century Chesapeake and Lowcountry* (1998), winner of the Bancroft and Beveridge prizes.

PETER S. ONUF, of the University of Virginia, is the author of *Jefferson's Empire: The Language of American Nationhood,* forthcoming from the University Press of Virginia.

JACK N. RAKOVE, of Stanford University, was awarded the Pulitzer Prize in history for his *Original Meanings: Politics and Ideas in the Making of the Constitution* (1996).

JOSHUA D. ROTHMAN is a doctoral candidate at the University of Virginia; he is completing a dissertation on race relations in antebellum Virginia.

WERNER SOLLORS, of Harvard University, is the author most recently of *Neither Black nor White yet Both: Thematic Explorations of Interracial Literature* (1997).

LUCIA STANTON is Shannon Senior Research Historian at the Thomas Jefferson Memorial Foundation (Monticello).

DIANNE SWANN-WRIGHT is the director of special programs at the Thomas Jefferson Memorial Foundation (Monticello).

CLARENCE WALKER, of the University of California, Davis, is the author of numerous works, including the forthcoming *Been There, Done That: Afrocentrism and Black American History.*

GORDON S. WOOD, of Brown University, is the author most recently of *The Radicalism of the American Revolution* (1992), which was awarded the Pulitzer Prize in history.

INDEX

Abram, 120, 122
Absalom, Absalom! (Faulkner), 10, 19–20, 24, 32, 205
Adair, Douglass, 76
Adams, Henry, 196, 200–201
Adams, John, 37, 210–11, 212
  and Abigail, 43
  Callender attack on, 91
  on evils of slavery, 75
Adams, John Quincy, 211
adultery, interracial, 62, 96
African Americans
  Callender's detestation of, 95, 99
  class distinction among, 26, 163
  community network of, 98
  deportation of, 211, 217, 220–21, 223
  Jefferson on freedom for, 44
  Jefferson's rejection of, 114–15
  loss of identity of, 237
  oral history of Monticello's, 161–81
  oral tradition of, 27
Age of Enlightenment, moral values of, 218
Albemarle County, interracial families in, 66
Alice (Custis slave), 53, 54
American Dilemma, An (Myrdal), 225
American Indians, Jefferson's interest in, 35–36, 47
American Protestantism, and sinfulness of slavery, 233–34
Anderson, Anna, 242
Ashby, Matthew, 55
Ashlin, Joseph, 68
Ashton, Father John, 63–64
Auschwitz, 228

Bacon, Edmund, 98–99, 142
Bakari, Harvey, 125
Bakhufu, Auset, 193
Baltimore Sun, 204–5

Bankhead, Anne Randolph, 134–35
Bankhead, Charles, 134, 135
Banneker, Benjamin, 45
Barker, Bill, 125
Barrett, Cyrus, 68
Barrett, Frances, 68
Barrett, Salley, 68
Barrett, William, 68
Beckett, Eleanor, 64, 65
Beckett, William, 65
Beckett-Norris clan, 65
Bell, Mary Hemings (Sally's sister), 66, 104, 179
Bell, Robert Washington, 66
Bell, Sarah Jefferson, 66
Bell, Thomas, 66, 104, 179
Benjamin (Ben; former Wythe slave), 57, 58
Bennett, Winifred, 242
Betsy (Judah slave), 60
Billy (Brown slave), 59
Billy (Jarvis slave), 68
Binah (Prestwood slave), 73–74
biography, as genre of history, 38
biracial society, problem of creating, 221–22
blacks. *See* African Americans
blackface, images of, 162–63
blackness, identification with, 171–72
Blair, John, 53, 55
Boyd, Julian P., 38, 75–76
Broadnax, Lydia, 56–57, 58, 59
Brodie, Fawn M., 6, 11, 25, 78, 212, 239, 241, 251
  on "family denial," 136
  on Jefferson at Monticello, 41
  transcription of, 249
  on Wythe's alleged miscegenation, 58
Brown, Ann, 59
Brown, Michael, 57, 58–59
Brown, Nancy, 59
Brown, Robert, 59
Brown, William Wells, 193, 202

Jeffersonian America

❦

Jan Ellen Lewis and Peter S. Onuf, editors
Sally Hemings and Thomas Jefferson: History, Memory, and Civic Culture

Peter S. Onuf
Jefferson's Empire: The Language of American Nationhood